BENIGN ANARCHY

Benign Anarchy

Alcoholics Anonymous in Ireland

SHANE BUTLER
Trinity College Dublin

IRISH ACADEMIC PRESS
DUBLIN • PORTLAND, OR

First published in 2010 by Irish Academic Press

2 Brookside,
Dundrum Road,
Dublin 14, Ireland

920 NE 58th Avenue, Suite 300
Portland, Oregon,
97213-3786, USA

www.iap.ie

British Library Cataloguing in Publication Data
An entry can be found on request

ISBN 978 0 7165 3063 3 (cloth)
ISBN 978 0 7165 3064 0 (paper)

Library of Congress Cataloging-in-Publication Data
An entry can be found on request

Printed by The Good News Press Ltd, Ongar, Essex

In memory of Barry Butler
(1948–2006)

Contents

List of Abbreviations

AA	Alcoholics Anonymous
AAAD	Alcoholics Anonymous Archive Dublin
AAANY	Alcoholics Anonymous Archive New York
INCA	Irish National Council on Alcoholism
JAD	Jesuit Archive Dublin
PTAA	Pioneer Total Abstinence Association
PTAAUCD	Pioneer Total Abstinence Association Archive, University College Dublin

Acknowledgements

My interest in Alcoholics Anonymous (AA) has grown, over many years, out of my wider academic and professional interest in addiction issues. I have generally been encouraged by those with whom I have discussed this project, not least by those who were openly sceptical of my capacity to bring it to any kind of fruitful completion: some on the basis that academic disdain would make it impossible for me to treat AA with any degree of fairness, others on the basis that I had become an apologist for AA to such an extent that I had lost all critical distance from this unusual institution! I chose the title 'Benign Anarchy' (a phrase used by Bill Wilson, one of AA's co-founders, in a letter to Sackville O' Conor-Mallins in Dublin) because it struck me as such an apt description of AA's approach to governance and administration; and because as I got deeper into the research, it became clear to me that the fellowship's blueprint for administration (The Twelve Traditions) was equally important to its programme of recovery (The Twelve Steps).

I should make it clear from the outset that this is not an authorized history of AA in Ireland, and that AA – as is its wont – has no corporate view on the value or validity of what I have written. However, the research could not have taken place without the cooperation and assistance of AA, both in Ireland and the USA, for which I am deeply grateful. The Archives Committee of the General Service Board of AA in Dublin gave me full access to its archives, and I was assisted in this task by members of the committee as well as by administrative staff at its General Service Office. I was also given permission by the Trustees' Archives

Committee of the AA General Service Office, New York, to consult its extensive collection of early correspondence between members in Dublin and staff at the Alcoholic Foundation in New York. I would particularly like to thank Michelle Mirza, assistant archivist at the New York archives, for her courtesy and assistance on this project. It appears to be generally accepted within AA that the convention of anonymity does not apply posthumously, and I have, therefore, named a small number of the early members of the fellowship in Ireland. I trust that this will offend nobody, and that members who read this history will recognize that I have tried scrupulously to balance academic objectivity with respect for the unique culture of AA.

I should also like to thank the following: Bernard Meehan, Keeper of Manuscripts at Trinity College Dublin, and his colleague Ellen O' Flaherty, for allowing to me check the official record of Sackville O'Conor-Mallins' attendance at TCD; David Sheehy and Noelle Dowling at the Dublin Diocesan Archive for help in locating relevant documents from the McQuaid Papers; staff at the University College Dublin Archive for giving me access to and advice on the papers of the Pioneer Total Abstinence Association; Fergus O'Donoghue, S.J., and Damien Burke at the Irish Jesuit Archive for background information on Father John Mulligan, S.J. The papers of the now-defunct Irish National Council on Alcoholism (INCA) do not, unfortunately, appear to have been preserved intact in any accessible way, but I have managed over the years to acquire some relevant INCA papers which I have drawn on for this project. In addition to having access to much of the correspondence of Sackville O'Conor-Mallins, I was fortunate to meet and interview two people who knew him well – his nephew Denis Murphy and a fellowship member, the late Paddy K. – for whose assistance I am most grateful. Cathal O'Háinle, Professor Emeritus of Irish at TCD, advised me about the meaning of the name 'O'Conor Don'; and Seán Freyne, Professor Emeritus of Hebrew, Biblical and Theological Studies at TCD, drew on his memory of working with Archbishop Joseph Walsh of Tuam so as to help me gain understanding of a key figure in the Catholic Hierarchy who supported AA without reservation. I was helped in my efforts to understand the contribution which Sean O'Riordan, the Redemptorist theologian, made to AA in Ireland by two moral theologians – Raphael Gallagher of the Accademia Alfonsiana in Rome and Ronan Murtagh of St Patrick's College, Maynooth – who are familiar with O'Riordan's work.

My greatest individual debt is to my colleague Tony Jordan, tutor in Addiction Studies at the School of Social Work and Social Policy, TCD, whose M.Litt. thesis on AA I supervised some years ago and with whom I collaborated on an earlier journal article on this topic. Tony was generous in making available to me the audio-tapes of interviews with early AA members which he made in the late-1990s, and in addition to this he has read this book carefully in draft form and advised me on all aspects of the research. He did not agree with all of my interpretations, but his patience, wisdom and good humour have made my task considerably easier. Another of my former graduate students, John MacHale, has also been consistently helpful, allowing me to draw on his considerable knowledge of this topic and lending me books and papers relevant to my task.

All of my colleagues at the School of Social Work and Social Policy have been supportive of this venture, but I should like in particular to thank Marguerite Woods for reading early drafts of the text, and Pam Isaacson for administrative support throughout this project. I am also grateful to Ann Hope (former National Alcohol Policy Advisor to the Department of Health and Children) who periodically assured me that the history of AA in Ireland was a story worth telling. Throughout the period of researching and writing this book, Eoin O'Sullivan allowed me to draw on his vast knowledge of the historical evolution of health and social services, and particularly of the role played by voluntary and religious groups in service provision. Two other colleagues with addiction interests, Barry Cullen and Paula Mayock, have also advised and encouraged. Within AA there is a great emphasis on the importance of *ego deflation*, which in ordinary language means not getting too big for your boots, and my colleague Helen Buckley has worked tirelessly to ensure that this fate should not befall me.

Left to my own devices I would have struggled to come up with an appropriate image for the book's cover, but Eddie McParland, recently retired from Trinity's History of Art Department, was generous with advice, as well as linking me to others in the art world who were equally helpful. David Britton of Adam's Fine Art Auctioneers suggested that a Micheal Farrell painting 'Alcool de Serpent' (1980), which was in the Trinity art collection, might suit this purpose; John Taylor of Taylor Galleries helped to secure copyright permission from Meg Early, Micheal Farrell's widow, and Catherine Giltrap, curator of Trinity's art collection, completed the practical arrangements.

The photograph of Sackville O'Conor-Mallins during his army days in India and the flyleaf of the second edition of the Big Book (inscribed by Bill Wilson for Sackville) were provided by the family of the late Paddy K; the photograph of Sackville's Papal audience was provided by Denis Murphy; and all other images used as plates in this book were provided by the Archives Committee of the General Service Board of AA in Ireland. Brian McGovern of the Photographic Centre at Trinity College Dublin prepared all of these images for publication.

Lisa Hyde of Irish Academic Press has been consistently supportive of this venture and has generally helped in bringing it to completion.

On a personal level, I'd like to thank my wife Phil, and our children Emer, Gráinne and Kilian for their support throughout the research and writing of this book. I especially appreciate the time and effort which Emer put into proof-reading the book in draft form, thereby helping me to eliminate errors and improve the overall clarity of the text. It's good to know that, whatever about the alcoholic gene, the pedantic gene flourishes!

I have dedicated this book to the memory of my brother Barry Butler, whose sudden and premature death in December 2006 was a huge emotional blow to his wife Anna, their children Una, Eoin, Clare and Jo Anne, and to all of us in the extended family. By virtue of his status as a lifelong teetotaller Barry was not really eligible for AA membership. However, he would intuitively have understood what I have tried to describe in this book and he would certainly have appreciated the AA sense of humour.

Shane Butler
Trinity College Dublin
September 2009

List of Plates

Chapter One

Introducing AA

Alcoholics Anonymous (AA) was the first of the modern *self-help* or *mutual-help* movements: those health-based associations that emerged during the twentieth century – particularly in the area of mental health – to assert explicitly that 'sufferers' could be a valuable source of help to one another and to challenge implicitly the therapeutic monopoly previously claimed by the medical profession. AA was founded in Akron, Ohio, in 1935, and spread throughout the USA largely through the work of its New York headquarters. After the end of the Second World War it was diffused internationally so that it is now to be found practically all over the world. AA established its first Irish group in Dublin in late 1946, but during its first year in this country it held less than a hundred meetings and had fewer than fifty members. Over the subsequent sixty years, however, the movement has enjoyed huge growth across the thirty-two counties of Ireland, estimating its membership for the year 2007 at about 13,000, spread across 750 groups, which between them hold 76,000 meetings per year.[1] Apart from its direct appeal to those who attend meetings in line with their desire to stop drinking, AA is obviously well known in popular cultural terms: one need go no further than the television cartoon series *The Simpsons*, with its frequent references to alcoholism and attendance at AA meetings, to get some sense of its global brand recognition, and in Ireland AA features regularly in both fictional and biographical writings that deal with the subject of drink.[2]

The aim of this book is to tell the story of how AA took root in Ireland, the first European country in which it was established.

This necessitates exploring the movement's origins in post-Prohibition USA, as well as the social and cultural forces either supportive of or – potentially at least – opposed to its introduction to Ireland in the 1940s. The difficulty with such a summarized account of the movement's origins, diffusion and growth is that it might easily create an impression of AA as just another American-based corporation, which, through the strategic skills of its management, has globalized its activities, establishing franchises in virtually every country in the world. Drawing on Weberian theory, the American sociologist George Ritzer has written extensively on what he refers to as the 'McDonaldization' of society, by which he means the global proliferation of large bureaucratic organizations which – regardless of national or local contexts – use standardized means or instruments to achieve agreed ends.[3] While it might seem tempting to consider the global dissemination of AA in terms of its fit with this paradigm – with AA seen as marketing 'contented sobriety' in much the same way as the eponymous fast-food corporation markets its products globally – there are compelling reasons for rejecting such a thesis. For a start, there is the linguistic problem immediately confronting writers on this topic as to how their subject should properly be described; if one refers to AA as an 'organization', which on the face of it would appear to be a reasonable epithet to cover all of the activities summarily described above, one becomes quickly and uneasily aware of the contradictions inherent in such a description. Unusually, perhaps uniquely, AA appears to pride itself on the avoidance of bureaucracy and on being positively disorganized. Tradition Nine of its administrative philosophy, the Twelve Traditions,[4] says explicitly that 'AA, as such, ought never be organized', and the Traditions generally make the point that what its members usually refer to as the 'fellowship' is a non-hierarchical, leaderless movement, in which authority resides at the level of individual groups rather than at the level of a corporate board or chief executive.

While it may seem an odd comparison, this 'cell structure' of AA has more in common with the Fenians of nineteenth-century Ireland or contemporary terrorist organizations, than it does with globalized business corporations. By adhering to its Traditions, particularly those which espouse anonymity and the avoidance of the accumulation of wealth or property, the fellowship has largely avoided distraction and succeeded in keeping its focus on what it sees as its sole purpose – which is to carry its message to alcoholics who wish to stop drinking. It would appear, therefore, as though AA is one of those rare social movements that contravene Michels' 'iron law of oligarchy', a sociological maxim which argues that, however democratically well intentioned they may originally be, all organizations end up as oligarchies.[5] A corollary of this administrative emphasis on avoiding the creation of a centralized or hierarchical leadership structure was that AA activities outside of the USA should be allowed to develop as their own members saw fit, allowing for national differences and cultural diversity rather than being forced into conformity with a template laid down by 'head office'. This study will look *inter alia* at this aspect of the fellowship's early history in Ireland and at relationships between AA's first Irish members and its New York office, in the context of an institution which, almost from its beginning, had a sense of the importance of balancing unity against diversity.

Since AA is clearly not a commercial institution, concerned with making profits or paying dividends to its shareholders, social scientists and historians who set out to document how this fellowship has been diffused globally are faced with an initial problem of deciding how best to characterize it. Commonly, writers have depicted AA as occupying a hybrid terrain between the institutions of religion and medicine,[6] and it is this characterization which will be used to structure the present study of the fellowship's early history in Ireland. The value of presenting AA as an institution that bestrides medicine and religion is not simply that it offers a convenient framework for studying its establishment and growth in Ireland from the mid-1940s onwards, but also that it reflects precisely the historic ambiguity – in Ireland and elsewhere – as to how problems associated with alcohol consumption might best be conceptualized and managed. For the past two centuries, and particularly in those societies where the trend has been towards increasing industrialization and urbanization, there has been continuous political concern and public debate over the societal disruption caused by alcohol consumption and about the best means of preventing or responding to such disruption. It has been frequently observed that the definitive resolution of the 'drink question' has been thwarted by conflicting cultural values and norms: alcohol has been simultaneously perceived as a gift from God and one of life's great boons, but also as the work of the Devil and the enemy of all that is good in individual, familial and communal life. In the midst of such cultural confusion and ambivalence, however, the two institutions that have most consistently, if not always coherently, claimed to have a legitimate societal role to play in the management of alcohol-related problems are religion and medicine.

In the case of religion, beliefs and injunctions about alcohol and the avoidance of related problems have conventionally been thought of and discussed in terms of *temperance*; and in western countries temperance ideas have understandably been dominated by the Christian tradition. Although it might appear linguistically as though religious ideas presented under the rubric of temperance are primarily concerned with urging moderate or controlled alcohol consumption as opposed to total abstinence, such has not always been the case. Instead, as often as not, religious temperance movements have based their activities on a belief that alcohol is inherently evil and, acting on this basis, have either urged their adherents towards lifelong personal abstinence or have moved beyond the personal into the sphere of political lobbying for strict alcohol controls, if not complete prohibition. Social scientists and historians have by now subjected the differences between Christian temperance ideologies based on this fundamentalist antipathy to alcohol and Christian temperance ideologies which are less extreme in their views of alcohol to a good deal of critical scrutiny, and there is a large measure of agreement that these differences are explicable in terms of wider cultural differences between Protestants and Catholics.

Essentially, what has been argued is that in the post-Reformation period the Protestant worldview was one which placed huge emphasis on the individual and on the necessity for individuals to accept personal responsibility for managing their own lives and acting with self-restraint; by contrast, the Catholic worldview, both theologically and socially, remained more communitarian. Applying these ideas to debates about alcohol, scholars[7] have sought to explain Protestant temperance ideas as being rooted in a fear that individuals who drink alcohol – regardless of how much or how little the volume consumed – could no longer guarantee that they were in complete charge of themselves or capable of acting with the desired degree of self-restraint. On the other hand, it has been suggested that Catholic teaching on temperance is less extreme ideologically, seeing alcohol as a Divine gift – albeit one that can be abused – rather than as something inherently immoral or evil. Ireland's most famous temperance movement, the Father Mathew crusade of the 1840s, was notable both for its apparent success in persuading half of the adult population to take a pledge of total abstinence and for the vehemence of its antipathy to alcohol.[8] The fact that this crusade was led by a Catholic priest who worked in harmony with Protestant clergymen might be taken as disproving the general thesis that Catholic temperance has been more ideologically moderate than its Protestant counterpart. However, very few of those initially swayed by Father Mathew's charismatic leadership style appear to have kept their pledge; the Catholic hierarchy, always ambivalent about his Protestant-like attack on alcohol, did nothing to institutionalize his campaign but waited for half a century after his death before replacing it with its own strictly Catholic and ideologically moderate temperance organization – the Pioneer Total Abstinence Association.[9] Previous studies of the global diffusion of AA have argued that it was most readily intelligible and acceptable within Protestant 'temperance cultures',[10] so it seems important for this present study to look in detail at how the fellowship became established in Ireland at a time when this country already had a strong Catholic temperance organization and when, in the phrase of Tom Inglis, the Catholic Church generally enjoyed a 'moral monopoly' here.[11]

One of the most striking aspects of AA is the extent to which it makes explicit use of religious concepts and terminology, although what is even more striking perhaps is the care it takes to avoid being caught up in debate or controversy of a sectarian nature. The Twelve Steps, the fellowship's suggested programme of recovery, conclude by describing members who follow these steps as 'having had a spiritual awakening', reflecting the general tendency amongst its members and in its literature to speak of AA as a 'spiritual programme' rather than as a 'religious programme'. Similarly, references to God in the Steps and Traditions are carefully framed, so as to avoid either incorporation by or alienation of any specific religious tradition, including those who would define themselves as agnostic or atheist: references are to 'a

Power greater than ourselves' (Step Two), 'God as we understood Him' (Steps Three and Eleven) and 'God as he may express Himself in our group conscience' (Tradition Two). A more detailed account of the evolution of AA's ideas about spirituality, set against the historical background of American religious ideas of the 1930s, will be presented in Chapter 3 below. Suffice it to say, at this point, that while the fellowship's founders were heavily influenced by the tenets and practices of the Oxford Group, an evangelical Protestant movement that saw itself as recreating the spirit of first-century Christianity, they quickly distanced their fledgling movement from this and from all other sectarian associations in their efforts to make it acceptable to people of all religions and people of no religion.[12] It would appear that AA generally succeeded, during the period that it was establishing itself in its country of origin, in avoiding conflict with or incorporation by the major churches. However, tensions associated with the fellowship's religiosity have persisted and over the past twenty years it has become increasingly subject to attack on the basis that it is – or has become – a cult which brainwashes and demands life-long and complete loyalty of its members. In the words of one of its critics, 'AA has become America's quasi-official religion.'[13] Whether such criticisms are warranted, or whether they reflect misunderstanding and a confusion of AA with other therapeutic ideas and practices – particularly professional services which describe themselves as operating a Twelve-Step Programme – is a question that will be returned to at various points throughout this study.

Chapter 4 of this book will look in detail at the establishment of the fellowship in Ireland in terms of its relationship with the then dominant Catholic Church, focusing on the fears of early AA members that the spirituality or religiosity of its recovery programme might evoke a hostile reaction from the Catholic hierarchy – especially since the Pioneer Total Abstinence Association might well be seen as already catering adequately for any church members experiencing difficulties with alcohol. The man who was the Catholic archbishop of Dublin when AA established its first group there in 1946 was Dr John Charles McQuaid, who held this office from 1940 to 1972. At a time when the political culture of Ireland was generally subject to persistent and direct influence from the Catholic Church,[14] McQuaid

stood out nationally as the most forceful and articulate member
of the Catholic hierarchy and, within his own diocese, as an energetic provider of educational, health and welfare services.
However, whatever his commitment to the broad field of social
service provision, there is no doubting McQuaid's theological
conservatism, intolerance of Protestantism and dislike for interdenominational activities.[15] The fact that the origins of AA were
to be found within the evangelical Protestant tradition of the USA
would automatically have made it suspect in McQuaid's eyes, and
given his absolute belief in the Catholic Church and its spiritual
efficacy, he might reasonably have been expected to query the
necessity for any other institution which claimed to play a role in
bringing about a spiritual transformation in the lives of its members. It also seems unlikely that he could ever be happy with a
movement which had adopted such an anarchic approach to
organizational authority and which took what would now be
referred to as an à la carte approach to its organizational beliefs,
even to the extent of allowing its members to define God as *they*
understood Him. In short, AA was exactly the kind of movement
most likely to be attacked by Archbishop McQuaid. The fact that it
never was attacked by him is, on the face of it, puzzling. Chapter 4
will look in detail at this fact in the context of a broader discussion
of how early members of the fellowship in Ireland negotiated a
relationship with the Catholic Church.

If we switch our attention to the medical management of alcohol-related problems, the other side of AA's hybrid philosophy, the
main historical developments that proved influential date from the
late eighteenth century and reside in the context of the broader
Enlightenment. While the term *alcoholism* appears to have been
coined in the mid-nineteenth century by a Swedish doctor, Magnus
Huss, the most influential medical writers on this topic were
Benjamin Rush (1743–1813), the renowned American physician
who was also a signatory of the Declaration of Independence, and
Thomas Trotter (1760–1832), a Scottish naval physician.[16]
Essentially, these and other doctors who developed an interest in
this area argued that, rather than attributing problems to the wilful
misbehaviour of drinkers, the phenomenon should be seen as a
disease or addiction characterized by progressive loss of control by
drinkers over this drug. Medical discourse of this kind overlapped
substantially with the moral views of the religious temperance

advocates, contributing on both sides of the Atlantic to the creation in the late nineteenth and early twentieth centuries of specialist inebriate asylums outside of the larger lunatic asylum networks of this era. These inebriate asylums constituted a short-lived experiment at helping problem drinkers to become abstinent, since it was believed that lifelong abstinence was the only remedy for the disease. There was, however, one major difference between the nineteenth-century understanding of alcohol addiction and the so-called 'disease concept of alcoholism' which was to emerge in the USA in the post-Prohibition years of the 1930s. The earlier understanding located the source of the disease in alcohol itself, which was seen to be an inherently addictive substance; the implication being that all who persisted in drinking were at serious risk of losing control over their habit. On the other hand, the post-Prohibition version, while proclaiming that 'alcoholism is a disease', took the view that alcohol itself was an essentially harmless substance for the vast majority of its consumers and, instead, located the source of the disease in the as yet unspecified vulnerabilities of a minority of defective or 'diseased' consumers.[17]

The difference between the nineteenth-century view of alcoholism as disease and the disease concept that emerged in the USA during the 1930s and 1940s – before gender inclusivity became normative – was popularly and pithily summarized in the phrase 'the problem is in the man, not the bottle'. In other words, problems could be attributed to the predisposition of a minority of individual consumers rather than to any negative properties inherent in alcohol as a substance. Chapter 3 will look in some detail at how this disease concept, which largely exonerated alcohol from the problems traditionally attributed to it, gained popularity and came to dominate public policy in the context of a society attempting to move away from what was widely seen to have been an ideologically extreme and practically ineffective experiment at ridding itself completely of alcohol. Disillusionment with the moralism of Prohibition fostered enthusiasm for a more scientific approach to alcohol policy, and the disease concept of alcoholism seemed tailor-made for this situation. The effect of the broad public 'disease concept' policy was to undermine the rationale for tough alcohol control policies, since it was assumed that the prevalence of alcoholism in any given society was limited to a minority of vulnerable drinkers and would not be affected in any way by changes in consumption levels in the population as a whole. Put simply, the belief was that alcoholism was a disease confined to a small number of biologically predisposed individuals, whose disease process was triggered by any degree of exposure to alcohol; members of this minority could not be protected from their sad destinies by alcohol control policies, while the majority of 'normal' or 'social' drinkers could drink more or less with impunity and had no need of alcohol control strategies.

From a health service provision perspective, the main implication of the disease concept was that people with clearly established drinking problems should no longer be viewed moralistically, as though they were personally culpable for behaviour now seen as symptomatic of a discrete illness or disease, but should instead be provided with non-moralistic and technically effective treatment services. In the USA, particularly from the early 1940s, a broad coalition of interests dedicated to the idea of alcoholism as disease lobbied to have this idea culturally accepted and enshrined in public policy.[18] While it might have been assumed that AA would happily participate in a movement which appeared to reflect most, if not all, of its own beliefs and values and which was aimed at reducing stigma and improving treatment services for alcoholism, this did not prove to be the case. As the 1940s progressed and as the fellowship formalized its administrative traditions, it adopted an unequivocal stance on avoidance of all forms of political lobbying or involvement in public debate. In the words of its Tenth Tradition, 'Alcoholics Anonymous has no opinion on outside issues; hence the AA name ought never be drawn into public controversy': in other words, AA would continue to focus solely on helping people who wished to stop drinking. Whatever individual members might think about it or do in their private capacities, AA as an institution would do nothing to lobby for the public acceptance of the disease concept and would express no corporate opinion on policy issues – such as licensing legislation, health care policy and practice on treatment of drinking problems, advertising and promotion of alcohol, drink-driving or other such matters. There will be a fuller exploration in Chapter 3 of the reasons why AA's founding fathers took this decision to distance themselves from the realm of policy and politics in the USA; in Chapter 5 these issues will be revisited in detail in relation to the role of AA in Ireland, at a time when a national organization, the Irish National Council on Alcoholism, was established to lobby for the public acceptance of the disease concept and its incorporation into official health policy.

Chapter 5 of this book will look at how early AA members in Ireland negotiated working relationships with members of the medical profession, particularly with psychiatrists who had – and to a large extent still have – a dominant role in the health care management of drinking problems. Just as the fellowship's use of spiritual concepts and practices had the potential to bring it into conflict with the Catholic Church, its ideas about disease and recovery had the potential to bring it into conflict with the medical profession: particularly since there was no tradition of self-help at this time and AA might well have been seen as challenging what is pompously referred to as the *sapiential authority* of the medical profession. Although neither the Twelve Steps nor the Twelve Traditions contain a statement to the effect that *alcoholism is a disease*, this is a view that is commonly seen as a core belief of AA. As the journalist John Waters puts it, 'It is an article of faith in Alcoholics Anonymous that alcoholism is a disease.'[19] However, the complexity and ambiguity of this state- ment is amply demonstrated when Waters goes on to say that alcoholism is a disease that can only be cured by spiritual transformation – rather than by conventional medical or surgical interventions. What this latter statement makes clear is that the fellowship's use of terminology ostensibly borrowed from med- ical science should neither be taken as evidence of deference on its part to the medical profession, nor of uncritical acceptance of a 'medical model' of alcoholism.

Instead, what emerges from a study of AA literature and practice is a sense that the fellowship, while eager to work collaboratively with the medical profession, sees alcoholism within its own frame of reference, which is primarily spiritual rather than biomedical. It is not so much that AA members have an antipathy to diagnostic systems, but rather that they have no real interest in such matters; people are accepted into the fellowship on the basis that they attend meetings and – explicitly or implicitly – express a desire to stop drinking, not because they have satisfied diagnostic criteria set down by medical scientists or have been diagnosed by appro- priately qualified clinicians. From an AA perspective, alcoholism is a spiritual disease and the only diagnosis that really counts is self-diagnosis, arising from a process of self-searching and acceptance of defeat by or powerlessness over alcohol. Similarly, the fellowship's ideas about treatment differ significantly from those of conventional medicine, most markedly perhaps in that AA sees its recovery programme as a lifelong spiritual process for people who are always 'in recovery' but never 'recovered': this manifests itself clearly in its conviction that life is to be lived 'a day at a time', that long-term abstinence offers no guarantee against relapse, and that in many AA groups the person deemed to have the longest period of sobriety is the person who got up earliest on that day.

Contemporary discourse on medicine and health care, a decade into the new millennium, is dominated by an understandable emphasis on advancing scientific research and on the importance of applying research findings to clinical practice, so that treatments offered to patients have a demonstrable 'evidence base'. AA, however, does not reflect this preoccupation with evidence-based practice, in that it shows no particular interest in outcome studies and does not modify or update its practices and suggested programme of recovery to take account of research findings. Instead of adapting its techniques of recovery to take account of the most up-to-date findings of alcoholism treatment outcome studies, AA has stuck with its own approach to recovery, an approach that crystallized during the years when the fellowship was becoming established in Ireland. Since it has no pretensions to being scientific and does not seek to pit itself against the medical profession, AA neither promotes its programme of recovery aggressively nor suggests in any way that it has a monopoly on understanding and helping alcoholics. Instead, in a spirit of pragmatism that reflects its American origins, existing members seek to attract new members simply by describing their own experiences in AA and suggesting that these experiences might be of interest to others who wish to stop drinking. The only advice given to new members is that they consider following the example of well-established members by attending meetings and starting to 'work the programme'.

Some of the main features of the Twelve Step Programme have already been touched upon and will be elaborated further throughout this book, but it is also important to make some preliminary remarks about the nature of AA meetings. The fellowship regularly organizes *open meetings* which may be attended by non-members who wish to find out more about AA, but the vast majority of meetings are *closed meetings* which are intended only for those who define themselves as members and who attend because they have a desire to stop drinking. While both open and closed meetings vary and some meetings focus on the Steps, the core activity in all AA meetings is storytelling: essentially what happens is that members take turns in telling their own stories or their personal narratives of their alcoholism and recovery. Unlike conventional forms of individual psychotherapy or group psychotherapy, in which, to a greater or lesser extent, clients can expect to be questioned, confronted or advised – and perhaps have their problems interpreted or explained – AA meetings are structured so as to avoid any such conversational style; and there is a clear, albeit implicit, rule against what is referred to as 'cross-talk'. In other words, meetings are structured so as to discourage members from responding to one another or offering one another feedback, and the resultant format might best be characterized as a series of monologues or a collective monologue rather than dialogue between members. Makela and colleagues, in an attempt to summarize the 'rules of speech' implicit in AA meetings in Finland, have provided the following account which would appear to be valid for AA meetings globally:

1. Do not interrupt the person speaking.
2. Speak about your own experiences.
3. Speak as honestly as you can.
4. Do not speak about other people's private affairs.
5. Do not profess religious doctrines or lecture about scientific theories.
6. You may speak about personal problems in applying the AA program but do not attempt to refute the program.
7. Do not openly confront or challenge previous turns of talk.
8. Do not give direct advice to other members of AA.
9. Do not present causal explanations of the behavior of other AA members.
10. Do not present psychological interpretations of the behavior of other AA members.[20]

Members who feel in need of individual advice or support are encouraged to receive this through the common practice of *sponsorship*, whereby newcomers to the fellowship are mentored outside of meetings by other members whose recovery is deemed to be somewhat more advanced. Despite the importance of sponsorship, regular attendance at meetings is recommended and it appears to be the case that personal narratives change and evolve over time, so that the style of story told by a fellowship old-timer is usually quite different from that told by a relative newcomer.[21] The idea that storytelling can be therapeutic – insofar as it helps people to externalize their problems and to reshape their self-images over time – became popular with professional therapists, particularly family therapists, in the 1980s and 1990s,[22] half a century after AA had put storytelling at the centre of its own therapeutic practices. One stereotype of the Irish is that they have an inordinate fondness for alcohol and an unusually high prevalence of related problems, and this is a stereotype that will be explored in Chapter 2 and returned to in Chapter 7. A second stereotype, however, is that the Irish are good storytellers, and on this basis, it might be argued that the centrality of narrative rather than analysis in AA might have made it attractive to Irish sensibilities.

This, therefore, is a book about how AA, a loosely structured and largely leaderless institution composed entirely of self-professed 'drunks', made the transition from its place of origin in post-Prohibition America to Ireland in the aftermath of the Second World War. This history of AA in Ireland is presented thematically rather than chronologically, and makes no attempt to deal with events after the late 1970s.[23] The remainder of the book will be structured as follows. Chapter 2 will review the general topic of alcohol and the Irish – looking at the prevalence of alcohol-related problems in the country and the stereotypical view of the Irish as being inordinately fond of drinking, as well as at changing cultural and public policy ideas about which institutions should accept 'ownership' of drinking problems. Chapter 3 will focus on AA's origins within the evangelical Protestant tradition of the United States of America and how the fellowship's co-founders and early leaders worked at designing an institution which would have broad appeal to problem drinkers and would avoid becoming mired in political or religious controversies as had happened to earlier temperance movements. Chapter 4 will present a detailed account of AA's establishment in Ireland, focusing on the fellowship's religiosity, the potential for conflict with the then dominant Roman Catholic Church, and the efforts made by early members to prevent such conflict. Chapter 5 will trace AA's history in Ireland in relation to the medical profession and health care institutions, exploring its working relationships with medical doctors and hospitals, as well as its subtly changing position on health policy on the subject of alcoholism as disease or illness. Chapter 6 will look at how AA in Ireland gradually evolved from its original Dublin group to become a nationwide movement, making no distinction between North and South but remaining administratively separate from AA in Great Britain. Finally, Chapter 7 will offer an overview of the history of AA in Ireland, emphasizing the robustness and adaptability of this institution across changing social, political and economic circumstances, but focusing throughout on the question of what the fellowship can contribute to a drinking society.

Chapter Two

Managing Alcohol Problems in Ireland in the Nineteenth and Early Twentieth Centuries

'QUITE BLUNTLY NO ONE KNEW HOW TO CURE A DRUNK'[1]

The main aim of this chapter, by way of providing a context for the detailed presentation of AA's early history in this country, is to explore how alcohol-related problems had been conceptualized and practically managed in the century or so prior to the coming of AA to Ireland in 1946. Irish drinking habits and attitudes towards alcohol have long been regarded as extreme, and the stereotype of the drunken Irish is one that seems to have general recognition abroad and to cause periodic disquiet at home. There has been much popular and academic debate as to the validity of this stereotype or, if its validity is conceded, as to when and how the Irish developed such a problematic relationship with alcohol. A poem attributed to St Bridget, one of Ireland's early Christian saints who is believed to have died in the early sixth century, envisages Heaven as a lake of beer around which the Heavenly Family sit drinking for all eternity,[2] suggesting that at least at this time alcohol consumption was seen as non-problematic and consonant with religious values. Whether changing perceptions of alcohol and the problems deemed to stem from its consumption were significantly associated with the introduction to this country of distillation and the availability of much more potent forms of beverage alcohol (probably in the fourteenth century) is unclear; in any event, from the early nineteenth century onwards the idea that alcohol consumption was socially, economically and morally problematic was one which was persistently expressed and which gave rise to a range of public policy and religiously motivated activities and institutions.

RELIGIOUS TEMPERANCE

As mentioned in Chapter 1, the idea of temperance appears, linguistically at least, to be concerned with the promotion of moderate alcohol consumption, but as historians of Irish nineteenth-century temperance movements have shown,[3] there were serious and ongoing tensions between those who favoured such moderation and those who were unequivocally opposed to alcohol and argued for what was commonly known as *teetotalism* or total abstinence from alcoholic beverages. Concerns about alcohol – and its alleged contribution to crime, to economic loss, to child neglect and to a general decline in family life – were voiced by many groups in mid-nineteenth-century Ireland, prominent among them the Dublin Statistical Society, which during the 1850s changed its name to the Statistical and Social Inquiry Society of Ireland (SSISI), the name by which it is still known. This society became greatly concerned with the question of alcohol consumption and its associated problems, and attempted, using the somewhat primitive social science concepts and methods of this era, to provide support for the religious temperance groups which were emerging at this time. The most active SSISI member on this issue was the Quaker philanthropist James Haughton who, between 1849 and 1858, read six papers on alcohol to the society. In an 1849 paper, in which he argued that 'drink was at the root of all crimes', Haughton was at pains to refute any suggestion that he and his colleagues were 'mere enthusiasts': 'We support our argument not by the crude theories of mere enthusiasts, but by the coolly expressed opinions of those best fitted, by station and education, to testify in our favour.'[4] This claim has much in common with the claims of present-day social and biomedical scientists that they are ideally placed to provide an objective 'evidence base' for public policy on alcohol, but SSISI members appear to have made little impact on either public attitudes or state responses in an arena dominated by the various Christian churches.

While there was a great proliferation of religious temperance movements in nineteenth-century Ireland, by far the largest and best known of these was that of Father Theobald Mathew, a Capuchin monk. Father Mathew, who died in 1856, was most active in his religious temperance work in the late 1830s, a decade or so prior to the devasting famine which so dramatically transformed Irish social and political life. It has been difficult for historians to establish reliable membership figures for the Father Mathew movement and there certainly appears to have been some exaggeration of such statistics as do exist; nonetheless, there is agreement that the scale of this temperance campaign was vast, with perhaps up to half the adult population of Ireland taking a pledge of total abstinence from its leader.[5] What was most significant ideologically about the Father Mathew temperance movement was the virulence of its antipathy towards alcohol and the fact that it espoused total abstinence or teetotalism, a position which was generally more reflective of Protestant attitudes towards alcohol than mainstream Catholic views on this matter. What was significant organizationally, however, was that Father Mathew was, in the classic Weberian sense, a charismatic rather than a bureaucratic leader. He was widely regarded as a miracle worker and had the personal ability and the communication skills, whether addressing small church congregations or open-air 'mass meetings', which rivalled the Repeal meetings of Daniel O'Connell, to persuade thousands of people to take a pledge of lifelong total abstinence from alcohol. He lacked, however, the administrative skills to set in place the formal organizational supports necessary to maintain such a commitment. It was not surprising, therefore, that the long-term impact of Father Mathew's temperance movement was relatively slight; he left behind him no structured organization to continue his work, and many – perhaps most – of those to whom he administered the pledge were 'backsliders' who quickly reverted to alcohol consumption. Father Mathew was at odds both with the deep-rooted cultural commitment to drinking in Ireland and with the Catholic hierarchy which – because of the vehemence of his denunciations of alcohol and because of his willingness to work in an interdenominational way with Protestant clergymen – was, at best, ambivalent about his work. The strongest and most explicit attack by a Catholic bishop on his activities was that delivered by Archbishop MacHale of Tuam (the legendary 'Lion of the West'), who referred to Father Mathew as a 'vagabond friar'.[6] Following his death, the Catholic Church in Ireland made no attempt to perpetuate his ideals or to institutionalize the campaign which he had initiated, and it was not until the end of the nineteenth century that a new and specifically Catholic temperance movement – the Pioneer Total Abstinence Association – was established in this country. If one looks at the political impact of Father Mathew's work, in relation to the pressure it generated directly or indirectly for legislative and other public policy measures to reduce alcohol-related problems, it again becomes clear that despite its scale and popularity it left behind no significant legacy which might compare, for instance, with the political influence exerted by the Woman's Christian Temperance Union (WCTU) in the campaign for alcohol prohibition in the USA.[7]

In 1898, almost half a century after Father Mathew's death, the Pioneer Total Abstinence Association (PTAA) of the Sacred Heart was established by Father James Cullen, a Jesuit priest based in Dublin.[8] The Pioneers, as they were usually referred to, differed both ideologically and organizationally from their predecessors. While Cullen's antagonism towards alcohol may well have been every bit as bitter as that of Mathew, he realized that frank expression of this antagonism would be imprudent; as Malcolm (1986) put it, 'Only by moderating his essentially hard-line teetotal views could Cullen hope to retain the approval of the hierarchy.'[9] This realization had clearly contributed to Cullen's long-term strategy to get and retain the approval of the bishops, as Malcolm points out in a reference to the publication of Cullen's *Temperance Catechism* some years prior to the founding of the Pioneers:

> During the controversies surrounding the centenary of Father Mathew's birth Archbishop Walsh's [of the archdiocese of Dublin] suspicious attitude to teetotalism became well known. In publishing his *Temperance Catechism* in 1891, Cullen sent copies of the proofs to Walsh in order to gain his imprimatur. But the archbishop's letter of acknowledgement, while it praised the work, at the same time clearly revealed Walsh's reservations regarding teetotalism. He commended Cullen for not 'exaggerating' the importance of total abstinence. 'It is no small merit', he wrote, 'that your catechism is free from every trace of that aggressiveness

which unfortunately so often forms a prominent feature in the writings of would-be temperance reformers'.[10]

The Pioneers were managed from the outset in a conventionally bureaucratic style by the Jesuit order. This was done, however, on behalf of and with the approval of the bishops so that, unlike the Father Mathew movement, they were an integral part of official Catholic Church structures in Ireland. It was also significant that the Pioneers clearly opted to work only with Catholics and to eschew all forms of interdenominational work; this was strikingly symbolized by their full title and by the fact that members wore a badge or 'pin' depicting the Sacred Heart of Jesus, devotion to which was a specifically Roman Catholic practice. Pioneers could and sometimes did lobby, individually or collectively, for change in relation to alcohol policy and legislation, but such lobbying was rarely independent of the bishops, and the movement was generally more ideologically moderate than that of Father Mathew. In the view of the Pioneers, alcohol was a gift from God and was therefore inherently good but, as with other Divine gifts, it could be abused; the Pioneer association primarily saw itself as providing structured spiritual support for those who voluntarily pledged themselves to abstain from alcohol for life. The decision to take this pledge was envisaged as being for a relatively elite group of Catholics, hence the name 'Pioneers'; and it was clear that even amongst the clergy alcohol consumption was the norm and was not be regarded as undesirable or as an impediment to preferment within the church's hierarchical system.[11]

In trying to summarize the impact of religious-based temperance movements on both drinking habits and alcohol policy in Ireland, it is useful to draw on Levine's (1992) influential paper on 'temperance cultures', a term he used in reference to 'those societies which in the nineteenth and early twentieth centuries, had large, enduring temperance movements'.[12] Levine identified nine such temperance cultures (the USA, Canada, the UK, Australia, New Zealand, Finland, Norway, Sweden and Iceland) and suggested that the most important common factors in these countries were, firstly, that they were predominantly Protestant societies and, secondly, that they were societies in which people drank a major portion of their alcohol in the form of spirits – or distilled liquor. Levine also developed an elaborate theoretical explanation of how the ethic of individual discipline and self-control, which was a central feature of Protestant culture, was seen as inevitably compromised by alcohol consumption, thus leading to the emergence of explicitly anti-alcohol forms of religious temperance in these societies. Applying this model to Ireland, it would seem that some at least of the urgency associated with official and popular disquiet about alcohol consumption in the country in the nineteenth century reflected fears about spirit drinking (and especially the drinking of *poitín*, an illicitly distilled whiskey); however, the country was predominantly Catholic, had a communitarian rather than an individualistic ethic, and Catholic Church leaders generally confined themselves to urging moderation while avoiding explicit denunciation of alcohol per se. In short, Ireland was not a temperance culture as defined by Levine, and, if one accepts these ideas, it is not surprising that neither the Father Mathew movement nor any of the smaller temperance movements of the nineteenth century left any lasting impression on public policy or legislation.

LUNATIC ASYLUMS, PRISONS AND INEBRIATE REFORMATORIES

Given that the dominant religious perspective on alcohol was somewhat ambiguous – seeing alcohol consumption as potentially rather than inherently immoral or sinful – it should come as no surprise that institutional responses to individuals deemed to be problem drinkers were equally confusing. The individuals in question, who resembled those at whom AA was aimed a century later, were not those who got drunk occasionally or who because of their drunkenness occasionally fell foul of the law; rather, they were those who appeared to have lost all ability to control their drinking and who, as a result, habitually created social disruption or failed to fulfil social obligations. Throughout the nineteenth century these problem drinkers, in Ireland as elsewhere, were subjected to a range of institutional regimes intended to either punish them for the vice of drunkenness or cure them of what was sometimes described as a disease. Contrary to the grand theoretical studies of the expansion of custodial state institutions (for instance, Foucault[13]), which emphasized the increased role of expert knowledge and institutional differentiation in societal management of deviants, attempts to categorize and segregate problem drinkers in nineteenth-century Ireland failed signally in their attempts to bring ideological or organizational clarity to this issue. As will now be reviewed here, the problem – most commonly referred to as *habitual drunkenness, inebriety,* or *dipsomania* – remained stubbornly intractable throughout the Victorian period.

Throughout the nineteenth century the courts and the prison system continued to deal with large numbers of offenders whose criminal behaviour was related to alcohol, but the creation and expansion of a lunatic asylum system during this century offered an alternative ideological and institutional framework for the public management of troublesome drinkers. Although what is now St Patrick's Hospital had been established as a private lunatic asylum in 1746, with money bequeathed for this purpose by Dean Jonathan Swift,[14] it was not until 1815 that a public asylum was first opened. This institution in the northern inner-city district of Dublin, which was later to feature prominently in attempts to establish AA in Ireland, has been variously known as the Richmond Lunatic Asylum, Grangegorman Mental Hospital and, most recently, St Brendan's Hospital.[15] In 1817, due to the work of Robert Peel, Chief Secretary for Ireland, a parliamentary committee was appointed to 'inquire into the relief of the lunatic poor in Ireland',[16] and this led to the establishment over the next half-century of a network of district lunatic asylums throughout the country. What was most remarkable about the evolution of these public asylums was the unanticipated scale of an enterprise originally expected to be small and static, since it was presumed that the numbers of lunatics – and particularly 'dangerous' lunatics – would be quite limited. For instance, Finnane's history of the public asylums reports that the Richmond Asylum, which had 257 beds when it was opened in 1815, had by 1904 been expanded to accommodate 3,218 inmates; similarly, the Ballinasloe Asylum was opened in 1833 with beds for 150 inmates, but by 1904 (when the population of its catchment area had been greatly reduced by the Famine and subsequent emigration) had been expanded to cater for 1,084 inmates.[17] Such expansion could be regarded as evidence, to use more recent concepts and terminology, of a high incidence and prevalence of mental illness in Ireland; most writers on this topic have seen it, however, as simply reflecting the vagueness and ambiguity of the concepts of 'insanity' or 'lunacy' and have tended to the view that, in the absence of authoritative working definitions of these concepts, the lunacy system in Ireland simply proved to be a generous host to an assortment of difficult, disabled and generally deviant people, all of whom were involuntarily detained.[18]

As in other countries, the original establishment of Ireland's lunatic asylums took place without reference to the medical profession, which was seen as having neither the scientific capacity to identify precisely ('diagnose') those appropriately confined within these new institutions, nor a legitimate claim to a leadership role in their management. The management of asylums was initially placed in the hands of laypeople and was based on the concept of 'moral treatment': a commonsense notion which suggested that inmates whose behaviour was disturbed and disturbing could best be helped back to normality by being treated 'morally', that is with kindness and ordinary human consideration. Gradually, however, the medical profession lobbied to have lunacy seen as a form of illness or disease, which was primarily amenable to medical treatment, and, accordingly, to have asylum management regarded as a medical monopoly.[19] From the mid-nineteenth century onwards, lunacy management in Ireland (as elsewhere) resided firmly in the hands of the medical profession, giving rise to the emergence of the modern specialism of psychiatry, while asylum attendants moved somewhat more slowly towards the professional status of psychiatric or mental health nursing. This displacement of the 'moral managers' by doctors reflected a fundamental shift from a moral to a scientific approach: the medical profession had succeeded in persuading government (and perhaps to a lesser extent the public) that the deviant behaviour and irrationality of asylum inmates was, in fact, a form of illness, the underlying causes of which would sooner or later be revealed by scientific research, thereby leading to technically effective treatment. Since this 'mental illness' primarily affected its victims' rational faculties, it was not surprising that frequently they failed to recognize their need for treatment and thus had to be compulsorily detained and treated. The historical and social science literature is virtually unanimous, however, that this medicalization of lunacy resulted from the political skills and relatively high status of medicine within nineteenth-century society, rather than from any demonstrable scientific progress or evidence of effective treatment technologies at this time. Indeed, almost two centuries later, the medical model of mental illness and the legitimacy of medical ownership is still greatly contested.[20]

From the perspective of the present study's focus on alcoholism treatment, however, what is most relevant is that, across the broad spectrum of behavioural problems which were medicalized within the asylum system, alcohol problems appear to have created a unique sense of unease in relation to the smooth transition from a moral to a scientific model of management. Valverde,[21] who has studied the management of alcohol problems within the asylums of nineteenth-century Britain and North America, concluded that the attempt to medicalize alcoholism failed and that this occurred primarily because it was thought to involve a 'disease of the will' rather than a disease of the mind. In other words, problem drinkers – at least when sobered up – frequently appeared to asylum staff to be quite rational and, therefore, categorically different from other lunatics. For this reason, there were persistently recurring debates as to whether habitual problem drinkers should be categorized as lunatics and managed in the asylums, or whether they might not more appropriately be categorized as criminals and managed by the courts and the prisons. Underlying all of this doubt was a fatalistic belief that scientific medicine could do nothing to alter destructive drinking patterns if the drinkers involved had no wish to change. From the time of their establishment, the Irish lunatic asylums were regularly called upon to manage inmates whose primary problems appear to have been alcohol-related, and Finnane has calculated that at the end of the nineteenth century approximately 10 per cent of annual admissions were being attributed to 'intemperance in drink'. There was little evidence, however, that admission to the asylum achieved anything other than a temporary respite for these drinkers, their families and the wider community, and what was notable about them was that they went in and out of the asylum much more frequently than other inmates, in a pattern which would later be described as a 'revolving door'.[22]

If the Resident Medical Superintendents and their staffs were ambivalent about the legitimacy and effectiveness of trying to cure 'inebriates' or 'habitual drunkards' within the Irish lunatic asylum system, then prison authorities were equally unconvinced of the value of constantly imprisoning such drinkers in the country's prison system. Smith (1989) notes that 'As late as 1895, the

[General Prisons] Board estimated that at least half of the prisoners in the local prisons were habitual drunkards',[23] so it is clear that this burden was significantly greater for the prisons than the asylums. Following protracted public and parliamentary debate involving religious temperance groups, prison authorities and others, the British Parliament enacted the Inebriates Act of 1898 which provided for the establishment of yet another form of institution. The institution in question, known as the *inebriate reformatory*, was neither a conventional prison nor a lunatic asylum but represented the first attempt at specialist treatment of recidivist problem drinkers. The legislation set in place a three-tier system of reformatories: one tier comprising of institutions financed entirely by the state and managed by the prison system; a second which was licensed, supervised and partially funded by the state; and a third which consisted of 'retreats' run by charities or private individuals for those who could pay for their own care. In Ireland a state inebriate reformatory was opened under the aegis of the General Prisons Board at Ennis in 1899 and two state-licensed reformatories were later established by voluntary groups at Wexford and Waterford.[24] In these, as in similar institutions in the United Kingdom and North America,[25] the aims were expressed idealistically in relation to the moral reform of inmates deemed to have lost control of their drinking. It was hoped that, through the experience of a structured and highly disciplined regime and the example of chaplains and specially selected attendants, inmates would rebuild their wills so that, when released back to society, they would abstain from alcohol. The Irish experience, essentially the same as that of other countries which set about this institutional process of moral reform, was that these inebriate reformatories proved to be no more successful than the lunatic asylums or the prisons, and by the time the Free State came into existence in 1921 all of the inebriate reformatories had been closed. While it might be argued that the functioning of the state inebriate reformatory at Ennis had been bedevilled by lack of funding and by tortuous legal processes, it is likely that few would quibble with Smith's conclusion (used as an epigraph to this chapter) that the fundamental problem was that 'Quite bluntly no one knew how to cure a drunk'.[26]

In summary, at the time of the establishment of the Irish Free State in 1921, attitudes towards people deemed to be habitual drunkards remained ambiguous and contested, and institutional responses to habitual drunkards reflected these attitudes. There appeared to be a broad consensus that people who regularly drank to such an extent that they were socially disruptive should be subjected to institutional confinement, if only to deprive them of access to alcohol, but there was ongoing confusion as to what type of institution was most appropriate. Whether problem drinking was a vice to be corrected in prisons or religiously structured institutions, or a disease to be treated in medically run institutions, remained a matter of controversy and contention.

THE INTOXICATING LIQUOR COMMISSION, 1925

The first detailed review of alcohol policy to be conducted in Free State Ireland was under the aegis of the Intoxicating Liquor Commission of 1925.[27] This commission was made up mainly of members of the Dáil and Seanad, with one representative from a temperance background but no representation from the drinks industry. It was primarily intended to review policy and legislation dealing with the sale and consumption of alcohol, and particularly with what was seen to be the excessive number of licensed premises in this jurisdiction. From an historical perspective, however, its report (based on seventeen sittings and the examination of fifty-three witnesses) provides a useful overview of the general alcohol policy debate during the period, largely confirming that none of the ideological or institutional ambiguities from the previous century had been resolved.

In its report, the commission dismissed as impractical the representations made to it by a number of temperance societies, which had lobbied for: 'complete Sunday closing; the reduction by one half of the number of licensed premises in An Saorstat [the Irish Free State]; the abolition of mixed trading [the practice of allowing alcohol sales in retail outlets which sold groceries, drapery or hardware]; the suppression of wine licences and the further restriction of registered clubs'.[28] The commission set out the general principles which it claimed to have applied in reaching conclusions and making recommendations: principles which obviously reflected its own awareness of the policy climate within which it was functioning, but which may also have reflected the somewhat negative views of Prohibition emerging from the USA at this time:

In the first place we desire emphatically to point out that temperance legislation has succeeded in the past only so far as the willingness of the community involved has permitted it to succeed. The essential functions of the law are to preserve order, maintain justice, and protect the community. It is not the function of the law to make people good. Whenever it tries to do so without general public support it fails.[29]

A reading of the oral evidence and cross examination of witnesses on the societal management of inebriates or habitual drunkards makes it clear that absolutely no progress had been made in resolving the conflicts discussed above, which had characterized this debate in the late Victorian era. Paradoxically, it was witnesses from the criminal justice sector who were most in favour of conceptualizing inebriety as a disease and managing it within therapeutic as opposed to custodial criminal justice settings. For instance, Mr Sean Troy, a District Justice in the South Tipperary–Waterford area, told the commission that he saw no merit in imposing heavy penalties in his court on habitual drunkards convicted of drunkenness: 'I look upon a man who is addicted to drinking like that as suffering more from a disease. I may be wrong.'[30] The vagueness of the terminology and the unlikelihood that common ground would be found amongst people of differing views may be discerned in the ensuing dialogue between Mr Troy and the commission's chairman, John Horgan, who was clearly sceptical of the value of medicalizing inebriety:

Chairman: But don't you see the effect of this disease is very serious for himself and for everybody else?

Mr Troy: So is cancer and consumption, and every disease of the kind.

Chairman: But is it not a moral disease, a danger to everything and everybody, like every other form of moral disease?

Mr Troy: I wonder?

An earlier witness from the criminal justice system, Mr Mark Cooper (described as a Senior District Justice for Dublin) had expressed sentiments similar to those of Mr Troy. He had agreed with the chairman's view that 'there is only one cure for the dipsomaniac, and that is enforced seclusion', but went on to argue for the revival of the inebriate reformatory system:

Chairman: Would you give power to a District Justice to put away persons of that kind, for a stated period, in a Home, in the same way that you imprison a man for a crime?

Mr Cooper: Well, first of all you would have to provide some kind of institution for them other than a prison.

Chairman: You mean that some kind of Inebriates' Home would have to be provided for them?

Mr Cooper: Yes, I certainly think it would be a wise provision if the Government were to do something on those lines.[31]

While no resident medical superintendent or other representative of the lunatic asylum system gave evidence to the commission, the frustration of trying to manage inebriates within this system was colourfully expressed by an Assistant Commissioner of An Gárda Siochána, who complained that

[They] get into a state of semi-lunacy and a doctor has got to certify them. They are put into an asylum, but they can get out soon again. They cannot be kept under the lunacy jurisdiction once they get sober. They get out, start off again, and the whole thing goes on in a vicious circle.[32]

The only medical witness to appear before the commission was Dr Arthur Shadwell, an English public health doctor who had studied the effects of alcohol controls introduced to Britain under the Defence of the Realm Act during the First World War. These controls had been selectively applied to locations where armaments and munitions were manufactured, but Dr Shadwell had become convinced of the value of continuing such policies so as to reduce the prevalence of alcohol-related problems in peacetime. His views were remarkably similar to those public health views that have been promoted by the World Health Organization since the 1970s,[33] in that he concluded that price (relative to disposable income) and access to retail outlets selling alcohol could be controlled in order to reduce consumption levels and associated problems. He did not, however, argue that the medical profession had a positive role to play in managing inebriates and appeared to have no belief in the efficacy of therapeutic intervention for such clients. When asked – in passing – about habitual drunkards, Dr Shadwell answered briefly: 'The habitual drunkard is impossible. You can do nothing with him.'[34]

The commission recommended some reduction in the number of licensed premises but, as already indicated, refused to countenance the demands made by religious temperance groups for radical restrictions on the sale of alcohol. In relation to societal management of inebriates, however, the commission reaffirmed the scepticism towards therapeutic options, which had been apparent in its questioning of witnesses:

> We are satisfied also that the present law concerning inebriates is entirely inadequate and hedged round by so many absurd requirements as to be practically unenforceable. Inebriate homes [reformatories] are at best degrading institutions, and we have not sufficient evidence to justify us in recommending the revival of the State home for inebriates. We think the only effective home for such people is a gaol, and the only suitable occupation plenty of hard labour. The only places where inebriates who have money cannot get drink are the gaol and the asylum.[35]

These hardline views on the management of inebriates had no discernible impact on policy or practice, and there were no legislative developments in this field until the Mental Treatment Act, 1945, appeared to signify a decisive policy shift towards the medicalization of drinking problems.

MENTAL TREATMENT ACT, 1945

The Mental Treatment Act, 1945, which remained in force until the end of 2006, was of great importance to Ireland's evolving mental health system. It was, for its time, a progressive statute which made provision for the voluntary admission of patients to institutions which were now coming to be referred to as 'mental hospitals', and which set in place a rudimentary system of legal safeguards against wrongful or unnecessary detention in these institutions. It also provided a statutory basis for the development of a range of outpatient psychiatric facilities, although such community-based services and facilities were not to be developed to any great extent for a further twenty years. In relation to the treatment or management of inebriates, the Mental Treatment Act was important because it made specific provision for both the voluntary and involuntary admission to hospital of 'addicts'; in the context of mid-1940s Ireland, one has to assume that this word primarily referred to those deemed to be addicted to alcohol. This legislation defined addicts as follows:

In this Act – the word 'addict' means a person who –

(a) by reason of his addiction to drugs or intoxicants is either dangerous to himself or others or incapable of managing himself or of ordinary proper conduct; or

(b) by reason of his addiction to drugs, intoxicants or perverted conduct is in serious danger of mental disorder.[36]

This inclusion of addiction to drugs or intoxicants as a form of pathology which might appropriately be dealt with within what was now coming to be described as the mental health system took place at a time when the so-called disease concept of alcoholism (which will be discussed in some detail in Chaper 3) was being heavily promoted in the USA. It might, therefore, be inferred that Irish policy on the management of inebriates was finally and unequivocally coming down on the side of the 'medical model'. Such an inference is not supported by a study of the background to this legislation, however, which reveals that support for the treatment of alcoholism within the mental health system was at this time tentative and equivocal. Although the Mental Treatment Bill, 1944, had been in preparation for several years, it contained no specific addiction provisions when first introduced by Dr F.C. Ward, parliamentary secretary at the Department of Local Government and Public Health. Indeed, one could speculate that these provisions might never have been included were it not for the intervention of the Irish Medical Association, which in an editorial on the bill critically noted that it made no reference to alcohol problems:

There is no mention in the Bill of methods for the control and treatment of drug addicts and alcoholics. This is an important, and in itself, a very difficult question. It bristles with legal difficulties, apart altogether from the medical aspects of the condition and, of course, any doctor be he a general practitioner or a psychiatrist, knows how urgent this matter is. Much suffering and misery is caused particularly by the chronic alcoholic who cannot be controlled and who cannot be fully treated under the present system.[37]

Following consultation with the Irish Medical Association and the Medico-Psychological Society (the professional association for the country's psychiatrists), the parliamentary secretary introduced the addiction clauses as an amendment at the committee stage of the legislative process. In introducing this amendment to the Dáil, Dr Ward began by referring to his own work as a general medical practitioner, which had given him direct experience of the difficulties involved in managing inebriates within the mental hospital system. He went on, however, to point out that this addiction amendment did not reflect any policy intent on his part to have the mental hospitals routinely used for the management of such clients; instead, he suggested that this part of the legislation would only be invoked in emergencies, and that his preference was for the creation of some kind of specialist institutions for the care and treatment of problem drinkers:

> I should tell the House that, at this stage, we can only provide the necessary [legal] machinery, and that until such time as suitable institutions are available we cannot deal adequately with the problem that this amendment is intended to deal with. It will only be in case of urgency, or particular emergency, that addicts will be received in the ordinary institutions. In the course of time it is hoped that we may be able to provide special institutions.[38]

Opposition deputies were highly critical of the amendment, arguing that the phrase 'ordinary proper conduct' was extremely vague and would put the hospitals and admitting psychiatrists under pressure to detain troublesome drinkers in a way or to an extent that might be deemed undesirable. Underlying these criticisms, which Dr Ward disregarded, was a suspicion that the addiction amendment had not been fully thought through; as one opposition deputy put it, 'it would seem to be a complete afterthought, although there were five years' consideration'.[39] Subsequent events largely vindicated Dr Ward's critics. The suggestion that 'special institutions' might be provided does not appear to have been raised again. The fact that the Mental Treatment Act provided a statutory basis for the admission and treatment of alcoholics, along with the growing acceptance of the disease concept of alcoholism, led to the emergence of a situation where the mental hospital became, in the words of Dr Dermot Walsh, the 'preferred locale'[40] for dealing with alcohol problems in Ireland. By the mid-1980s such admissions accounted for a quarter of all annual admissions to the country's mental health system.[41]

CONCLUSION

Although the terms *alcoholism* and *alcoholic* were coming to be used to some extent in mid-1940s Ireland, the use of this terminology did not in any way signify a resolution to ongoing controversy about the management of people whose drinking was a constant source of societal disruption. In sociological terms, 'ownership' of drinking problems was still a contested affair, with no agreement as to whether habitual problem drinkers should be categorized as victims of a disease and processed through health care institutions, or as weak-willed degenerates who should be processed through criminal justice institutions or exposed to some kind of religious reformation.[42] While there appeared to be a degree of consensus that the only way to handle problem drinkers was to subject them to some kind of institutional confinement, neither health care nor the criminal justice institutions were particularly keen on accepting this responsibility. Psychiatrists seemed ideologically unconvinced that alcoholism was a genuine mental illness for which they had any useful remedy, while judges, police officers and prison authorities were equally unconvinced of the value of processing alcoholics through their own institutions. This, then, was the Ireland into which AA arrived in 1946: a country which had avoided the ideological extreme of Prohibition, but also a country in which the management of alcohol-related problems continued to be a highly contentious social function.

Chapter Three

Alcoholics Anonymous: Origins, Beliefs and Practices

> In a score of ways, Alcoholics Anonymous was at least by association as American as baseball, apple pie, hot dogs, and the Fourth of July.[1]

This quote from Kurtz (1991), author of what is to all intents and purposes the authorized history of AA, gives some indication of how rooted in its country of origin the fellowship was, and this chapter will explore AA's origins in post-Prohibition 1930s USA. From the perspective of this present study of AA's diffusion to Ireland, however, it is equally if not more important to identify those features of AA which – despite these strong American roots – facilitated its introduction to other societies and cultures and which have allowed it to survive globally for three-quarters of a century. This chapter will, therefore, draw on historical accounts of the establishment of AA in an attempt to present the main characteristics of this unusual 'fellowship', which held its first European meeting in Dublin in November 1946.

Following the outline presented in Chapter 1, the present chapter will focus on the following characteristics of AA: its importance as the first-ever 'mutual-help' movement in the realm of mental health; the centrality of themes of spirituality or religiosity in its programme; its relationship to the wider disease concept of alcoholism; and, finally, its unusual organizational culture and structure. Before looking at these specific aspects of AA, however, it seems useful to offer a summarized account of its establishment and early years. While historic accounts of the founding of AA may vary slightly in tone,[2] there is almost total agreement about the factual details of its establishment in 1935 by its two co-founders, Bill Wilson and Dr Bob Smith.

Bill Wilson (1895–1971), a native of Vermont, has been generally described as a sensitive, self-conscious adolescent who was greatly upset by his parents' divorce and later by the sudden death of his first girlfriend. Having failed in his ambition to secure a place at the Massachusetts Institute of Technology, he attended Norwich University, a military college in Vermont, but once America entered the First World War, in 1917, he was called up by the army and never returned to finish his degree. Wilson was commissioned as a second lieutenant after further training at an officers' training camp in New York State, and in mid-1918 was shipped to Europe, spending time in England and France but arriving too late to see any real military action. His military career, despite its brevity, gave some inkling of the drive and capacity for leadership which he would later demonstrate in his work for the establishment and maintenance of AA. Wilson appears to have had misgivings about the wisdom of starting to drink, reflecting his awareness of a familial tendency towards drinking problems, and his account of his first alcoholic drink – taken at the age of 21 when he was in the army – resembles what would later come to be stock AA descriptions of first exposure to alcohol. Essentially this describes the first experience of alcohol as wonderfully and positively transformative, quickly followed by a realization of the difficulties caused by and the problems involved in maintaining control over this magic substance: 'Well, my self-consciousness was such that I simply had to take that drink', he recalled.

> So I took it, and another one, and then, lo, the miracle! That strange barrier that had existed between me and all men and women seemed to instantly go down. I felt that I belonged where I was, belonged to life; I belonged to the universe; I was a part of things at last. Oh, the magic of those first three or four drinks! I became the life of the party. I actually could please the guests; I could talk freely, volubly; I could talk well. I became suddenly very attracted to those people and fell into a whole series of dates. But I think, even that first

evening, I got thoroughly drunk, and within the next time or two, I passed out completely. But as everybody drank hard, nothing too much was made of that.[3]

Having left the army after the war, Wilson dabbled in a number of ventures before going to work as a stocks analyst on Wall Street in New York, achieving considerable financial success before being badly hit by the stock market crash of 1929. By the early 1930s, however, he had fallen on hard times, not solely because of the parlous state of the stock market but also because of his inability to control his drinking. Like many other Americans, Wilson had been a heavy drinker throughout the Prohibition years – 1920 to 1933 – but by 1934 he could neither sustain any prolonged period of abstinence nor drink in a controlled way. His drinking pattern appears to have been of the 'loss of control' variety, in the sense that he could abstain for variable periods of time but once he resumed drinking he drank incessantly, until his money ran out or he physically collapsed. This pattern of drinking was disastrous both for his work life and for family relationships, although his wife Lois remained supportive and tolerant throughout the years of his worst drinking escapades. Having had a few unsuccessful hospitalizations, Wilson was influenced by a former schoolmate and drinking friend, Ebby Thacher, who, in turn, had been influenced by another apparently hopeless drunk, Rowland Hazard, a patient of the famous Swiss psychiatrist, Carl Jung. Jung's opinion, conveyed to a sceptical and essentially irreligious Wilson, was that the only hope of freeing those who became addicted to alcohol was through a 'spiritual awakening'. In December 1934, Wilson was readmitted to Towns Hospital in New York after another disastrous binge and, while there, he had a dramatic conversion experience, following which he remained abstinent for the rest of his life.

During the early months of his abstinence, Wilson drew heavily on the support of the Oxford Group, a Protestant evangelical movement committed to recreating the ethos and practices of the early Christian church and which offered a structured spiritual programme thought to be appropriate to the needs of recovering alcoholics. In May 1935, however, while on a business trip to Akron, Ohio, he felt dangerously close to taking a drink and through Oxford Group contacts was put in touch with Dr Bob

Smith (1879–1950), a medical doctor some fifteen years Wilson's senior who was also struggling with a huge alcohol problem. Wilson and Smith spoke for hours, and while Smith did have one further drinking bout, he quickly became and remained abstinent following this establishment of a relationship with Wilson. Both men were struck by the value which they derived from simply talking to one another about their shared experience of alcoholism, and following Wilson's return to New York they maintained contact and worked collaboratively on the creation of a support network which would primarily draw on this potential for mutual aid between recovering alcoholics. While Smith continued with his medical career, Wilson effectively devoted the rest of his life to this new venture, which – following its separation from the Oxford Group in 1937 – came to be known as Alcoholics Anonymous. Wilson edited and wrote much of the book *Alcoholics Anonymous* (usually known in AA circles as the 'Big Book'), which contained a summary of the fellowship's programme in the form of the Twelve Steps, as well as a collection of case histories or life stories of early members.[4] By the mid-1940s, Wilson was also working on what came to be known as the Twelve Traditions, a model of governance and administration which has guided AA ever since, both in the USA and throughout its global diffusion.[5] The growth of AA in the USA was initially quite slow and largely based on the two original groups in New York and Akron, but following the publication of a highly positive article by the journalist Jack Alexander in the *Saturday Evening Post* in March 1941 there was a huge spurt of interest and growth which made it imperative that the fellowship address the question of governance.[6] The preamble to the Steps and Traditions is perhaps the most succinct, available summary of what AA is and how it sees itself:

> Alcoholics Anonymous is a fellowship of men and women who share their experience, strength and hope with each other that they may solve their common problem and help others to recover from alcoholism.
>
> The only requirement for membership is a desire to stop drinking. There are no dues or fees for AA membership; we are self-supporting through our own contributions. AA is not allied with any sect, denomination, politics, organization

or institution; does not wish to engage in any controversy; neither endorses nor opposes any causes. Our primary purpose is to stay sober and to help other alcoholics achieve sobriety.[7]

AA AS MUTUAL HELP

The fact that an informal meeting which took place between Bill Wilson and Bob Smith in Akron in June 1935 is usually regarded as the first ever AA meeting, indicates the importance members attach to the mutual help aspect of their fellowship. As far as members are concerned, AA is first and foremost a vehicle that allows alcoholics to help one another through a system of meeting, talking and psychological identification. This latter concept of *identification* refers to the process whereby group members, prone to regarding themselves as unique in their inability to control their drinking or manage their lives, recognize both that others have had a similar experience and that others have succeeded in turning their lives around. Given the subsequent proliferation of mutual-help or self-help organizations in the health sphere (as well as the more recent trend on the part of public health providers to regard service users as 'consumers' whose views should be sought and taken into account in planning and delivering services[8]), one could easily overlook just how radical this perspective was in the 1930s and for many subsequent years. In effect, the establishment of AA represented the first coherent expression of the view that people with emotional and behavioural disorders could help one another, and that such people were not solely and passively dependent upon the technical expertise of professional therapists.

Historically, as was made clear in Chapter 2, the main debating point was whether those problem drinkers coming to be described as alcoholics might be best helped by medical doctors or by clergymen – in circumstances where it was generally assumed that alcoholics could neither help themselves nor others, and where institutional confinement appeared to offer the only real prospect of sustained abstinence. AA, however, while careful to avoid controversy or the expression of ideas which might be construed as critical of doctors or clergymen, offered an alternative to this 'expert' approach, taking the view that nothing could match the unique quality of the help which one alcoholic could offer another. AA members saw themselves as primarily helping one another to remain abstinent, but the kind of abstinence being aimed at was commonly referred to as 'contented sobriety'; a phrase which indicated that becoming abstinent was intended to help alcoholics to improve the overall quality of their lives, rather than leaving them disgruntled or resentful at having to give up one of life's great pleasures. This help continued to be non-professional and, particularly within AA meetings, to be of an oblique nature, with members simply telling their personal stories – what they had been like when they drank, what they did with the help of AA, and how they were at present – rather than inter-acting with one another in the style of conventional group psy-chotherapy. What this means is that at standard meetings AA members tell their own stories or listen to the stories of others without questioning, replying, advising, confronting or interpret-ing: a style of participation sometimes describing as consisting of a 'ban on cross-talk'.[9] As mentioned in Chapter 1, it is recognized that 'old-timers' (that is, members who have sustained many years of sobriety within the fellowship) can serve as useful role models and act as sponsors to newer members outside of formal meet-ings; but there is also a strong egalitarian ethos to the fellowship, reflected in the commonly expressed view that life and sobriety are to be taken 'a day at a time' and that length of sobriety is no guarantee against relapse. This sometimes finds expression in the saying that at an AA meeting the member with the longest period of sobriety is the person who got up earliest on that day. Step Twelve of the fellowship's suggested programme of recovery ('Having had a spiritual awakening as a result of these steps, we tried to carry this message to alcoholics, and to practise these principles in all our affairs') is perhaps the most explicit statement of the importance of mutuality to AA members. There is an obvi-ous altruistic element to this step, which reminds members of the value of offering to others what they themselves have gained from affiliation to the fellowship, but 'twelve-stepping' is also seen as being positively advantageous to those who do it – in the sense that by helping others they also help themselves. This latter emphasis is described in a paradoxical AA saying that 'in order to keep it, you have to give it away'.

Despite this emphasis on AA's responsibility to be available to help what Tradition Five refers to as 'the alcoholic who still suffers', the fellowship also developed a keen sense of the folly and potentially counterproductive effect of any kind of 'hard sell' on the part of its members. In setting up AA as a specific support system for alcoholics quite separate from the Oxford Group, Bill Wilson was motivated, among other things, by a belief that alcoholics were likely to respond badly to being preached at, or to dogmatism or absolutism of any kind. He suspected that alcoholics would refuse to participate – as indeed he himself would – in any therapeutic enterprise which was coercive or which insisted that they *must* adopt any particular line of action, or *must* accept any particular set of beliefs. As will be discussed later in this chapter, the Twelve Steps were offered as a 'suggested' programme of recovery to be considered as an option by actual or potential AA members. This à la carte approach is exemplified in the common recommendation to members finding the programme in its entirety hard to follow, to 'take what you need and leave the rest'. At an administrative or organizational level, members are explicitly reminded in Tradition Eleven that 'Our public relations policy is based on attraction rather than promotion'. In the USA, and to a somewhat lesser extent in other countries, it would appear that the widespread use from the 1970s onwards of what is commonly known as the Minnesota Model (an alcoholism treatment model which draws substantially on elements of AA's programme, albeit within professionally run centres) has been confused with AA and has caused some observers to attribute to AA qualities of aggression and dogmatism that it would certainly disavow.[10] In summary, therefore, the mutual-help aspect of AA is central to the fellowship's overall functioning: members act on the basis that a sharing of experience and life stories by alcoholics is uniquely helpful, and that a central part of recovery is a willingness to make this experience available to other alcoholics still struggling with alcohol problems.

AA AS A SPIRITUAL MOVEMENT

Although AA members routinely speak of alcoholism as a disease or illness that has physical, mental, emotional and spiritual dimensions to it, it is clear from even the most superficial study of the Twelve Steps that it is the spiritual dimension which takes precedence in the fellowship's approach to recovery. In the Big

Book (and, incidentally, in a chapter of the Big Book entitled 'We Agnostics'), the primacy of spirituality is emphasized as follows:

> We hope we have made clear the distinction between the alcoholic and the non-alcoholic. If, when you honestly want to, you find you cannot quit entirely, or if when drinking you have little control over the amount you take, you are probably alcoholic. If that be the case, you may be suffering from an illness which only a spiritual experience will conquer.[11]

It is only in Step One that alcohol is actually mentioned and in none of the subsequent steps is there any reference to conventional medical or psychological therapies; instead, the steps as a whole outline a programme that starts from an admission of defeat and thereafter places primary emphasis on personal conversion to and reliance on a Higher Power (or 'God as we understood Him') in the quest for sobriety and sanity. In short, the Twelve Steps are suggested to potential fellowship members as a lifelong spiritual programme, as much perhaps an end in itself as a technical means to an end. In Ireland in the 1940s the Catholic Church was a dominant institution – theologically, socially and politically – and might well have been expected to resent this new fellowship, which had its origins in the Protestant evangelical tradition of the USA. Conventional Catholic teaching and practice in this pre-Vatican Two era was often antagonistic to ecumenical or interdenominational movements, tending to the view that the Catholic Church was uniquely efficacious as a channel of God's grace, thereby leaving it unclear why alcoholic Catholics should have any need of this new institutional link to a vaguely defined 'Higher Power'. In view of this potential for conflict or tensions between AA and the Catholic Church, particularly in Ireland, it seems useful to look here in more detail at Bill Wilson's original conversion experience and at the effort he subsequently put into ensuring that AA could retain its emphasis on spirituality, albeit in a way that would facilitate participation in the fellowship by atheists and agnostics and which would avoid antagonism with existing institutional religions.

Wilson's conversion experience in December 1934, about which he was subsequently reticent, was nothing if not dramatic. Having been readmitted to Towns Hospital under the care of Dr William Silkworth, a physician who specialized in helping alcoholics,

Wilson was overwhelmed by despair and frustration at his inability
to come to grips with his alcohol problem. He was 39 years old,
physically healthy and with the energy, experience and ability to
excel in a variety of occupational spheres; but, because of his loss
of control over alcohol, he was effectively broke and was rapidly
losing the trust of family, friends and work associates. One
prospect facing him was that, in order to prevent further health
and social decline, which appeared to be the inevitable consequence of his drinking, he would have to be admitted to some
kind of permanent institutional care. As he later described it,
his spiritual experience took place when he was on his own in a
hospital room, and commenced when he cried out in distress: 'If
there be a God, let him show Himself'.

> What happened next was electric. Suddenly, my room
> blazed with an indescribable white light. I was seized with an
> ecstasy beyond description. Every joy I had known was pale
> by comparison. The light, the ecstasy – I was conscious of
> nothing else for a time.
>   Then, seen in the mind's eye, there was a mountain. I
> stood upon its summit, where a great wind blew. A wind, not
> of air, but of spirit. In great, clean strength, it blew right
> through me. Then came the blazing thought 'You are a free
> man.' I know not at all how long I remained in this state, but
> finally the light and the ecstasy subsided. I again saw the wall
> of my room. As I became more quiet, a great peace stole
> over me, and this was accompanied by a sensation difficult
> to describe. I became acutely conscious of a Presence which
> seemed like a veritable sea of living spirit. I lay on the shores
> of a new world. 'This', I thought, 'must be the great reality.
> The God of the preachers.'[12]

It should be made clear that Bill Wilson did not expect that
such dramatic conversion experiences would be the norm for
alcoholics entering AA, and it is worth pointing out that his co-
founder Bob Smith had no such experience; neither did Wilson
expect that his own experience was sufficient to guarantee him
lifelong abstinence from alcohol. Unlike Father Mathew, who
appeared to believe that by taking the pledge which he administered to them, people would remain teetotal thereafter, Wilson
had a keen sense of the necessity to provide ongoing support for

those embarking on such a radical lifestyle change. In its immediate aftermath, there were two further events which helped Wilson to understand how he could use this experience both for his own continuing sobriety and as a means of helping other alcoholics. The first of these was when he asked Dr Silkworth whether what he had experienced was a psychotic episode, a hallucination which merely offered further evidence of his own deterioration into alcoholism and insanity. In reply, the doctor assured him that he was quite sane, that he had gone through a conversion experience which Silkworth could not pretend to understand but that the effect of this experience was a positive one, to be welcomed and nurtured: 'You are already a different individual. So, my boy, whatever you've got now, you'd better hold on to. It's so much better than what you had only a couple of hours ago.'[13]

The second event to influence Wilson was the serendipitous gift of a book from his friend Ebby Thacher, who had visited him in hospital just a few days after his conversion experience. The book, *The Varieties of Religious Experience*, had been written by the Harvard philosopher and psychologist William James (1842–1910) and was based on the Gifford Lectures series he had delivered at Edinburgh University in 1901 and 1902; it was primarily concerned with exploring the validity of religious *experience* as opposed to religious *ideas*. Amongst other things, James wrote at length about conversion experiences similar to that which Bill Wilson had just had. For Wilson, whose previous academic studies had included no philosophy or psychology, this cannot have been an easy read, but he appears to have read through it immediately and with considerable excitement, finding in it support and encouragement for his own continuing recovery from alcoholism as well as possibilities for the provision of help to other alcoholics. The two main aspects of the *Varieties* which appealed to Wilson were those most frequently noted by academic commentators,[14] namely its pragmatism and its pluralism. In the case of pragmatism, what James was espousing was a philosophy that assessed the validity of ideas not in relation to the extent to which they could be demonstrated to accurately mirror some objective reality, but in relation to their practical consequences or fruits. Menand has concluded that 'James's pragmatism was not a philosophy for policy makers, muck-rakers, and social scientists. It was a philosophy for misfits, mystics, and geniuses – people who believed in mental telepathy, or immortality, or God. James was never able to believe unreservedly in any of those things himself; but to the end of his life, he tried'[15] – a description which arguably could also be applied to Bill Wilson. From his reading of the *Varieties*, Wilson went on to see recovery from alcoholism as based on experience – what people did and continued to do, as opposed to what they believed or claimed to believe – and this would later be reflected in the nature of AA, which simply encouraged alcoholics to go to meetings and 'work' the programme. In relation to pluralism, Wilson found in his reading of James support for his own tendency to favour ideological and institutional diversity in the religious sphere, thereby avoiding the situation where recovering alcoholics were dragooned into believing that their recovery was dependent on acceptance of one specific theological system. From the *Varieties* Bill Wilson took the view that it would be foolish either to describe his emerging fellowship as having a monopoly on recovery from alcoholism or as a fellowship in which all members had to share precisely the same set of religious beliefs. In the Big Book the only academic source referred to is William James:

> The distinguished American psychologist, William James, in his book 'Varieties of Religious Experience' indicates a multitude of ways in which men have discovered God. We have no desire to convince anyone that there is only one way by which faith can be acquired. If what we have learned and felt and seen means anything at all, it means that all of us, whatever our race, creed or colour are the children of a living Creator with whom we may form a relationship upon simple and understandable terms as soon as we are willing and honest enough to try. Those having religious affiliations will find here nothing disturbing to their beliefs or ceremonies. There is no friction among us over such matters.[16]

Such was the influence of this book on Bill Wilson at this highly impressionable stage in his own recovery that it is not surprising that he would later say that – though long dead – William James was a founder of AA.[17]

Although it was to be almost thirty years after the fellowship's foundation before he made contact with the psychiatrist Carl Jung to acknowledge the influence which Jung's ideas had had on him, there is no doubt that Wilson was greatly struck by Jung's ideas – conveyed, admittedly, at third hand – on the primacy of spirituality in recovery from alcoholism. Writing to Jung in early 1961, shortly before Jung's death, Wilson explained how he had developed his hope that 'If each sufferer were to carry the news of the scientific hopelessness of alcoholism to each new prospect, he might be able to lay every newcomer wide open to a trans-forming spiritual experience.'[18] Jung responded very positively to this letter, concluding with a summary comment (which would later be much cited by fellowship members) on his view that spir-ituality represented the only real solution to alcoholism:

> You see, alcohol in Latin is 'spiritus' and you use the same word for the highest religious experience as the most depraving poison. The helpful formula therefore is: *spiritus contra spiritum.*[19]

As already mentioned, the early months of Wilson's recovery were spent in involvement with the Oxford Group, an evangeli-cal Christian movement to which he had been introduced by his friend Ebby Thacher. The Oxford Group was a non-denomina-tional movement which had been founded in 1908 by Frank Buchman (1878–1961), a former Lutheran pastor from Pennsylvania whose ambition was to recreate what he perceived to be the spirit and practice of first-century Christianity.[20] Buchman had concentrated his ministry on young people, partic-ularly young people within the university system, and his move-ment took its name from a somewhat tenuous connection to Oxford University. The Oxford Group, as developed by Buchman, was characterized by a return to fundamental New Testament religion, revolving around meetings of small groups of believers in private homes where members were encouraged to confess their faults to one another, to make reparation for hurt caused to other people and to surrender themselves entirely to God.[21] Wilson was greatly helped by one New York clergyman, the Reverend Sam Shoemaker, who ran a mission along Oxford Group lines, and he and Bob Smith initially seemed satisfied to view their work as constituting the 'alcoholic squadron' of the Oxford Group. However, within two years Wilson had severed his connection with the Oxford Group, and, while continuing to draw substantially upon the group's beliefs, he saw his work thereafter as aimed solely at helping alcoholics. The Akron group, while more reluctant to sever its connection with the Oxford Group, did so a little later.

The reasons why Bill Wilson left the Oxford Group and set up AA as a fellowship in its own right are relatively plain to see. Frank Buchman had always been a controversial character, and remarks he made in 1936 in support of Adolf Hitler did nothing to persuade Wilson that he should continue to hitch his wagon to this particular star. Buchman persisted in seeing the Oxford Group as having the potential to have a positive impact on international affairs, and in 1938 he changed its name to Moral Rearmament, a name it retained until 2001. As Wilson's ideas gradually evolved, he had become increasingly and more explicitly clear that the purpose of AA should be the modest one of helping alcoholics to stop drinking; it should avoid involvement with ambitious schemes aimed at global transformation. On a more practical level, however, it was the Oxford Group's insistence on 'absolutes' (such as, for example, the group's belief in absolute honesty, absolute purity, absolute unselfishness and absolute love as goals for its members) and the aggressive style of its evangelization which ultimately proved too much for Wilson, who, despite his own dramatic conversion experience, continued to be extremely wary of all organized religions. It was not that he objected to the ideals of the Oxford Group, but rather that he – and he suspected most alcoholics – were put off by their use of the word *absolute*: 'when the word "absolute" was put in front of these attributes, they either turned people away by the hundreds or gave a temporary spiritual inflation resulting in collapse'.[22] Wilson was also conscious of the fact that the Oxford Group, while tolerated by the more mainstream Protestant churches, was considered highly suspect by the Catholic Church, and that this would make it difficult, if not impossible, for Catholic alcoholics to become part of the alcoholic squadron of the Oxford Group: 'Since there are plenty of alcoholic Catholics, why deprive them of their chance by being dogmatic, when experience shows that is entirely unnecessary?'[23]

The consequences of leaving the group are reflected most clearly in Wilson's drafting of the Twelve Steps. The *content* of the Steps is very obviously based on the Oxford Group's programme of spirituality and contains all of the familiar references:

human helplessness and the necessity for absolute reliance on God; confession of sin; restitution where possible; regular prayer and meditation; proselytization. The *language* of the Steps, however, demonstrates the influence of William James in its determination to encourage potential AA members to define God and spirituality in their own way: for example, 'a Power greater than ourselves' (Step Two) and 'God as we understood Him' (Steps Three and Eleven). The intent was to retain the central emphasis on spirituality, but to do so in a way that would be as inclusive as possible and might be acceptable to people from all sectarian religious backgrounds, as well as to atheists or agnostics who could define their Higher Power without reference to conventional theistic beliefs. The pragmatic influence is also clearly revealed in the style in which Wilson wrote the Twelve Steps, all of which are written in the past tense and with no use of the imperative; it is as if early AA members are simply saying 'We did this and found it helpful', the implication being that other alcoholics, should they choose to do so, were free to try this course of action.

Despite having removed his fledgling fellowship from its immersion within a fundamentalist Protestant grouping, Wilson appears to have remained acutely aware of the risk of antagonism – or worse – on the part of Catholic Church leaders. For example, when the Big Book was in draft form in 1939, one of the few Catholic members of the fellowship, Morgan R., was asked to use his contacts within the New York Archdiocesan chancery to read an advance copy and see whether it contained anything objectionable from a Catholic perspective. This was not a formal attempt to gain the *imprimatur* of the Archbishop of New York, which would almost certainly have proved off-putting to many non-Catholic readers, but Wilson was greatly relieved to hear that Morgan's contact had thoroughly approved of the book and had found nothing in it which could be deemed offensive to Catholic sensibilities.[24]

In 1940 an Irish-American Jesuit, Fr Ed Dowling, who was based in St Louis, Missouri, visited Wilson in New York and began what was to be an important friendship, which lasted until Dowling's death in 1960. Dowling was not an alcoholic, but he had become interested in the Twelve Steps and intrigued by what he perceived as their resemblance to the Spiritual Exercises of Saint Ignatius Loyola. The fact that Wilson knew nothing of

Catholic spirituality and had never heard of Ignatius Loyola amused Dowling, and seems to have whetted his appetite for further exploration of the common features of these two programmes – particularly the shared paradoxical belief that power and strength could only arise from admission of total powerlessness.[25] Influenced by Dowling and others, Wilson began in 1947 to take instruction in the Catholic faith from the well-known Monsignor Fulton Sheen, but, despite finding many aspects of it attractive, he ultimately baulked at conversion to Catholicism. He later suggested that he had feared that his conversion would be damaging to AA, but Kurtz tends to the view that – as with his reaction to the Oxford Group – his decision was primarily influenced by an inability to cope with the absolutism of religious dogma; in a letter of 1948 to a friend, Wilson wrote: 'The thing that still irks me about all organized religion is their claim how confoundedly right all of them are.'[26] At no point did the hierarchy of the Catholic Church in the USA give AA its unequivocal blessing, and there were occasional attacks or criticisms from individual clergymen,[27] but AA made many influential friends within American Catholicism and no church leader argued that membership of AA was incompatible with membership of the Catholic Church.

AA AND THE DISEASE CONCEPT OF ALCOHOLISM

If, as has been discussed, AA had a primary focus on spirituality while refusing to be pigeon-holed in terms of any of the conventional sectarian religions, then its adherence to the disease concept of alcoholism – and what this implies about its relationship to the medical profession – is even more complex and ambiguous. Stated simply, what came to be known as the 'disease concept' of alcoholism had its origins in post-Prohibition America and essentially consisted of a belief that alcoholism existed as a discrete, unitary disease, the primary symptom of which was loss of control and the primary cause of which was some, as yet to be specified, biological vulnerability or predisposition.[28] A central tenet of the disease concept is that alcohol is *not* the cause of alcoholism, since only a minority of drinkers become alcoholic, and, implicitly at least, the disease concept argues that alcoholism is a treatable condition which should be managed in a non-moralistic way within the health care system. Unlike nineteenth-century versions of the disease concept, which had either seen alcoholism as the inevitable consequence of continued alcohol consumption or had argued that it was a 'disease of the will' and best left to religion, this 'modern' disease concept appeared to be a good cultural fit for a society that was coming to see its temperance movements and its legal Prohibition of alcohol as old-fashioned and moralistic. The new scientific approach, which was how its adherents sold the disease concept, offered no succour to moralists who would deny well-informed adults the right to drink alcohol, and it also implied that the treatment of alcoholism was subject to the same relentless progress of medical science as was to be found in other areas of the health care system.

In a much cited book on the disease concept of alcoholism published in 1960, E.M. Jellinek commented on those involved in promoting the disease concept:

> Around 1940 the phrase 'new approach to alcoholism' was coined, and since then this phrase has been heard again and again, every time that the Yale Center of Alcohol Studies, the National Council on Alcoholism, Alcoholics Anonymous, or individual students make an utterance to the effect that 'alcoholism is a disease'.[29]

Within the social science and historical literature on this topic, there is broad consensus that there was indeed an alcoholism movement in the USA – including the National Council on Alcoholism (NCA) and the Yale Center referred to by Jellinek – but there is no evidence to support the implication that AA was part of this coalition of stakeholders. Nowhere in what might be considered AA's core texts – the Big Book, the Twelve Steps and Twelve Traditions – is it stated unequivocally that alcoholism is a disease, and, as the 1940s proceeded, the fellowship took the view that debate about the status of alcoholism was a matter of scientific controversy on which it had no view. This stance was explicitly supported by Tradition Ten, which says: 'Alcoholics Anonymous has no opinion on outside issues; hence the AA name ought never be drawn into public controversy.' What prompted AA to take such a clear stance of neutrality on this issue was the controversy surrounding the establishment in 1944 of the NCA by Marty Mann, one of the very early women members of the fellowship. Members were initially uneasy that, by identifying herself as an alcoholic as part of her lobbying activities, Marty Mann was breaking the tradition of anonymity, but much more unease followed when Bill Wilson and Bob Smith became members of the advisory board of the NCA, allowing their names (albeit without reference to AA) to appear on NCA letterheads. When the NCA began a public appeal for funds in 1946, implying in the process that it was linked to or approved by AA, this sparked a mass revolt from the AA grass roots, following which Wilson and Smith severed all connections with the NCA.[30] The decision to break with Marty Mann and the NCA reflected the fellowship's broader organizational policy, as reflected in the Twelve Traditions, not to become involved in political lobbying of any kind lest such activities would 'divert us from our primary purpose' (Tradition Six) – which was to offer help to alcoholics. This is not to say that AA members were antipathetic to the aims of the NCA, particularly the aim of providing help for alcoholics in a style that was non-moralistic and non-stigmatizing, merely that they judged lobbying of this kind to be a distraction best avoided. In practical terms, what this has meant is that, from this time on, AA as a fellowship has never become involved in lobbying for the incorporation of the disease concept into public policy and has also refrained from expressing opinion on licensing legislation, alcohol taxation, advertising and promotion of alcohol, alcoholism treatment policy or any other aspect of public policy on alcohol.

Just as AA strove to form positive relationships with all religious groupings while insisting on retaining absolute independence in relation to its own programme of spirituality, its relationship to the health care system is similarly marked by a desire for collaboration, albeit in the context of maintaining its own independence. Fellowship members have always spoken, and continue to speak, of alcoholism as a disease or an illness, but such descriptions are highly ambiguous and appear to be in the realm of metaphor rather than science; members primarily see themselves as suffering from an illness 'which only a spiritual experience will conquer'. All through its history, AA has tried to co-operate with medical doctors and with professional alcoholism treatment systems – principally by running meetings in detoxification and rehabilitation centres – while resolutely keeping away from debates about alcoholism and its diagnosis. Whether or not its members have been medically diagnosed as alcohol dependent has always been immaterial, since what counts within the fellowship is self-diagnosis: members are those who have a desire to stop drinking and who attend meetings. Again, one can discern the influence of pragmatism in the sense that AA has little or nothing of a scientific or ideological nature to say about *alcoholism*: instead, its concern is to offer a programme of action for *alcoholics*. This approach might in religious terms be described as favouring *orthopraxy* over *orthodoxy*: that is, doing the right thing rather than holding the right beliefs. It has meant that the fellowship has remained largely unchanged over the decades, displaying no interest in conventional scientific research or in modifying its approach to incorporate new research findings. The message which it seeks to convey to potential members is virtually unchanged from that worked out in the first decade of its existence: 'if you're an alcoholic and wish to stop drinking, then you're welcome to attend our meetings and work our programme'. It is understandable, however, that in the public mind AA has contributed to the popularity of the simple idea that 'alcoholism is a disease'. Kurtz, in a summary comment on the complex relationship between AA and the disease concept, concluded that

> On the basic question, the data are clear: Contrary to common opinion, Alcoholics Anonymous neither originated nor promulgated what has come to be called the disease concept of alcoholism. Yet its members did have a large role in spreading and popularizing that understanding.[31]

The decision of AA to maintain an official position of neutrality in relation to the disease concept of alcoholism proved, as will be shown in some detail in Chapter 5, to be a shrewd one. Social science and biomedical research did not, as had been expected, provide unequivocal support for the basic tenets of the disease concept, thereby rendering redundant all moral discussion and policy controversy on these matters. Instead, historical and sociological writers helped to clarify how the initial enthusiasm for the disease concept had reflected the particular circumstances of post-Prohibition USA rather than any significant scientific progress in this sphere. In 1962, for example, an American sociologist, John Seeley, had expressed reservations about the uncritical way in which its advocates had promoted and publicized the notion that 'alcoholism is a disease', since this 'conceals what is essential – that is, that a step in public policy is being *recommended*, not a scientific discovery *announced* [italics original]'.[32] By the mid-1970s and persuaded by what it saw as the compelling weight of the epidemiological evidence, the WHO had effectively dropped all support for the disease concept, reverting to a public health position which was that alcohol – due to its toxicity, its addictive properties and its capacity to intoxicate – had a risk potential for all its consumers, and that increased levels of consumption in any given population would inevitably be reflected in an increased prevalence of a range of alcohol-related problems.[33] In other words, alcohol was not – as proponents of the disease concept tended to argue – a threat solely to those born with a predisposition or 'allergy' to this substance, and the policy implication was that the state was entitled, if not obliged, to implement public policies that would reduce or stabilize societal consumption. Such policies (which included the use of fiscal measures to keep alcohol prices high and a range of licensing strategies aimed at restricting public access to retail outlets) seemed scientifically justifiable to the public health community, but to the drinks industry they were a form of 'neo-Prohibitionism'. In the face of this continuing policy controversy and moral debate about the role of the state in preventing alcohol-related problems, the decision of AA not to adopt any official position on the disease concept would seem to have been organizationally prudent.

AA: ORGANIZATIONAL CULTURE AND STRUCTURES

It was noted in Chapter 2 that the Father Mathew temperance movement in nineteenth-century Ireland had, despite the dramatic successes it initially enjoyed, failed to survive its founder because no organizational structures had been set in place. From a relatively early stage of his work with AA, however, Bill Wilson appears to have been acutely aware of the dangers of charismatic leadership – of turning the fellowship into the 'Bill Wilson movement'; it was, he believed, necessary to create organizational structures which would ensure AA's long-term survival following his own resignation, death or relapse into active alcoholism. He gradually became convinced of the necessity to create a style of governance which would reflect the content of the fellowship's Twelve Steps, clearly believing that it would be incongruous to have a spiritual programme based on personal humility and service to others housed within a corporate structure based on top-down, hierarchical relationships. Although Wilson continued to play a major leadership role in the fellowship until the 1955 'coming of age' conference in St Louis, he had by 1946 – the year that AA came to Ireland – drafted and got agreement for the Twelve Traditions, which encapsulate the fellowship's commitment to its unique style of governance. The main features of this style, which will now be looked at in some detail, were: an emphasis on anonymity; the establishment of a non-hierarchical or bottom-up leadership; the commitment to remaining non-professional; and the singularity of the fellowship's focus on helping alcoholics, while eschewing all involvement with public policy on alcohol or endorsement of any external organizations working in the field of prevention or treatment.

The principle of anonymity refers to the tradition whereby AA members are enjoined not to publicly acknowledge or disclose their membership of the fellowship and, even with fellow members, are encouraged to stick to the custom of identifying themselves primarily by first names, or by first names and the first initial of their family names – as in Bill W. or Bob S. Since the fellowship is Alcoholics *Anonymous*, this self-evidently is a key principle and as such deserves some explanation. The first and perhaps most obvious explanation is that members are urged to preserve anonymity as a means of protecting themselves against the stigma which has been commonly associated with alcoholism, and there is undoubtedly some validity in this explanation. The dominant explanation to emerge from the historical literature, however, is that anonymity was set in place so as to encourage recovering alcoholics to keep a low personal profile, lest they become complacent and egotistical, thereby putting their recovery at risk and, in the process, bringing the whole fellowship into disrepute. Bill Wilson saw the AA programme (and particularly Steps One and Two, which speak of powerlessness and reliance on a Higher Power) as starting from the experience of 'deflation at depth',[34] by which he meant the painful and humiliating acknowledgement for alcoholics that – left to their own devices – they could not control their drinking. His fear was that in recovery they might, should they personally identify themselves as members of AA and start to proselytize, become so egotistical that this would lead to relapse:

> Excessive personal publicity or prominence in the work was found to be bad. Alcoholics who talked too much on public platforms were likely to become inflated and get drunk again. Our principle of anonymity, so far as the general public is concerned, partly corrects this difficulty by preventing any individual receiving a lot of newspaper or magazine publicity, then collapsing and discrediting AA.[35]

Bill Wilson took the principle of anonymity very seriously with regard to his own role in AA, and it was not until after his death that fellowship members began to use his full name; indeed there are still members who insist on referring to him as Bill W. Wilson turned down an offer of an honorary degree from Yale on the basis that even if he accepted it as Bill W., co-founder of AA, this would contravene the fellowship's principle of anonymity, and he also refused to appear on the cover of *Time* magazine – even though the proposal was to photograph him with his back to the camera.[36] While some of the earlier biographical writing tended to be hagiographical, recent studies of Wilson[37] have presented a 'warts and all' account of his life, work and personality. His failure to deal with his own heavy smoking habit, which undoubtedly contributed to his death from emphysema, was already well known, as were his periodic struggles with depression; what was less known was his obsession with spiritualism and his frequent use of a ouija board, and – most shockingly for those who saw him as a great spiritual leader – his numerous sexual infidelities throughout a long married life. Had he been confronted about these oddities and shortcomings, Wilson would almost certainly have pointed out that the work he did on establishing AA's administrative structures and culture was precisely aimed at saving the fellowship from people like himself. He would probably also have pointed out that he had never claimed to be a saint or put himself forward as a model of perfection, and that he as an individual is unimportant to AA: as the Twelfth Tradition puts it, 'Anonymity is the spiritual foundation of all our traditions, ever reminding us to place principles over personalities.'

The second aspect of the fellowship's governance style or

administrative culture to be looked at here is its commitment to a democratic style of leadership and the avoidance of hierarchical authority and centralized control systems. This is clearly manifest in the Traditions, particularly the following:

> *Tradition Two*: For our group purpose there is but one ultimate authority – a loving God as He may express himself in our group conscience. Our leaders are but trusted servants; they do not govern.
>
> *Tradition Four*: Each group should be autonomous except in matters affecting other groups or AA as a whole.
>
> *Tradition Nine*: AA, as such, ought never be organized; but we may create service boards or committees directly responsible to those they serve.

This creation of what would in the early twenty-first century be described as a 'leaderless organization'[38] may have owed something to Bill Wilson's conservative political roots in Vermont and his suspicions of 'big Government'. Primarily, however, as revealed in his writings on the Traditions in *The Grapevine* and elsewhere, it reflected his belief that alcoholics would not accept a conventional, corporate style of governance in which a ruling elite handed down detailed instructions as to what members should do and what they should believe. As the fellowship had grown, disputes at local level had frequently been referred to Bill Wilson for adjudication, but he had discovered that 'heavy-handed assertion of my personal authority always created confusion and resistance',[39] and so he had gradually moved towards the position that individual groups had to use their own 'group conscience' to resolve conflicts and controversies. Such conflict resolution within AA groups did not necessarily presume that a consensus would emerge, nor did it favour taking votes to establish the majority view; where a compromise position could not be achieved, it was accepted that dissident members could simply start an alternative group. This latter option gave rise to another well-known AA witticism that all one needs to start a new group is 'a coffee pot and a resentment'. In practice, what this means is that even in a small town in rural Ireland where one AA group would be quite sufficient, a disgruntled member has the option of renting the hall on nights not already taken by the original group, thereby starting an alternative group, which has precisely the same status as the town's first group.

In a strongly Catholic culture such as that of Ireland in the 1940s, it is likely that the old Latin phrase *servus servorum Dei* (servant of the servants of God), used as a description of the Pope, would have some currency. How convincing such a description was, given the doctrine of papal infallibility and the generally ultramontane style of Catholic Church leadership, is a moot point, but certainly the contrast between this type of leadership and the style of leadership of AA – with no 'visible head' and no centralized teaching authority – could not have been more stark. The third aspect of AA to be looked at here, its decision to 'remain forever non-professional' (Tradition Eight), is one which evolved slowly. All of the histories provide accounts of how Bill Wilson, Bob Smith and other early members, in the first flush of enthusiasm and ambition for their new fellowship, entertained the idea that members would be paid for their work with other alcoholics and that AA would go on to run its own hospitals and clinics. As early as 1937, Wilson himself had been offered a job as a therapist in Towns Hospital (the scene of his own conversion experience), but despite being broke and in serious need of financial stability, he had conceded to the 'group conscience' of his New York AA peers that such a move would not be in the best interests of the fellowship, and so he turned down this offer.[40] At about the same time, in an attempt to put AA on a more stable organizational footing and to professionalize its activities, he had looked for philanthropic support and had been put in touch with the millionaire John D. Rockefeller, Jnr. Rockefeller was highly impressed with what he saw and heard, but took the view that this uniquely spiritual enterprise would be spoilt by money and so gave only very limited amounts to facilitate the creation of a foundation to oversee its survival and growth.[41] Ultimately, Wilson and the fellowship generally came to the conclusion that Rockefeller was right: that members should not be paid for their Twelve Step work and, furthermore, that AA should neither create its own hospitals and clinics nor become involved in acquiring properties or building up monetary assets. The view taken, as set out in Tradition Six, was that 'problems of money, property and prestige' might 'divert us from our primary purpose'. Tradition Seven simply says: 'Every AA group ought to be fully self-supporting, declining outside contributions.' In keeping with these traditions, AA operates a simple system of mutual support for its members, with minimal formal organization and without making any demand or request for funding from statutory health or social service authorities. In that it doesn't seek statutory or philanthropic financial support and doesn't engage in any other form of voluntary fundraising, AA is unusual if not unique amongst voluntary health and social service systems.

Finally, AA decided at an early point in its evolution to concentrate solely on helping alcoholics and not to become involved in lobbying or in policy activities relating to wider alcohol policy issues. Again, it is clear from Wilson's writings[42] that early members were tempted to develop the fellowship as a high-profile organization that would claim expertise in all aspects of alcohol policy. What changed their minds, however, was an awareness of how earlier movements, particularly the Washingtonian movement, which had achieved spectacular success in helping alcoholics in mid-nineteenth century USA, had been distracted and terminally damaged through involvement in contentious public debates on the wider 'alcohol problem'. It remained open, of course, to individual AA members to commit themselves in either a voluntary or professional capacity to working with societal alcohol issues, so long as in doing so they retained their anonymity and did not draw the fellowship into public controversy. In practice, what this meant was that as AA became established in Ireland it was unlikely to express views on or lobby for policy or legislative developments relating to alcohol, and the fellowship was unlikely to seek or accept representation on committees set up to advise on any aspect of alcohol policy.

CONCLUSION

While AA continued to evolve until the 1960s, its basic structures and unique organizational culture had been substantially formed by the time it was established in Ireland in late 1946. It was, as Kurtz observed, a very American institution, particularly by virtue of its pragmatic *modus operandi*: it had no pretensions of a scientific or philosophical kind in relation to defining or explaining alcoholism, but merely offered a suggested programme which some alcoholics at least had found helpful and which its members thought was likely to be helpful to others. It was pluralist, in the sense that it curbed the enthusiasm of any members who might be tempted to say that their way of recovery was the only way, or that within the fellowship there was just one acceptable approach to spirituality. From the perspective of governance, AA obviously reflected an American political suspicion of hierarchy, a strong egalitarian tendency and a preference for maximizing democratic participation in human institutions. In considering its likely impact on the Irish scene, there are obvious difficulties and pitfalls which can be readily envisaged in relation to the two institutions, health care and religion, with which it was most associated.

From the perspective of the health care system, AA was puzzling in that its emphasis on mutual help – the idea that one alcoholic could help another – was previously unknown and could well have been seen as a threat to the hegemony of the medical profession: a particular threat of course to psychiatrists who, however unwillingly, had been given and accepted institutional responsibility for the management of drinking problems within the Irish health care system. It remained to be seen how Irish AA members would negotiate working relationships with psychiatrists, a professional group more accustomed to seeing alcoholics in terms of incompetence and irresponsibility than in terms of an allegedly unique therapeutic potential for mutual aid. Brendan Behan is usually credited with the saying that when any organization is formed in Ireland, the first item on the agenda is the split; when, as in this instance, organizational membership is solely based on a personal history of alcoholism, it must surely have occurred to some of the professionals involved that this organization had little chance of remaining intact or avoiding major internal conflicts and splits. That AA, which from its early days in this country, saw itself as a 32-county institution, has never experienced either an internal split or major conflict with the medical profession is remarkable.

On the religious side, the coming of AA to Ireland – a country that arguably already had a surfeit of religiosity – was not without its problems. If the fellowship's founders had worried about how the Catholic Church in the USA would react to this new movement, which placed such emphasis on spirituality, then early Irish members could be expected to be even more anxious about the reaction of church leaders in this country. In a society in which the Catholic Church played a dominant role in health and social service provision, as well as exercising what Tom Inglis has called a 'moral monopoly'[43] in broader cultural terms, it could not be seen as unduly paranoid of AA members to fear attack from church leaders. The fact that the fellowship was first established in Dublin during the Primacy of Archbishop John Charles McQuaid gave even greater cause for concern, given McQuaid's overall controlling instincts and his antagonism towards ecumenical activities.[44] McQuaid might well have objected to the centrality of spirituality within the fellowship, a spirituality which from his perspective was already adequately catered for by the Catholic Church. Given his own authoritarian tendencies, he might also have been puzzled by the absence of identifiable leadership within AA, a fact that to him might have smacked of anarchy. What will be explored in some detail in the next chapter, therefore, is how early fellowship members perceived this threat of attack from Catholic Church authorities and the measures they took to counter this.

Finally, and on a positive note, it can be seen that despite being clearly rooted in American history and culture, AA was eminently suited for global diffusion because of its style of governance. There was no question of American members, or administrators in its emerging foundation office in New York, laying down the law and telling Irish members precisely what they could and could not do. In keeping with its respect for the autonomy of individual groups, one could expect that the New York office would simply offer non-prescriptive advice and support to the new Dublin group and to other Irish groups that were subsequently formed. This was a style of governance which accepted that within the basic unity of the fellowship there was room for considerable diversity; how AA took root and flourished in Ireland will be looked at in detail in the pages that follow.

Chapter Four

Alcoholics Anonymous in Ireland: Peaceful Coexistence with the Catholic Church

Alcoholics Anonymous got started in Ireland in 1946 when Connor [*sic*] F., an AA tavern owner from Philadelphia decided to go on a vacation with his wife to the Emerald Isle. When they got to Dublin they both said, 'Never mind the vacation: let's start a group here'. So they made their way to a local mental hospital, the one endowed by the author-clergyman Swift, and there they found their first man, Richard P. And so AA began to take root in Ireland. The Dublin group, by the way, has achieved special renown because of its world correspondent, Sackville M., the group's honorable secretary. When it comes to helping alcoholics by mail, he is no doubt the world's champion.[1]

GETTING STARTED

This folksy summary of how AA came to be established in Ireland was originally presented by Bill Wilson in 1955, during the fellowship's 'coming of age' convention at St Louis, Missouri. The fellowship's establishment here was, however, by no means as uncomplicated as Wilson implies, and the present chapter will look in detail at the difficulties experienced by its founding members in Ireland, focusing particularly on their efforts to avoid being drawn into conflict with the leaders of the Catholic Church.

In the AA archive in New York the first reference to its establishment in Ireland dates back to 1944, when Bobbie (Roberta) Burger, who was at this time secretary to the Alcoholic Foundation (a trust which had been set up in New York to manage AA publications and act as a clearing house for information on the fellowship), replied to a query from Father Senan Moynihan, a Dublin-based Capuchin priest and editor of the *Capuchin Annual*:

> Thank you for your letter of July 13th expressing interest in the work of Alcoholics Anonymous ... We are sorry indeed to advise you that there is no AA group in your vicinity at the present writing. However, since our work is spreading so rapidly we hope for some developments there in the near future at which time we will get in touch with you.[2]

The Capuchins – the order to which Father Mathew had belonged a century earlier – had continued to have an interest in alcohol problems, so it was unsurprising that one of their number should be the first to query whether AA had, or was about to, set up an Irish group. Priests who are members of religious orders are subject to their own 'chain of command', traditionally enjoying much more pastoral and theological latitude than diocesan priests, and the Capuchins were especially noted for their independent thinking in political and cultural matters. It should be made clear, therefore, that this expression of interest by Father Senan could not be regarded as reflecting the official view of the Catholic Church in Ireland, much less a formal invitation from the Archbishop of Dublin. Neither, of course, did AA function like a commercial enterprise that devised and implemented annual business plans, including the targeting of potential new markets; instead, its growth and diffusion as a voluntary body was an organic and somewhat unpredictable process, largely dependent on the activities and travel arrangements of existing members. The reality, underlying Bobbie Burger's vague reference to the fact that there was no AA group in Father Senan's 'vicinity', was that at this time in 1944 there was no AA group anywhere in Europe.

It was to be a further two years before any attempt was made to start an AA group in Ireland, and on this occasion the initiative again came from a priest. In late 1946, Father Tom Dunlea, an Irish priest home on holiday from Australia, gave an interview to the *Dublin Evening Mail*; although the interview was mainly about his work with a Boys' Town project in Sydney, Father Dunlea also spoke of the newly established AA group in Sydney and suggested that the fellowship would be a welcome addition to Ireland.[3] This *Evening Mail* interview – which appears to have been the first reference to AA in the Irish media – came to the attention of Conor Flynn, a 49-year-old Roscommon man who had been living in Philadelphia but who was then home on holiday and staying with his wife's family in Derry. Conor had been in AA for about three years and, with what appears to have been a rather vague idea of introducing it to Ireland, had brought several copies of the Big Book and some other fellowship literature with him. Prompted by the Dunlea interview, he came to Dublin, where he gave an interview to the *Evening Mail,* announced his intention of starting an AA group and gave a box number where he might be contacted.[4] These activities took place during November 1946 and were marked by a sense of urgency on Conor's part, since he was scheduled to return to Philadelphia in January 1947. His first attempts to attract potential members through use of the media were largely unsuccessful, as were his plans to use priests as sources of referral to AA. Accounts of these initial failures and the type of response encountered by Conor became part of the lore and tradition of Irish AA, as recalled, for instance, in the booklet published to mark the fellowship's fortieth anniversary here:

> He got busy visiting doctors, priests and others. He was assured that no Alcoholics existed south of the Border and was advised not to waste his time in Dublin but to look for them in the North of Ireland. He was told that if alcoholics wanted to stop drinking all they had to do was to join The Pioneer Association – Ireland's great temperance society. He was most often told that they had no wish to waste time on the usual crazy and short-lived ideas thought up by Americans. In short, he got nowhere very fast, and his time was running out.[5]

This retrospective account of Conor's initial failures may be interpreted, as it still appears to be by some fellowship members, as clearly indicative of prejudice or antipathy on the part of those initially contacted by him. However, in light of the historical review of attempts to understand and respond to drinking problems in Ireland presented in Chapter 2, it might be more reasonable to conclude, firstly, that the concept of alcoholism was largely unknown here at this time, and, secondly, that the subtlety of the AA perspective needed more time to impress itself on people. As will become clear throughout the remainder of this and in subsequent chapters, there is little or no evidence of any deep-rooted ideological or practical objections to AA during the years that it was becoming established in Ireland.

Having failed to make progress through his contacts with priests and through media overtures to potential members, Conor's next idea was to use the city's psychiatric hospitals as a point of contact with alcoholics being detoxified there. Since there was a long history of alcoholics being admitted to these institutions and since the Mental Treatment Act of 1945 had given statutory 'ownership' of alcohol dependence to the mental health system, this seemed like a very practical idea.

Conor first visited Ireland's oldest and largest public mental institution, which, reflecting ideological changes and shifting aspirations, had at various times since its establishment in 1815 been known as the Richmond Lunatic Asylum, Grangegorman Mental Hospital and latterly St Brendan's Hospital.[6] This institution, which was located in the north inner city of Dublin, was colloquially known as 'Grangegorman' (or in the abbreviated, Dublin version simply as 'the Gorman') and at the time of Conor's visit it housed approximately two thousand inmates.[7] In the 1940s clinical directors of public mental hospitals still luxuriated in the Victorian title of Resident Medical Superintendent (RMS) and still enjoyed an unusually autocratic style of authority over both patients and staff in these vast institutions.[8] Historical and sociological studies of the performance of public lunatic asylums[9] during the nineteenth and much of the twentieth centuries have shown that these institutions were generally characterized by low staff morale and, more importantly, by a dismally poor quality of life for their inmates. This institutional bleakness, usually attributed to the lack of effective treatment technologies, coupled with public indifference to the lot of asylum inmates and inadequate funding, was, however, occasionally punctuated by bursts of reforming zeal on the part of newly appointed Resident Medical Superintendents.

In 1946 the RMS of Grangegorman was Dr John Dunne, who occupied this position from 1937 until 1965. Dunne was a man of considerable stature in Irish psychiatry: he was the first person appointed to a Chair of Psychiatry in the Republic of Ireland and in the mid-1950s he went on to serve as President of the Royal Medico-Psychological Association, which at this time was the specialist professional body for psychiatrists in Britain and Ireland. Reynolds, in his detailed history of Grangegorman, portrays John Dunne as a psychiatrist who, like many of his predecessors, had seen an initial energy and enthusiasm for reform gradually give way to therapeutic nihilism and conservatism.[10] His successor, Dr Ivor Browne (a much younger man who obviously worked with him as Dunne came close to retirement) is singularly disparaging, however, describing Dunne as someone who spent a great deal of his time playing golf, cynically telling friends that in order to preserve his own sanity he spent as little time as possible in the institution of which he was director.[11] Conor Flynn's experience, when John Dunne was less than a decade into his long career as RMS at Grangegorman, certainly does not reflect well on Dunne's performance in this role.

As Conor recalled it, his first visit to Grangegorman was full of promise. John Dunne was welcoming, expressing interest in AA and suggesting that he had several patients currently under his care for whom it might be suitable; the meeting ended amicably with Conor lending a copy of the Big Book to Dunne and arranging to meet him a week later. On his return visit, however, the reception was very different: 'I was met with a scowl. He gave me a tongue-lashing ... humiliated me ... he asked me to take my books and literature and never come back.'[12] Conor was aware, of course, that doctors were unaccustomed to the idea of sharing therapeutic power with laypeople, and conscious of the fact that an Irish psychiatrist of this era might not be open to the idea that one alcoholic could be uniquely helpful to another. He suspected, however, that his aggressive dismissal was not primarily a considered, professional response as much as an impulsive reaction by an autocratic RMS who, ironically, appeared to have been drinking prior to their second meeting. Conor had detected what he described as the 'full-bodied aroma of Powers Gold Label' and suggested that 'had I half the amount he had, I possibly would have been an overnight guest in the Bridewell for assault and battery on an eminent psychiatrist'.[13]

Conor Flynn's next attempt to introduce AA to the Irish mental health system took him to a private institution, the St John of God Hospital in Stillorgan, run by a Catholic religious order – the St John of God Brothers. His contact here was a religious Provincial, since at this time the hospital had no full-time medical director. Again, Conor had a preliminary meeting at which he described the work of the fellowship and expressed interest in starting a group for alcoholics being detoxified at St John of God's. Having lent AA literature to the Provincial, he arranged to return for a second meeting the following week. While the tone of both meetings in St John of God's was a good deal more cordial than had been the case in Grangegorman, the net result was the same; the Provincial politely returned Conor's literature, explaining that it was of no interest to him because 'they never did have alcoholics and never would have alcoholics'.[14] Conor was puzzled as to why the Provincial should have said that the hospital never admitted alcoholics, since his understanding was that St John of God's, like all Irish mental hospitals, regularly admitted such patients. The feeling of having been duped was compounded by a conversation he had with a friend he had made at the hotel in which he was staying. Eva Jennings, a teacher from Galway who stayed during term-time at the Abbotsford Hotel on Harcourt Street, had become friendly with Conor and aware of his interest in starting a Dublin AA group. She expressed incredulity on being told what the Provincial had said about his hospital never admitting alcoholics, telling Conor that 'there is now somebody very close to me who is being at this moment dried out in that very institution'.[15]

While there are no survey data available from the mid-1940s to confirm that, in the public mind, the St John of God Hospital at Stillorgan was closely associated with alcoholism treatment, this would certainly seem to have been the case. For instance, there is a suggestion in Joyce's *Ulysses* that as early as 16 June 1904 (Bloomsday) the hospital was synonymous with alcoholism treatment; the following dialogue takes place early in the Cyclops episode, when an unnamed narrator meets Joe Hynes and they go for a drink to Barney Kiernan's pub in Little Britain Street:

Are you a strict t.t.? says Joe.

Not taking anything between drinks, says I.

What about paying our respects to our friend? says Joe.

Who? says I. Sure he's in John of God's off his head, poor man.

Drinking his own stuff? says Joe.

Ay, says I. Whiskey and water on the brain.[16]

It is difficult in the absence of documentary evidence[17] to reach any definitive conclusion on the motivation underlying this denial of involvement with alcoholism by the religious director of St John of God's. The most plausible interpretation is that, having noted the centrality of spirituality in the AA programme of recovery, the Provincial may have feared that support for this fellowship might involve him in theological controversy and incur the displeasure of his ecclesiastical superiors. Dr Desmond McGrath, who was appointed as the hospital's first medical director in 1955, noted many years later that – despite a decision at the time of its establishment in 1882 not to admit cases of inebriety – the St John of God's Hospital had in fact 'became very much associated with alcoholism and more particularly with the idea of "drunken priests"'.[18] While it might have been difficult to explain why lay Catholics who became alcohol-dependent had need of AA to facilitate a spiritual awakening and a recovery, it would have been highly embarrassing if not virtually impossible in the cultural milieu of 1940s Ireland to explain why alcoholic priests should need such help. It may simply have been the case that the Provincial, fearing controversy or embarrassment on this issue, cut short the discussion and was less than honest in describing his hospital's work to Conor. A more benign, but somewhat implausible, interpretation is that the confusion between Conor Flynn and the Provincial was based on semantic differences. It could be argued that St John of God's, like the Irish mental health system as a whole, had not explicitly accepted the disease concept of alcoholism at this time; if so, patients with alcohol problems may have been predominantly conceptualized and managed in relation to coexisting mental health problems – with the alcohol component seen as secondary to a primary mental illness. If this latter explanation is accepted, then the Provincial was reflecting a commonly shared ambiguity rather than deliberately misleading Conor.

Although understandably deflated, Conor persevered with his efforts to introduce the fellowship into the Irish mental health system, and was successful when the third institution he visited welcomed him, gave him access to an alcoholic being treated there and effectively facilitated what was to be Europe's first AA meeting. The institution in question was another private hospital, St Patrick's Hospital in James's Street, Dublin, which had been founded in 1746 with money bequeathed for this purpose by Jonathan Swift, Dean of St Patrick's Cathedral.[19] Dr Norman Moore had been appointed as Medical Director of St Patrick's Hospital in 1946, shortly before Conor's visit, having worked for the previous six years at Crichton Royal Hospital in Dumfries, Scotland, where he had been greatly influenced by Professor Willi Mayer-Gross, a leading figure in European psychiatry during the early twentieth century. Moore, who was generally regarded as being open-minded and progressive in his approach to psychiatry, specifically recalled that, following a visit to the USA to catch up on developments there during the war years, Mayer-Gross had spoken very positively about AA. This meant that when Conor called to see him he already had some knowledge of the fellowship and was predisposed to working collaboratively with it.[20] Moore himself later described what Mayer-Gross had said about AA and how this had influenced his meeting with Conor:

> On his [Mayer-Gross's] return he held a staff meeting and told us that the most impressive therapeutic advance he had encountered in his travels was at a meeting of an organisation called Alcoholics Anonymous, run by patients suffering from alcoholism and exclusive to sufferers from this tragic disease. A few months later on return to Dublin, I was requested one evening to see a member of this organisation. He proved to be a cheerful, burly American who introduced himself as Conor, his first name, in conformity with the rules of his organisation. He told me that he had come over especially from America to the land of his forebears to spread the news about Alcoholics Anonymous. After some discussion and on the strength of Mayer-Gross's recommendation, I introduced him to a recently admitted patient with a long history of alcoholism and personal disaster. He was named Richard Percival [*sic*] and that week, along with Conor, he

formed the first Alcoholics Anonymous group in these islands and, I believe, in Europe.[21]

There is some confusion about the precise dates of the first closed meeting (that is a meeting for alcoholics only) and the first open meeting (that is a meeting for both alcoholics and interested non-alcoholics), but these are recorded in the Golden Jubilee anniversary booklet as being, respectively 18 November and 25 November 1946.[22] The first open meeting was held in the Country Shop, a shop run by the Irish Countrywomen's Association on St Stephen's Green in Dublin, which was to play host to AA for more than thirty years. There is no confusion or disagreement, however, about the significance of the help offered by St Patrick's Hospital and the importance of the role played by Richard Perceval (1902–82), the fellowship's first Irish-resident member.

Conor was conscious from the outset that having its origins in St Patrick's Hospital, which in the parlance of the times would have been known as a 'Protestant hospital', might not be the most auspicious start for AA in a jurisdiction where the Catholic Church had such a profound influence on all aspects of the health care system, and in a city where the Catholic Archbishop was intolerant of Protestantism and generally hostile towards inter-faith activities. He was deeply appreciative of the help offered and risks incurred by Norman Moore in allowing him access to one of his patients, but never concealed the fact that St Patrick's had been his last choice: 'And finally, the place that I didn't want to go – possibly it was the last port of call, the last resort – was St Patrick's Hospital. I knew I came from the other side of the fence when I talked to Dr Moore.'[23] The fence in question, of course, was a religious fence, and the risk was that the Catholic bishops might take exception to AA: seeing it as a form of proselytization by an organization that had originated within the evangelical Protestant tradition and which had been introduced to Ireland through a Protestant hospital – which, incidentally, had strong links to the medical school at Trinity College Dublin, a university which was a specific irritant to Archbishop McQuaid. The fact that his overtures to St John of God's, a Catholic hospital, had been rejected would almost certainly have added to Conor's anxieties about religious tensions arising in relation to the intro-duction of AA to Dublin.

Richard Perceval was born in 1902 into a well-to-do Protestant family at Saintfield House near Downpatrick, Co. Down; he was a boarder at Radley College in Oxfordshire, then went up to Trinity College, Oxford. While at university he developed a serious alcohol problem which caused him to leave Oxford without completing his degree, and he eventually drifted into a skid-row-type of existence in London. He returned to Ireland, but despite many efforts by his family to help him, he continued to drink; his hospitalization in St Patrick's in late 1946 appeared to have been primarily motivated by a desire to escape legal problems, stemming from his liberal approach to writing cheques for which he had no supporting assets.[24] He was happily surprised by the fact that Conor did not lecture or advise him, but simply told of his own experience of alcoholism, and this style of communication seems to have made an immediate impact on Richard. Following this meeting, Richard Perceval remained abstinent for the remainder of his life, working on a voluntary basis with AA and later in a number of paid positions with organizations promoting the disease concept of alcoholism in Britain and in Ireland. As Conor undoubtedly appreciated, and certainly as he himself appreciated, Richard Perceval's involvement with AA in Ireland was complicated by the fact that he was a Protestant. Another potential complication, although it may not have been widely known at the time, was that Richard had divorced his first wife and was to remarry soon after joining AA: given the strength of Catholic views on this subject, and the constitutional prohibition of divorce in Ireland at this time, it might not have helped AA's cause had it been public knowledge that its first Irish group was chaired by a Northern Protestant divorcé.

Since Conor was due to return to the USA a few weeks later, Richard assumed the role of secretary of the Dublin group, setting about the task of acquiring AA literature and learning as much as he could about how meetings were structured and how the fellowship functioned. He wrote immediately to the AA Foundation in New York, informing it of the establishment of the Dublin group and requesting that it send him some literature.[25] Following a reply from Bobbie Burger, Richard again wrote to New York in early December 1946, telling Bobbie of the progress being made: 'We have now fifteen real members of AA – by "real" I mean members who attend all the meetings and are staying dry.

I do not know whether fifteen members in 3 weeks is good or not, but we are growing at the rate of about two per week and that seems to be a good sign.'[26] In this second letter, Richard also voiced for the first time what were to become standard anxieties about how religious tensions in Ireland might hinder the fellowship's growth here:

> The first [problem] is accommodation. It is very hard to find a suitable room or hall for private or public meetings. There is, as you probably know, very strong religious feeling in Ireland, and most public halls are connected with some Church or other. A Catholic member would not wish to go to a Protestant hall or house and 'vice versa'. Personally, although I am a Protestant, and nearly all the other members are Catholic, I do not mind where I go, but many of the others have strong views on the subject.[27]

Bobbie Burger's response to these concerns about the religious culture of Ireland and its potential impact on the fellowship reminded Richard explicitly that AA had no interest in engaging with, or bringing about change in, broader political or cultural issues. What was equally important perhaps was the tone of her letter, which implied that AA in Ireland could and would find solutions to its own difficulties, and that the New York 'headquarters' had no intention of prescribing or imposing solutions to problems experienced by the fellowship in other countries:

> I know that Ireland is steeped in rather hard and fast tradition and I am sure that AA, as you are now doing, will have to go along with existing conditions. We do not intend to, nor could we, change a basic mode of life, but rather fit ourselves into things as we find them.[28]

In fact, even prior to writing to New York about the difficulties involved in finding a neutral venue for AA meetings in Dublin, Richard and Conor had cleverly solved this problem by renting a meeting room at the Country Shop on St Stephen's Green in central Dublin; the Irish Countrywomen's Association (ICA), which ran the Country Shop, was one of the few non-sectarian voluntary groups in Ireland at this time, and as such was likely to be acceptable to AA members regardless of religious affiliations. The Country Shop not only provided a meeting room for the first

Dublin AA group, but for many years also acted as an informal headquarters for the fellowship as it evolved and grew. In 1949, Sackville O'Conor-Mallins, who had replaced Richard as secretary of the Dublin group, commented to an American friend on the generosity of the ICA:

> They really treat us very well in this joint. In fact when I come to think of it, almost unbelievably well, considering that when we began, I'm told, they often had to wait for the rent. Now, of course, we pay a month in advance. There wouldn't have been too many places willing to hire rooms to a bunch of what they thought might be rowdy drunks a year or so ago. Now we've educated them into realising that alcoholics, providing they are not actively so, are rather good and steady clients.[29]

Apart from this kindness on the part of the ICA, the first few months of the fellowship's existence in Dublin appear to have been generally marked by interest and support from relatives and friends of the early members. Eva Jennings, who had befriended Conor Flynn at the Abbotsford Hotel, attended open meetings of AA at the Country Shop and continued to encourage the early members to persevere following Conor's return to the USA. Eva's own reminiscences about this period are interesting in that they convey a sense both of how financially straitened circumstances were in Dublin in the late 1940s and of the style of informal help offered to the early AA group. She recalled, for instance, the send-off given to Conor and his wife as they began their journey back to Philadelphia: a journey which, in the days before air travel was the norm, began at Heuston (then Kingsbridge) Station:

> The early days of any organisation are very challenging and exciting. We were full of energy and enthusiasm and all became close friends. Conor and his faithful wife, Margaret remained until after Christmas. I still remember the great send off they got from Heuston station. Everyone turned up but as it was January 1947 few had transport. That is why Conor's cousin, Eddie Garvey, made a great contribution. Eddie was then a Garda Inspector, later Commissioner and his support and help were invaluable. The Dublin First Group owe him a big debt of gratitude. He was one of the few with a car in those days.[30]

Following Conor's departure for Philadelphia, Richard continued to work actively as secretary of the Dublin group, while worrying constantly that the Catholic Church might actively oppose the fellowship or ban Catholics from joining it. In May 1947 he again wrote to Bobbie Burger in New York, explaining that his attempts to publicize AA had been stymied by fears on the part of some journalists that the Catholic Church disapproved of it; he wondered whether there had been any public statements of approval by American Catholic leaders which he might use to counter such fears. To illustrate his difficulties he quoted at length from a letter received from a journalist whose help he had sought; in part, this letter reads as follows:

> If any way can be devised by which the queer suspicions about AA which I find exist in many quarters can be dissipated, it will give a great impetus to the movement. Because the movement originated in America – 'the land of freak religions' – there is a dumb feeling that it resembles in some way the 'Moral Rearmament' campaign which has been completely discredited, I think, across the channel as well as in this country.
>
> In view of the strictly non-sectarian nature of the AA movement, it would not be advisable to have ministers of any denomination patronise it in this country, I believe, but it is possible that they have come out openly in its support in the United States. If this has happened, it would be very effective, I think, if some of their utterances were published over here – particularly any words of cheer and encouragement that were spoken by Bishops or priests of the Catholic Church. In the existing situation I am debarred – through no fault of my own – from giving you the Press support that I would like to give, and I am anxious that this barrier should be removed.[31]

While the journalist who wrote this may have considered it 'dumb' to compare AA to Moral Rearmament, the truth of the matter was that AA had grown out of this movement, albeit under its earlier Oxford Group name (as described in Chapter 3). It is interesting that, at such an early stage in its Irish history, its critics should have had detailed information of this kind, which suggests that fears of attack by Catholic authorities were not solely based on paranoia. In replying to this letter, Bobbie Burger pointed out that AA had never had any formal split with any religious grouping in the USA, although she recalled that 'In the early days of AA in this country there was a little fear on the part of some Catholic heads that we were a "new religion".' Once again, she was disinclined to offer an American solution to what appeared to be an Irish problem. She did not think that endorsement of AA by American Catholic authorities would necessarily be of any help to its members in Ireland, and instead suggested to Richard that it might help to cultivate relationships with Irish Catholic leaders who could be persuaded to become familiar with and express approval of the fellowship.[32] As a Protestant, Richard was obviously not best placed to develop such relationships and, in any event, he had limited time to do so – being 44 years old, about to remarry and in need of a full-time job. Although he continued to be deeply committed to AA, he was replaced as secretary of the Dublin group some months later by Sackville O'Conor-Mallins, a retired British army officer who was to have a huge impact on the development of AA in Ireland for the next thirty years.

ENTER SACKVILLE

As discussed in Chapter 3, AA is a paradoxical institution which, amongst other things, suggests that for those with severe alcohol dependence success is often related to an admission of failure. Another central paradox is that the historic evolution of AA – an institution which emphasizes anonymity and the primacy of 'principles before personalities' (Tradition Twelve) – cannot be understood without focusing, at least for some parts of its history, on a small number of key players. Just as the establishment of the fellowship in the USA cannot be understood without reference to Bill Wilson, so, too, would it be impossible to offer any meaningful account of its history in Ireland without looking in detail at the personality and work of Sackville O'Conor-Mallins, who joined AA in April 1947 and who devoted the next thirty years of his life to ensuring its survival and success.

Sackville (1897–1979)[33] was born at Raglan Road, Dublin, the son of Frederick Mallins, a Dubliner who was an officer in the British army, and Elizabeth O'Conor, one of the O'Conor Don family from County Roscommon who were reputedly descendants of the last High Kings of Ireland. In his correspondence with AA friends in various parts of the world, Sackville occasionally commented on his family background: usually discussing his mother's family of which he appeared to be quite proud, but referring much less frequently to his father, who died when Sackville was just 7 years old. He explained to Joe D., an AA friend in Chicago, in a letter written in 1948:

> O'C stands for O'Conor. Note that there is only one N in the name. It shows my direct descent from the last King of All-Ireland, Rhoderic Dhu O'Conor. Dhu has been corrupted into Don, the title assumed by the head of the family. I believe I am 3 or 4 away from it, but haven't bothered to find out, as it is a different branch of the family at present. My mother was an O'Conor before her first marriage. My father died in 1904. I have a stepfather alive still, aged 83 I think.[34]

Many years later, he told this same correspondent in Chicago about his mother's brother, Roderic O'Conor, an impressionist painter and close friend of Gauguin: 'My uncle and Godfather Roderic O'Conor the artist is coming in again for publicity in the British papers. He has now been adopted by them apparently and is referred to as a British artist. This is a good old English custom.'[35] From his father's side of the family he inherited a military tradition, describing himself in his Big Book entry (where he is identified simply as 'The Career Officer') as coming from 'one of the Irish families who, more or less traditionally, sent their boys to the British armies'.[36] What is most significant in relation to his later AA membership, however, is that Sackville grew up a Catholic: the O'Conor Dons being especially proud that through the difficult Penal Law years of the eighteenth century – even if it meant that they were to be dispossessed of their lands – they had remained Catholic.

Sackville went to Stonyhurst, the Jesuit public school in Lancashire, subsequently returning to Dublin where he registered for a degree in science at Trinity College Dublin. Like Bill Wilson, with whom he was later to form a close friendship, Sackville left university without finishing his degree, opting instead to go to military college for accelerated officer training. In 1916 he left Trinity College and went to Sandhurst Military College, from which he was commissioned some eight months later. His only brother – Claude, a lieutenant in the Connaught Rangers – had been killed at Ypres in November 1914 at the age of 21. There is no record of Sackville sustaining any injury, and following the ending of the First World War he decided to make his career in the British Army. Many years later, he summarized his military career in a letter to Joe D. in Chicago as follows:

> I went to the Royal Military College (cf. your West Point) in 1916, got commissioned in the Connaught Rangers in 1917, France ... Belgium ... Silesia ... Rhine up to 1924, becoming a Lieutenant in the process (and also a developed alkie ...) India 1924–1931, including a Frontier War, Home in England 1931–1933, India again to 1935, Egypt and Palestine to 1938 (another 'War'), Cyprus 38–39, Egypt, Sudan, home and retirement 1941. I 'went' on March 12th officially 1941. From the point of view of being on the active payroll, you could say I retired at 001 13th March 1941. One reason why the war went on so much longer![37]

Sackville appears to have enjoyed army life, and despite his own accounts of problem drinking all through his army years his career was highly successful and he was also heavily involved in sport – particularly hockey, at which he excelled and with which he kept up an active involvement as coach and referee during his AA years.[38] Although he was given many responsible postings (the last of which was Officer in Command of British troops in Cyprus in 1938) and attained the rank of major, he insisted that he had been an alcoholic for all of his army life: 'My alcoholic career lasted well over 30 years, and during that time I was in about 30 hospitals and a couple of homes, and 40 different doctors had me through their hands.'[39]

Having been retired on medical grounds, Sackville returned to Dublin, where he lived for six years at Pembroke Road with his elderly mother while continuing to drink in the manner that had led to his effective dismissal from the British Army. In April 1947, following discussions with other family members, his mother decided that she could no longer cope with his drinking and that she was throwing him out. This threat, which Sackville took seriously ('She really meant business this time'[40]), had an immediate salutary effect on him, since it seemed to him that the prospect of

ending up as a vagrant alcoholic on the streets of Dublin was ter-
rifyingly real. He recalled having read about AA in the *Evening
Mail*, and bargained with his family to be allowed to continue living at home if he succeeded in tackling his drinking with its help.
On 28 April 1947, Sackville – by his own admission still quite
intoxicated – attended his first AA meeting in the Country Shop:

> My mind was too screwy to able to understand much of what
> was being said. But I did understand this eventually, that
> these people had been through a lot of drinking experiences
> just as I had, and had managed to make a job of it. What
> struck me most was that they all seemed to be quite pleased
> with having made a job of it and having stopped drinking.
> That gave me my first bit of hope. I thought that if these kind
> of ordinary people can do it, a man of my brains ought to
> find it much more easy, and I joined. I suppose I had reached
> my spiritual gutter that night, but I have never had what you
> could call a real urge to drink again.[41]

Sackville himself liked to joke that at the end of this meeting, when
he went up to tell the established members that he had decided to
join them, they were not as overwhelmed at this joyous news as he
had expected. Ruth Perceval (Richard's second wife, who although
not an alcoholic herself was heavily involved in AA activities during these early months) confirmed that the Country Shop AA members were neither convinced by this immediate commitment nor
instantly enamoured of their new member. As she recalled: 'Nobody
expected to see Sackville ever again, because he was so odd and so
rude to everybody. Little did they know.'[2] But see him they did: not
only did Sackville stop drinking from that night, but he quickly took
over as Secretary of the Country Shop group and went on to play a
leadership role in AA in Ireland and internationally which lasted for
almost three decades.

   If Richard Perceval's background could be deemed potentially
unhelpful to the AA cause in Ireland, then it also has to be acknowledged that Sackville's background seemed less than ideal in neutral,
'post-Emergency' Dublin.[43] He was, after all, a retired British army
officer with a suspiciously British first name and a double-barrelled
family name, educated at Stonyhurst, Trinity College Dublin and
Sandhurst, and continuing to speak with an English accent.Personal
reminiscences and anecdotes from AA members who remember

Sackville generally agree that he was shy and socially awkward, often concealing these traits under a military-style brusqueness that was initially off-putting to new acquaintances. He was particularly irritated, for instance, by members who he deemed to be long-winded during meetings, and his letters to AA friends indicate that he regarded visiting Americans as frequent offenders on this score. Most of those who continued their acquaintance with Sackville, however, appear to have been won over by the sincerity of his commitment to helping others and, despite his somewhat bombastic exterior, by his obvious humility and lack of ego. In the words of one of the many AA members for whom he performed this role, he was 'the world's best sponsor'.[44] In life-cycle terms, Sackville was a real godsend for the fellowship in Ireland because, unlike Richard Perceval, he had an adequate income from his army pension and felt free to devote all of his considerable energies to working on a voluntary basis for its promotion. In terms of his other personal attributes, there are two traits in particular which stand out as being of central importance to his work for AA and which – explicitly or implicitly – will feature in the remainder of this chapter and in Chapters 5 and 6: his organizational ability and his spirituality.

In his biographical entry in the second edition of the Big Book, Sackville commented with apparent surprise on the fact that 'right through to the end of my twenty-six years in the Army, I was still being offered very good and important jobs in spite of the fact that my superiors must have known that I wasn't thoroughly reliable'.[45] Perhaps the most obvious explanation for this is that he had superb organizational skills and, despite recurring difficulties with alcohol, may well have performed competently for much of his time as an army officer. He seemed to thrive on administrative work and his nephew, with whom he lived during his final years, recalled Sackville as saying that had World War One not intervened, his preferred career choice would have been the Indian Civil Service rather than the army.[46] What emerges with great clarity from his correspondence and the many other writings about AA he left behind him is that Sackville – in the language of modern management – was a *strategic manager*. By August 1947, just four months into his own recovery, he had taken over from Richard Perceval as secretary of Ireland's first AA group and had already begun to think systematically about what needed to be done to secure the fellowship's survival and expansion. It is also noteworthy that Sackville's organizational skills were not rooted immutably in his military experience; it is difficult to imagine a greater disparity than that to be found between the hierarchical leadership style of the army and the anarchic, leaderless style of AA, but Sackville seems to have made this transition in a relatively effortless way. In an informal history he left at the AA General Service Office in Dublin, and which has been subsequently quoted in commemorative booklets, Sackville recorded his initial impressions of what needed to be done:

> Two things were evident from the start: (a) either the Catholic Church in Ireland was made an ally or AA in Ireland was sunk; and (b) either AA publicised itself in Dublin or it would perish of dry rot.[47]

The work done by Sackville and others to publicize the fellowship will be looked at in Chapter 6; the remainder of this chapter will look at the steps that were taken to build alliances between AA and the Catholic Church in Ireland. Before embarking on this in detail, it is important to comment briefly on the other key trait of Sackville referred to above: his spirituality. What comes through clearly from his writings, including those where he was obviously in strategic mode, is that – at least during his years in recovery from alcoholism – there was nothing nominal about Sackville's religious beliefs and practices: he was a profoundly spiritual man and a devout Catholic. This is not to say that he was uncritical of Roman Catholicism or of church leaders, but the obvious sincerity of his beliefs and practices undoubtedly helped in the delicate negotiations which went on over many years and which were aimed at making AA acceptable to potentially hostile church leaders. While his recovery from alcoholism, which began in the Country Shop on St Stephen's Green, lacked the drama of Bill Wilson's conversion experience in 1934, Sackville maintained a sense of his own recovery as a miraculous release from dependency, for which he was eternally grateful. However, knowing the Catholic Church as he did, he was fearful that some church leaders would see AA's spiritual practices as incompatible with conventional Catholic beliefs and practices, hence his ongoing efforts to form alliances with church authorities.

THE MAYNOOTH CONNECTION

Staff at the AA Foundation offices in New York quickly became aware that in Sackville the fellowship had found an organizer of unusual skill and energy: someone who wrote to them with such frequency that they were hard pressed to keep pace with all his comments and queries; and someone who was also busily making contact with AA groups all over the world. Sackville himself explained that his initial burst of organizational energy had been inspired by fears that the fellowship in Dublin might not survive until its first birthday, since Conor had gone back to Philadelphia and Richard was quite limited in the amount of time which he could devote to voluntary work: 'When I took over as Secretary the Group was at a standstill and rather in the doldrums; so I thought it my job to infuse some self-respect and interest into it.' [48] In his letters to New York, and especially in his letters to Bill Wilson, with whom he appears to have struck up an immediate rapport, Sackville touched constantly, indeed almost obsessively, on what he perceived to be the importance for AA of gaining the approval of the Catholic Church in Ireland.

To an uninformed observer it might seem that the most obvious step would be for AA members to approach the Archbishop of Dublin, in whose diocese the first Irish group had been established, and seek his blessing and approval for the fellowship's work in the country. To do so, however, might have run the risk of incurring a public attack on AA, and it is not surprising – given Archbishop McQuaid's reputation as a conservative, ultra-orthodox and controlling prelate – that early AA members opted not to go down this route. The fact that McQuaid maintained a public silence on AA is in itself quite remarkable, and this will be discussed later in this chapter.

Instead, the primary strategy devised by Sackville from 1949 onwards was to establish links with St Patrick's College, Maynooth, the country's national seminary, in the hope that, with the collaboration of academic theologians and others involved in the pastoral formation of priests, Irish priests might come to see AA as an institution whose beliefs and practices were fully consonant with those of the Catholic Church. In a letter to Bill Wilson, written in early 1950, Sackville commented happily on the news that the Franciscan University of Steubenville, Ohio, had awarded its Poverello Medal to Alcoholics Anonymous, something that Sackville believed would help him cement relationships with Irish Franciscans. In the same letter he also told Wilson: 'At present, I am endeavouring to soften the clerical influence, which is a big factor in this country. I have a promise of a short article in the leading priests' paper produced by Maynooth College, the great Catholic seminary.'[49] It is clear, however, from his letters to his Chicago friend Joe D., that the task of writing and publishing an article about AA in the *Irish Ecclesiastical Record* proved to be quite a tortuous process. Sackville had written a short article which, through the influence of his own parish priest (who was also an auxiliary bishop), was submitted to this theological journal at Maynooth, in the confident hope that the editors would publish it as written. However, as he told Joe D. in a letter written in December 1949:

> Maynooth will NOT publish my article because they are afraid if they did they would be giving 'Episcopal sanction' to AA, a thing not done even in America yet. However, they have said that if I send in a query to their Theological section they will print an answer and have asked to keep the article. They were very sympathetic, and some of them had heard a lot about it before without knowing any details of how AA goes to work [capitals in original][50]

In March 1950 the *Irish Ecclesiastical Record* published what seems to have been the first ever discussion of AA in a Catholic theological journal in this country; it was a short article, perhaps drawing on Sackville's original contribution and purporting to provide an expert theological answer to the question 'What is to be thought of the Fellowship of Alcoholics Anonymous, whose avowed purpose is "to help the sick alcoholic if he wishes to recover"?' The discussion contrasts help which alcoholics can get from AA and which is deemed to be in the 'natural' sphere, with help which alcoholics can get through reception of the Catholic sacraments, deemed to be in the 'supernatural' sphere. Presumably, most AA members would not agree that invocation of their Higher Power could be dismissed as being entirely in the natural sphere, but, most significantly, this short piece contains the sentence: 'We see nothing in the programme which need conflict in any way with Catholic principles.'[51]

Following this initial foray into the world of theological publishing, Sackville further developed his contacts with Maynooth, becoming especially friendly with two professors – Father J.G. (Jerry) McGarry, Professor of Pastoral Theology, and Father Sean O'Riordan, Professor of Moral Theology – who were to prove consistently helpful to AA's cause. Although a fast learner in these matters, Sackville made no pretence of familiarity with the various aspects of theology represented by his new friends; in a letter to Joe D. in Chicago, written in early 1952, he explained:

> I spent Sunday last at Maynooth College with Richard [Perceval], interviewing the grave and reverend Professors of Pastoral and Moral Theology on AA. They were very approving and inquisitive. I asked them the difference between Pastoral and Moral Professorships, and the Pastoral explained that Moral told the priests what to do, and he (Pastoral) told them how to do it. So, no doubt, they will shortly receive word to support AA.[52]

McGarry had been the founding editor in 1950 of *The Furrow*, a theological journal which was aimed at priests, religious and laypeople involved in various forms of pastoral work, rather than at academic theologians. *The Furrow*, which was generally regarded as an influential and progressive journal that helped an otherwise conservative clergy to adapt to the radical changes later ushered in by the Second Vatican Council, was, predictably, looked on with suspicion by John Charles McQuaid – not least perhaps because its editor took advantage of ecclesiastical law which permitted him to submit it for the *imprimatur* or doctrinal approval of the Bishop of Kildare and Leighlin, in whose diocese it was printed, although Maynooth was in the Archdiocese of Dublin.[53] Similarly, Sean O'Riordan, who was a member of the Redemptorist Order, had a reputation as a liberal theologian with the courage to tease out complex moral issues, rather than confining his academic work to the restatement of theological orthodoxy or the appeasement of church authorities.[54] In early 1952 *The Furrow* published an article on AA which was written by O'Riordan and which offered a detailed study of how the fellowship worked and, most provocatively, how AA's Twelve-Step Programme provided an effective remedy for dependent drinkers whose practice of the Catholic religion did not appear to be nearly as helpful in this regard.[55] This article took the form of a review paper comprising O'Riordan's summary and comment on a paper entitled 'Science, Religion and Alcoholism', which had been published some months earlier in an American Catholic magazine. One can only surmise that this somewhat oblique format was adopted lest any critics attack O'Riordan, who, it could be argued, was essentially reporting and commenting on somebody else's ideas rather than aggressively promoting AA in his own right. It appears, however, that nobody responded negatively to the O'Riordan paper, even though in its enthusiastic endorsement of the Twelve Steps it quoted what might have been seen as a highly provocative statement of 'John Doe', the American author of the article being reviewed: 'The second reason I give for the success of AA is a rather shocking one. I offer it in humility and with all due respect. AA insists more vigorously on the practice of those principles of Christian ascetics and the spiritual life than do priests of the Church of Christ.'[56]

Sackville responded ecstatically to this publication, seeing it as the long-awaited stamp of approval for AA from the Catholic Church in Ireland, and arranging to reprint it in booklet form, complete with *imprimatur*. The Dublin group raised a loan to produce 6,000 copies of this booklet, which it proposed to sell both in Ireland and elsewhere, and in his correspondence with friends Sackville described, in what even then must have seemed like wildly exaggerated terms, the importance of this publication. His letter to Bill Wilson at the AA Foundation in New York is a good example of the almost manic glee of Sackville in relation to *The Furrow* article:

> This time I have an event of great importance to write about. I have asked Ann [a staff member at the AA Foundation] to show you the copy of The Furrow, a paper published by the Maynooth College over here, which holds an article on AA from the Catholic point of view. I consider this to be the GO AHEAD signal from the Catholic Church for AA and feel I cannot overestimate its importance to us ... Maynooth College is the headquarters of the Catholic Religion in Ireland and everything it produces is done after long thought, and is conveyed throughout the country to the priesthood. We cannot, and of course would not, publicise

the fact that we have their approval, but it will be inferred from the booklet, which incidentally they have promised to allow us their Imprimatur on [capitals in original][57]

Within days, however, Sackville himself sensed that he had been excessively optimistic about the O'Riordan article and what it might achieve for the fellowship in Ireland; he also became worried that, given the strictly non-sectarian nature of AA, the Foundation in New York might not be altogether happy that the Dublin group was publishing a booklet written solely from the Catholic perspective and carrying the *imprimatur*.[58] But, as was its custom, the AA Foundation offered no criticism and made no attempt to stop Sackville and his Dublin colleagues from going ahead with this publication; Bill Wilson made the mild suggestion that if *The Grapevine* (the newsletter issued by the Foundation in New York) publicized the booklet, it should do so cautiously and perhaps alongside the views of some other denomination – 'That would even matters up a little, denominationally speaking.'[59]

Perhaps what comes through most clearly from the archival material dealing with the 1950s is that Irish AA members became less convinced that any single master stroke could definitively resolve potential tensions between the fellowship and the Catholic Church, but now tended to see this as a matter to be whittled away at continuously. Throughout the 1950s Sackville continued his friendship with Professor McGarry and *The Furrow* continued to publish occasional articles on alcoholism and AA, with Sackville himself contributing one such article in 1953.[60] However, the article into which he put most effort and with which he appeared to be most pleased was one written under the pen-name I.G.S, on 'The American Church and AA' published in *The Furrow* in early 1957.[61] Once again, the content of this article reflected the hope, originally expressed by Richard Perceval, that if church leaders in Ireland could be made aware of how good relationships were between AA and the Catholic Church in the USA, this might once and for all bring to an end residual tensions between these two institutions in Ireland. The article refers explicitly to the work of two American Jesuits – Father John C. Ford, a moral theologian, and Father Ed Dowling, a close friend and confidant of Bill Wilson – sympathetic to AA, and also to the annual National Clergy Conference on Alcoholism (NCCA) – an annual event at which Catholic clergy in the USA met to discuss pastoral responses to the problem of alcoholism. It describes the establishment of specialist alcoholism wards in general hospitals in Ohio by an Irish-born nun, Sister Ignatia – a friend and former colleague of AA's co-founder Dr Bob Smith – and expresses the hope that some Irish nuns might be persuaded to train for and take on a similar role in Ireland. The article contains a lengthy quote from a letter received by Sackville from an unnamed chancellor of a large American archdiocese, and which is uniformly positive about AA; even arguing that the fellowship is more likely to bring 'lukewarm' Catholics back to the full practice of their religion than to act as a substitute for church membership.[62] The article's final sentence reads: 'In this spirit, and with this aim, the Irish groups of AA offer their services to any parish, diocese or seminary that may wish to avail of it.'[63]

While the text of this 1957 article presents an unambiguously positive picture of relationships between the American Catholic Church and AA, the background correspondence shows this to be a somewhat disingenuous exercise, with Sackville being fully aware that these relationships were more delicate and qualified than he depicted them to be. He had visited the USA twice, in 1954 and 1956, staying with Bill and Lois Wilson and visiting AA friends in several cities, and he continued to correspond with these American friends. He appears to have mulled over the idea of writing this paper for several years and, in doing so, to have consulted widely with people he trusted to help and advise with the project. The most detailed advice he received was from the Jesuit theologian John C. Ford, who in late 1955 had written to Sackville at some length on the question of how this article for *The Furrow* should be framed:

> With regard to your projected article on the Church and AA in the United States, I think you might get your ideas across better by going at it a bit obliquely and writing rather on the Church and Alcoholism in the United States. Actually there are only a few pronouncements of Bishops which directly encourage and approve AA – that is quotable pronouncements. As you say, the High-ups probably prefer not to commit themselves even though they want to make good use of the AA program and ideas.

I think that if you wrote an article on Catholic Church interest in alcohol problems and in the course of it kept coming back to AA, as if that were the indispensable basis, taken for granted as the best practical and pastoral approach you wouldn't have to commit yourself to any exaggerated statement of ecclesiastical approval over here ...

Well these are the thoughts that run through my Jesuitical mind – that you will do better by writing on the Church and alcohol problems and not make an explicit plug for AA, but mention it all the time, taking it for granted that priests and hierarchy are for it ...[64]

While Sackville took much of the general advice offered by Father Ford, he ignored this Jesuitical suggestion and his article was an unashamed and 'explicit plug' for AA in Ireland and for more collaboration between the fellowship and bishops, priests, nuns and seminary directors.

On one of his American trips he had travelled to Ohio, where he had met Sister Ignatia, the Mayo-born nun who had set up specialist alcoholism treatment wards in general hospitals. However, when he wrote to her in connection with his planned article for *The Furrow*, she seems to have been somewhat alarmed at the prospect of being drawn into theological controversy, replying that she did not 'feel that I would be qualified to even give you an opinion as to the attitude of the Church towards AA'.[65] Eventually, with editorial encouragement from Professor McGarry, who had read an 'outline of the more delicate part' of this article and judged it to be 'first class',[66] Sackville's paper on AA and the Catholic Church in America was published.

The archives reveal no specific developments arising from this paper and its invitation to Catholic clergy and seminary teachers to use AA as a resource, but there are general indications that AA contacts with the Catholic Church in Ireland continued to expand. More importantly, there is no evidence of any conflict between AA and Catholic Church leaders in Ireland. Sackville's *Furrow* article had some circulation outside of Ireland, resulting in requests for permission to translate and circulate it in two countries adjoining the USA where, it appears, Catholic suspicion of AA also existed. In April 1959 the Dublin AA group received the following request from a Canadian alcoholism rehabilitation centre:

> Ours is rehabilitation centre in the Province of Quebec, where the population is predominantly French-Canadian and Catholic.
>
> The medical director and I have been very much impressed by your pamphlet: 'The American Church and Alcoholics Anonymous'. As we are experiencing some difficulties in explaining to some of the workers that the AA Program is 'commendable and not condemnable', may we be permitted to translate your pamphlet and mimeograph same for limited and free distribution.[67]

Later that year, the secretary of an AA group in Mexico wrote to the Dublin group in praise of Sackville's article, which was considered to be 'full of the kind of information that is so badly needed here' and seeking permission to translate and print it in Spanish.[68] It must have been gratifying for Sackville that his article was appreciated in countries other than that at which it was primarily aimed, and perhaps he also took consolation from the fact that Ireland was not the only country in which AA members regarded themselves as being viewed with suspicion by Catholic authorities.

ARCHBISHOP MCQUAID: THE CURIOUS INCIDENT OF THE DOG THAT DIDN'T BARK?

It is clear, therefore, that during AA's first few decades in Ireland, Irish AA members were concerned, almost to the point of obsession, with building good relationships with the Catholic Church – or at least with the avoidance of conflict with church leaders. The reality, however, was that no clerical opposition of any kind ever materialized during these years, and the signals emanating from clerical Ireland were in fact highly supportive of the fellowship. The relationship set up by Richard Perceval and Sackville with Maynooth continued to flourish and, through *The Furrow*, AA continued to be presented in a very favourable light to this journal's largely clerical readership. AA speakers were regularly invited to address seminarians in Maynooth and soon afterwards in some of the other seminaries, thereby ensuring that young priests began their ministry with positive attitudes to the fellowship and with no concerns as to its compatibility with orthodox

Catholic teaching and practice. As AA began to establish groups outside of Dublin, Catholic priests encouraged alcoholics to attend and they made parish facilities available as meeting places.[69] Those religious orders, such as the Capuchins and the Cistercians, which had a tradition of working with alcoholics continued with this work, amending it only to the extent that they now recommended AA membership to their clients.[70] Sackville also built bridges with the Pioneer Total Abstinence Association, and from the 1960s onwards it was not uncommon for AA speakers to address Pioneer rallies.[71] One potentially problematic episode, in which AA appeared to be at risk of being drawn into internal Pioneer politics, is discussed later in this chapter.

In the AA archives in Dublin and New York there is little or no explicit reference to communication between the fellowship and individual Irish bishops, but what little exists is positive. The only archbishop (out of four Catholic archbishops in Ireland) to feature on a few occasions in the early AA records is Archbishop Joseph Walsh of Tuam. In July 1950, Sackville reported to his friend Joe D. in Chicago that he had written 'to the Archbishop of Tuam, in the West, yesterday to try to get him interested in AA. I believe he is, so I hope he will give us the green light for his See'.[72] A few months later, in preparation for the establishment of a group in Galway, Richard Perceval went to visit Archbishop Walsh and Sackville's account of this meeting was as follows:

> All seems to be getting set for the Galway meeting on December 8th. One of our members, Richard – a Protestant – went to call on the Archbishop of Tuam the other day. He apologised in advance for any mistakes he might make in addressing him, and pleaded that he was the first Archbishop that he had met. The Archbishop said quietly that he hoped that he himself would be able to maintain the standard and not let Archbishops be thought less of by him. Rather nice of him.[73]

Three years later, presumably at the instigation of Richard Perceval and Sackville, Eva Jennings – who had originally befriended Conor Flynn and had continued to remain involved with the fellowship – wrote to Archbishop Walsh, whom she knew personally, sending him AA literature. The archbishop's reply is worth quoting at some length, since its content is unequivocally positive about AA, and its informality (it is hand-written in green ink) suggests that this was a churchman who was more interested in doing something that might be practically helpful than in standing on his ecclesiastical dignity:

> My dear Eva,
>
> Thank you very much for sending the documents. I found them very useful. Please forgive my delay in writing – but a lot of things have turned up to keep me more than occupied. Since you wrote I received 'The Furrow' which contains an article 'Alcoholics Anonymous'. This is most interesting, well written and I think calculated to do a lot of good. I should like to see the article produced as a pamphlet, and I intend to write to Fr O'Flynn, Maynooth. He might induce the C.T.S. [Catholic Truth Society] to publish it ...
>
> One thing occurs to me in connection with the article. In all our towns we have a number of alcoholics. The number of these is small, and I fear these towns are too small to warrant the establishment of a centre of AA. Would it be possible to extend the centres on a County or parochial basis, so that these men in the smaller towns be taken in?
>
> Anyhow I am anxious to see a big extension of AA. It is capable of doing a great deal of good – so I shall be anxious to hear what you think.
>
> Kindest regards,
> Joseph Walsh[74]

In the light of this obvious goodwill and pleasant informality, one might wonder whether continuing fears about clerical aggression were not exaggerated or indicative of paranoia on the part of AA and its Irish promoters. While it remains at the level of surmise, the most likely explanation for this ongoing fear of conflict with the Catholic Church is that it was primarily based on the reputation of Dr John Charles McQuaid, archbishop of Dublin, in whose diocese AA had been first established in this country. Bearing in mind the nature of AA's programme of recovery as discussed in Chapter 3, there were several objections that might potentially have been raised by members of the Catholic hierarchy. The most radical objection might have been that, for its own members, the Catholic Church was the obvious institutional conduit for 'spiritual awakening' and, therefore, that Catholic alcoholics had no need of AA; less radically, it might have been argued that in an Irish context AA should have organized meetings which were confined to Catholics only and where the Higher Power was clearly identified as the Christian God. Although any or all of the Irish Catholic bishops might have raised such objections, in the context of church politics of the 1940s and the 1950s, the most likely source of such contention was Archbishop McQuaid of Dublin.

The only full-length biography of McQuaid, Cooney's (1999)[75] study, which in its subtitle describes McQuaid as the 'Ruler of Catholic Ireland', has been criticized as biased and unscholarly by McMahon, an academic historian who accuses Cooney of presenting 'McQuaid as a sort of episcopal prototype of J. Edgar Hoover, his tentacles reaching into every corner of the land that was the bleak Ireland of the 1940s and 1950s'.[76] Although specific aspects of Cooney's depiction of McQuaid – in particular a vague and unsubstantiated allegation of paedophilia – may validly be criticized, his overall portrait of an austere, conservative and authoritarian church leader is well documented and broadly in line with that presented by others who have written about McQuaid's long tenure as Archbishop of Dublin.

While Carty's (2007) book[77] – which draws both on archival material and on interviews with priests and religious people who knew and worked closely with McQuaid – has a specific focus on how McQuaid adapted to the radical theological implications of the Second Vatican Council, its overall depiction of the archbishop is not unlike that of Cooney. In particular, Carty highlights the difficulties which McQuaid experienced in reconciling his antipathy toward Protestantism with the emerging consensus within the Council that Catholics should work and pray with Protestants: recognizing the shared Christian heritage, rather than seeing all contacts with Protestants as aimed at converting them to Roman Catholicism. Similarly, Father Joe Dunn, who spent most of his priestly ministry involved in journalism and the production of television documentaries, wrote two books of reflection and reminiscence[78] in which *inter alia* he reflected on his relationship with McQuaid. In theological terms, Dunn was clearly in the liberal camp – a reader of *The Furrow* and an admirer of its founding

editor – but he managed his relationship with his superior pragmatically and with a certain degree of affection, summing it up
thus:

> I had a lot of dealings with Archbishop John Charles
> McQuaid. I became fond of him. I got on well with him, rela-
> tively speaking and judging by some of the stories that other
> priests tell ... That said, I must also say that there was no man
> that I feared more. He exercised absolute power over
> his priests which nobody in their right mind would dare
> question. The theology we were taught placed the bishop as
> pastor of the diocese and priests purely as extra arms and
> mouths and legs of the bishop. If it were possible to have
> clones of the bishop, then priests would be unnecessary.[79]

Dunn also confirms Cooney's view of McQuaid as someone who
combined strongly held proprietorial views about Dublin with a
somewhat lax attitude towards church–state boundaries: to the
archbishop, Dublin was 'my city'.[80] McQuaid had an undoubted
commitment to the creation and expansion of health and social
services in Dublin, but disliked interdenominational initiatives and
organizations which were completely outside of his own sphere
of influence. Cooney, for example, describes how an attempt to
create an interdenominational anti-tuberculosis organization in
1943 was effectively subverted by McQuaid, with this function
being assigned to the Red Cross Society, which was largely in
Catholic hands.[81] Similarly, Jordan discusses how proposals to
establish a Dublin branch of the Samaritans by a Church of Ireland
clergyman in 1969 evoked an uneasy response from Father E.F.
O'Doherty, a Dublin diocesan priest who was also Professor of
Psychology at University College Dublin, and who 'reading the
mind of his superior, distanced himself from the need for such an
idea for Dublin'.[82] This uneasiness surrounding the establishment
of the Samaritans exemplifies the anxiety experienced by Dublin
diocesan priests who, in a spirit of deference, tended to second-
guess how their superior might view new developments rather
than form their own judgements on such things.

In 1960 a four-day conference was held at St John of God's
Hospital in Stillorgan on the theme of 'The Priest and Mental
Health', and the conference proceedings were subsequently edited
for publication by E.F. O'Doherty and Desmond McGrath, the

hospital's medical director.[83] This conference was attended by priests and by Catholic mental health professionals and was primarily aimed at exploring how mental health concepts and practices could be of help to priests in their pastoral work. Three papers were read on the subject of alcoholism: one was by P.D. McCarthy, a consultant psychiatrist at St John of God's, which by now was openly acknowledging its commitment to alcoholism treatment; another was by Sean O'Riordan, who had moved from Maynooth to the Redemptorist Accademia Alfonsiana in Rome; and the third was by Sackville, who was simply described as 'A member of Alcoholics Anonymous'. The three presentations were generally in accord with one another and broadly supportive of the so-called 'disease concept of alcoholism', which at this time appeared to have the support of the medical profession and was also being promoted by the World Health Organization. O'Riordan's paper, which approaches the topic of alcoholism from a theological perspective, betrays a lingering nervousness about possible Catholic antagonism towards AA:

> Speaking as a priest, I should like to clear up one point about Alcoholics Anonymous and their methods of therapy. Some priests have been chary about invoking the help of this movement because of its undenominational character. Would not a similar movement but on specifically Catholic lines, they ask, be much better suited to our conditions and be more effective too, since then *all* the Church's sources of grace would be brought directly into play in helping the alcoholic back to sobriety and steady living? This might well be true in some cases: but the far-gone alcoholic, eaten up (as this type commonly is) with frustration and resentment – resentment against family and former friends, against priests and the Church, against life itself – just *cannot* be approached by a specifically spiritual or Catholic recovery agency.[84]

These remarks by Sean O'Riordan may be taken as reflecting a type of ideological limbo in which AA found itself in relation to the Catholic Church, almost fifteen years after its foundation in Ireland. Archbishop McQuaid, under whose patronage this conference was taking place, had not denounced the fellowship, but neither had he publicly supported it; so that, for its members, satisfaction with the fact that he had not attacked AA was mingled with anxiety that he might yet do so. Quite apart from McQuaid's theological misgivings about a fellowship which encouraged Catholics to mix with non-Catholics and to define their Higher Power without reference to the teaching authority of the Catholic Church, he could equally be expected to have grave reservations about its non-hierarchical leadership style. And, given the deference to which he was accustomed, he might well have felt resentment that AA had simply established itself in 'his' city without consulting with him, informing him or seeking his blessing. It is generally agreed that the archbishop was intellectually sharp and possessed of unusual stores of general knowledge, so it seems safe to assume that he was well informed about AA. It is also of interest to note that, in preparation for the Second Vatican Council, McQuaid had identified Moral Rearmament as one of the worrying developments which he thought the Council might address,[85] and again it is likely that he was aware of AA's origins in this movement in the USA.

Just as Sherlock Holmes famously observed the significance of the curious fact that the dog did not bark in the night, it is noteworthy that the archbishop made no public utterance about AA and that there is absolutely no reference to the fellowship in the McQuaid archival records, which are now available to researchers.[86] It is equally remarkable, however, that Sackville made no specific reference to McQuaid in the many and detailed letters which he wrote to AA friends – and particularly in his letters to Bill Wilson and the staff of the Alcoholic Foundation in New York. If one links these two facts and tries to explain them, the most likely explanation – and one which is part of the lore of AA in Dublin and corroborated by interviews with AA 'old-timers' – is that McQuaid had developed a grudging respect for the fellowship because some of his own relatives had joined and found it helpful. It would appear that a number of meetings took place between McQuaid and the early promoters of AA in Ireland. Ruth Perceval, for instance, recalled that her husband Richard had met McQuaid on several occasions, although she was unsure whether Sackville was also party to these meetings. However, Donal X., a fellowship member from the late 1950s, recalled visiting the archbishop with Sackville and hearing McQuaid say that while he appreciated AA's work, he could not publicly endorse it.[87] Another fellowship member, Paddy K., who first joined AA in the early 1960s, had been a drinking friend of one of the archbishop's relatives who also joined AA at this time; Paddy recalled that this relative of McQuaid would visit the archbishop, who encouraged his membership and constantly inquired as to how he was getting on in the fellowship.

Sackville's letters to AA friends in other countries were frequent, lengthy and gossipy, and a likely reason for not mentioning such an important figure as McQuaid (it should be noted that he showed no such reticence about other churchmen) is that to do so might breach the fellowship's tradition of anonymity: arguably this would have occurred had he revealed that his acquaintance with the archbishop had originally been focused on relatives of McQuaid who had attended AA meetings. The first reference to the archbishop to be found in Sackville's correspondence with Bill Wilson is in a letter dating from 1961, and this reference would seem to corroborate the belief that McQuaid was well disposed towards AA but felt himself incapable of publicly expressing his support:

> One of our city groups lost its rooms a couple of weeks back ... but they are now fixed up again most satisfactorily. The most satisfactory thing to my eye is that the owner is the Catholic Archbishop of Dublin who has asked for a very nominal rent of about four to five dollars a week for two good rooms and coffee making facilities. This will be a distinct feather in our caps, having him on the right side of the fence <u>openly</u> for the first time [underlining in original].[88]

It was not until 1967, however, that AA members were invited to speak to students in Holy Cross College, the seminary adjoining the archbishop's residence where students were prepared for ministry in Dublin. Writing to his friend Joe D. in Chicago, Sackville remarked: 'I crash the sound barrier into Holy Cross College on Sun. Feb. 12, as this is the first time the Archbishop of Dublin's own Dublin Diocesan Seminary has invited us in.'[89] This invitation may also have reflected McQuaid's growing understanding that priests could benefit from a knowledge of AA, not merely with reference to their pastoral work with problem drinkers but also because of their own alcoholic proclivities. It was generally accepted that despite his overall authoritarian approach to managing his priests, McQuaid was kind to priests who developed personal problems, including alcohol problems. As Big Eugene, an AA member, put it: 'He was very kind to alcoholics; did you know that? If you had an alcoholic priest now, McQuaid had a terrible soft spot for them.'[90] While it could never have been an easy admission for him, McQuaid may have gradually come to realize that the spirituality of AA – in all its Protestant vagueness – was helping some of his own diocesan priests to remain sober. However one views it – whether as paranoia on the part of Sackville or as a realistic assessment of the power wielded by John Charles McQuaid – the fact remains that, even as it celebrated its twenty-first birthday in Ireland, AA members continued to be aware of the fact that the Archbishop of Dublin had never given the fellowship his blessing, so that attack from this quarter could not yet be ruled out.

ALCOHOLICS ANONYMOUS AND THE PIONEERS

As discussed in Chapter 2, the Pioneer Total Abstinence Association (PTAA) had been founded in 1898 by a Jesuit priest, Father James Cullen, and the Jesuits had continued to manage the Pioneers on behalf of the Catholic bishops of Ireland. In ideological terms, the Pioneer movement reflected Catholic views on temperance and was considerably more moderate than that of Father Mathew; it will be recalled that in the mid-nineteenth century Father Mathew had conducted an aggressive anti-alcohol campaign, which had enjoyed astonishing albeit short-lived success. Father Cullen did not expect his organization to be comparable in scale to the Father Mathew movement; instead, as the name 'Pioneer' suggests, he envisaged it as consisting of an elite group of Catholics who would practise lifelong abstinence from alcohol for spiritual motives. Above all, Father Cullen was adamant that his association was neither intended for regular drinkers who wished to have a period of respite from their drinking nor for the rehabilitation of problem drinkers. Malcolm (1986) has quoted him on this topic: 'For chronic drunkards and periodic boozers, jovial tipplers, "weary wobblers", or even moderate drinkers, we keep no ordinary or reserved seats. They must travel by other trains – ours is a special.'[91] Despite such modest intentions, the PTAA expanded hugely, becoming an extremely

large and well-known institution within the wider Catholic community in Ireland; when AA began to establish itself in Ireland in
the late 1940s, membership of the Pioneers – signified by the
wearing of a distinctive lapel pin depicting the Sacred Heart of
Jesus – appears to have been close to half a million.[92] Although
the dominant motivation for membership continued to be one of
voluntary renunciation of alcohol for spiritual purposes, Pioneer
leaders by this time had deviated from Father Cullen's strictures
about not allowing drinkers on his 'special train', and were now
giving a temporary pledge to problem drinkers who sought to
join the PTAA as a means of resolving personal alcohol problems.
In the context of its general desire to foster good relations with
the Catholic Church, it was clearly important for AA that it
should – at a minimum – not be seen as being in any way critical
of, or in competition with, the Pioneers.

There is, in fact, relatively little direct reference to the
Pioneers to be found within the AA archives, and absolutely no
indication of tension or conflict between these two institutions,
which, while sharing a common concern with alcohol-related
problems, had different aims and different target groups.
Sackville had always cultivated good relationships with the
Jesuits, and may have been assisted in this task by the fact that his
first cousin, Father Charles O'Conor (who held the hereditary
title 'The O'Conor Don') was a Jesuit priest who served as
Provincial of the order in Ireland between 1959 and 1965.
Sackville also maintained contact with the long-serving director
of the Pioneers, Father Daniel Dargan, regularly sending him
copies of *The Road Back*, the newsletter of AA in Ireland which
he edited for almost thirty years.[93]

What the Pioneer archives[94] reveal, however, is that, throughout the 1960s internal organizational strains emerged within the
Pioneers in relation to attempts to modernize this Irish Catholic
temperance movement, with AA being cited (probably without its
knowledge and certainly without its consent) by the main propo-
nent of change as an example of the modern, progressive and
scientific approach to alcohol problems. Father John Mulligan
had originally studied at Clonliffe College and at St Patrick's
Maynooth with a view to serving as a priest in the Archdiocese of
Dublin, but then joined the Jesuits and was ordained a priest in
1954.[95] Father Mulligan appears to have been a lifelong Pioneer,

and in 1960 he was appointed spiritual director to the influential Saint Francis Xavier Council of the Pioneers (based in Pioneer headquarters at Upper Sherrard Street in Dublin) and – at national level – assistant director to Father Daniel Dargan.[96] Mulligan saw himself as a reformer whose task it was to shake the PTAA out of its lethargy and compel it, however unwillingly, to adapt to the world of the 1960s. His modernizing instincts were reinforced by the ethos of the Second Vatican Council, with its rhetoric of *aggiornamento* and its general openness to change and adaptation to the modern world. Prior to his appointment as its spiritual director, monthly meetings of the Saint Francis Xavier Council (as recorded in its handwritten minutes) were characterized by a quiet piety and a distinct lack of controversy, but all this was to change. Month after month, Mulligan harangued the council members on what he perceived to be their lack of understanding of alcoholism, their conservatism on all matters relating to alcohol and on the necessity for change. He was especially emphatic that problem drinkers seeking admission to the PTAA should be referred on to Alcoholics Anonymous, although it was far from clear that he really understood AA or its *modus operandi*. In February 1964, for instance, the council minutes noted:

> After the minutes of the previous meeting had been read and adopted Fr J. Mulligan discoursed on the attitudes which aught to be adopted by Councillors when dealing with people who have quite obviously a drink problem. They should be advised, he suggested, to go to AA. If they insist on taking a pledge it may be given (Temp. Pledge). In such cases they could be asked to read the series of questions presented by AA to all intending members of that Assoc. If they recognise in these questions their own special problems they are clearly alcoholics or at the very least [word illegible] a serious drinking problem.[97]

The minutes reveal that Father Mulligan was unrelenting in his presentation of views which showed the Pioneers up in a very negative light, while simultaneously praising AA members for their insight and general virtue, but some monthly meetings stand out for the strength of these views; and his opinions expressed in May 1966 were especially forthright:

Fr Mulligan initiated a discussion on Membership of the Pioneer Assoc. and the attitudes which should be shown by members of the Assoc. to Alcoholics and Alcoholism. Fr Mulligan holds the view that the attitude of Pioneers towards Alcoholism was not Christlike inasmuch as there was a great lack of charity shown towards such people. He urged that we Pioneers should have a very special interest in helping and assisting alcoholics and that it is only by doing this that we will be able to show a positive approach. He believes that much of the criticism of the Pioneer Assoc. has its roots in the 'holier than thou' attitude which, he believes, was held by Pioneers in the past. That must, he said, be shed if we are to get down to real lasting work. Continuing, he explained that this will not be possible until Pioneers become acquainted with the problem of alcoholism. If we are to help these people we must learn to understand their problems, he said.[98]

With the exception of the spiritual director, these meetings were attended by laymen (there were no women members on the council during the 1960s) whose attitude towards Father Mulligan, as reflected in the minutes, changed as the years went by: shifting gradually from pious acceptance to simmering resentment and finally to open mutiny. When the papers from the Second Vatican Council were published and came to influence his thoughts, Father Mulligan drew explicitly on these papers in support of his advocacy of modernization of the Pioneers. For instance, in May 1967 the minute-taker referred to a paper read by Father Mulligan: 'There was some discussion on his paper and it took a turn towards developing attitudes of Catholics stemming from Vatican II. The discussion was exhilarating 'though it did expose that some thinking Catholics were bewildered at developing trends in Church thinking.'[99] Father Mulligan's views, including his recommendation that the Pioneer pin be replaced, that Protestants should be admitted to the PTAA and that there should be a move away from devotion to the Sacred Heart, were generally regarded as unacceptable to the Saint Francis Xavier Council.

The meeting of May 1969 appears to have been the last straw as far as council members were concerned. The minutes of this monthly meeting record a discussion and vote on the merits of

sending a goodwill message from the PTAA to the Kilkenny Beer
Festival; a Kilkenny-based priest had already done this and Father
Mulligan thought that such a message reflected a mature and
modern attitude towards alcohol on the part of the Pioneers.[100]
One can only surmise that following this meeting council members
besieged Father Dargan with pleas to have their spiritual director
moved, because the next month's minutes simply recorded that
'Reference was made to the pending transfer of Fr John Mulligan,
S.J. ... The Council wished him every success in his future work
for God and His Church.'[101] The fact that Mulligan was not only
at loggerheads with the Saint Francis Xavier Council but also
with his religious confrère, Father Dargan, became clear when,
following his removal from all official Pioneer roles, he became
involved in a controversial exchange of letters with Father
Dargan in a Sunday paper concerning the future of the PTAA.
The Jesuit Provincial, Father Cecil McGarry, finally intervened to
bring to an end this public disagreement between two Jesuit
priests on the future of the Pioneers. Writing to Mulligan at the
end of September 1969, the Provincial had this to say:

> I know that your desire is to help the cause of temperance.
> I have been witness over the past few years of your interest
> and zeal to find ways in which this can be promoted in a way
> calculated to appeal to modern young people. I know of
> your interest to see that the PTAA does not become obsolete.
> It is my considered view, John, that further letters from you
> to the newspapers will not in fact further the very objects
> you have at heart.
>
> Quite a considerable number of priests, nuns and laypeople
> have commented to me and to other Jesuits these past weeks
> on the impropriety of the public fued [sic] you seem to be
> conducting through the newspapers with Father Dargan. I
> know this is not your intention but this is the impression
> that has been given. It is certainly not helping the PTAA to
> adapt itself or find new ways. If you were not till recently
> the Assistant Central Director the situation would be quite
> different ... I would ask you, therefore, John, not to continue
> this particular way of serving the cause, which I know is your
> desire and motive in these letters.[102]

This request from his Provincial effectively brought to an end

Father Mulligan's campaign to reform the Pioneers and, in particular, to persuade it to adopt some of the attitudes and practices
of AA – at least as Mulligan understood AA. Needless to say, AA
had not been consulted on any of these matters and would, in any
event, have refused to become involved in what were internal
matters of the PTAA and 'outside issues' as far as the fellowship
was concerned. While Father Mulligan's monthly homilies to the
Saint Francis Xavier Council can scarcely have endeared AA to
council members, there is no evidence of any lasting damage to
AA–PTAA relations. Big Eugene, an AA old-timer who knew Father
Mulligan, remembered him with amused affection, referring to him
as 'Buck' Mulligan (a Joycean reference) and concluding that 'he
was a terrible confused man in ways',[103] a description with which
many Pioneers of the time would presumably have concurred.

PAPAL AUDIENCE

The first European Convention of AA had been scheduled to take
place in Bristol during September 1971, with Bill Wilson lined up
to address this historic event. However, in January 1971 Wilson
died, and it is a measure of Sackville's standing in the global
fellowship that he was asked to address this convention in the
co-founder's place. The main organizer of the Bristol convention
was Travers C., an English Catholic who had invited the
Apostolic Delegate to Great Britain (equivalent to Ireland's Papal
Nuncio) to attend as a guest of honour. The Apostolic Delegate,
Archbishop Domenico Enrici, accepted this invitation, found the
experience interesting and subsequently discussed AA with
Sackville and Travers. As Sackville later explained it to Cardinal
William Conway of Armagh:

> Afterwards, he [Archbishop Enrici] expressed his opinion
> that a visit by AA members to the Vatican would be of great
> value, as he believed that very little was known there about
> the problem of alcoholism or the AA way of Recovery.
> Accordingly, he asked the convenor of the Bristol
> Convention and myself to go to Rome.[104]

How serious or enthusiastic the Apostolic Delegate was about this
visit to Rome is not clear from the archival records, but there is
absolutely no doubting Sackville's determination to grasp this

opportunity to, as he put it, 'convert Rome to AA'.[105] What also emerges with clarity from the records is that Sackville did not wish to consult with or involve Archbishop McQuaid in relation to this proposed trip. Archbishop Enrici had agreed to introduce Travers to contacts who might prove useful to him in Rome, and Sackville had requested that he also might be included in these introductions, specifically requesting that he be introduced to the Rector of the Irish College in Rome. Whether or not he was consciously seeking to avoid being drawn into Irish church politics, the Apostolic Delegate demurred, replying to Travers: 'With regard to the Irish College, it would be appropriate if Major Sackville Mallins were to obtain an introduction from the Archbishop of Dublin.'[106] Sackville, however, neither sought such an introduction nor informed Archbishop McQuaid of his planned visit to Rome.

Sackville left Dublin on 8 January 1972, travelling first to Bristol where he met Travers, with whom he travelled on to Rome. Their main contact in Rome was Father Cormac Murphy-O'Connor, rector of the Venerable English College in Rome (later to become the Cardinal Archbishop of Westminster), who performed wonders in introducing them to key figures in the Vatican and in the wider sphere of Catholic politics. They were invited to address the staff and students at the main English-speaking seminaries – the Beda, Irish, English, Scots and North American Colleges – and they also met with Father Pedro Arrupe, Superior General of the Jesuits, and with Cardinal Wright of the Congregation of Rites.[107] But the high point of their trip was a private audience with Pope Paul VI on January 19, which Sackville described in a hurried note written on that same day to his friend Joe D. in Chicago:

> Only 3 at it. This strikes me as an historic AA [*sic*] – first 2 members to be received by a Pope as AA members. He looked well, has beautiful eyes and hands and grace of movement – speaks poor English but understands it well. He began by thanking us for 'our' work (for our and your translate to 'AA') which he knew of (?) and thought a real Apostolate. He asked a few Q's about numbers and Catholics in it, then urged us to press on 'in our noble work'.[108]

No sooner was he back in Dublin than Sackville wrote a short account of his trip for publication in the March 1972 issue of *The Furrow*, reporting that:

> The Pope graciously greeted us not only for our own sakes, but for the work we were engaged on (i.e. Alcoholics Anonymous), which he described as fine work, a real apostolate. He urged us to press on with our work, gave it his blessing and told us that he would keep it and us in his prayers.[109]

It now seemed unlikely that, with endorsement of this kind from the Pope, any Irish bishop could ever contemplate mounting a serious attack on AA. But in many ways it could be argued that Sackville's papal audience was unnecessary and that, having survived twenty-five years without such attack, AA in Ireland had by now largely put itself beyond the reach of potential clerical critics. John Charles McQuaid's influence within the wider group of Irish bishops had apparently been waning for some years, as exemplified by the lifting in 1970 of the ban on Catholic attendance at Trinity College, Dublin. Then, on 4 January 1972, just a few days before Sackville set off for Rome, it was announced – quite unexpectedly– that the Pope had accepted Archbishop McQuaid's resignation and was appointing Father Dermot Ryan as his successor. Sackville's decision to write to Cardinal Conway of Armagh – and not to McQuaid – with an account of his Roman trip could be seen as simply reflecting this interim situation in Dublin, but it may also have reflected the fact that two years earlier Conway had publicly supported the fellowship by attending a national AA convention in Newry. Replying to Sackville's letter, which somewhat disingenuously explained that he had not given the Cardinal prior notice of his trip to Rome because it had been so hurriedly arranged, Conway was full of uncomplicated goodwill:

> Thank you so much for your kind letter and I am very pleased everything went so well for you on your visit to Rome. I have happy memories of our meeting in Newry and I wish you and the movement every blessing and success.[110]

While this papal endorsement may be seen as bringing to an end Irish members' fears of the legendary 'belt of a crozier', its somewhat ambiguous reception within AA circles in New York provides another example of the fellowship's unusual organizational style.

Almost immediately after returning from Rome, Sackville had written to the AA General Service Board at New York, describing the papal audience and enclosing a photograph of Sackville and Travers with Pope Paul VI, which was to be passed on to Lois Wilson, Bill Wilson's widow. The initial response from Robert Hitchins at the General Service Board was uniformly positive and enthusiastic, and offered to reimburse some of the expenses incurred by Sackville and Travers in making the trip.[111] The photograph was received with great delight by Lois Wilson: 'Upon returning home from my trip abroad I found the exciting picture of you and the Pope and Travers. How wonderful that you were able to tell him about AA in a private audience!'[112] Within a few weeks, however, staff at the General Service Board had begun to express reservations about the propriety of the papal audience and, more especially, about publicizing it through AA publications lest such publicity could be seen to violate the fellowship's Traditions. Ann MacFarlane, an old friend of Sackville's who was on the staff at the New York office, pulled no punches in explaining these reservations:

> For instance, much as we loved seeing your picture with the Pope, it is in violation of our Anonymity Tradition, even if your names were not used, unless it is to be used solely as a personal memento for you and Travers, and there is a further point that we are nonsectarian and that to involve us too closely with Catholicism might bring about a misunderstanding on the part of the general public, even if your visit was undertaken in the simple interest of providing information about our fellowship.
>
> At this time we have not attempted, for instance, to meet with the top people in the other major religions of the world ...
>
> Now that Ireland has its own Board [a General Service Office had been opened in Dublin in 1970] we would suggest that you bring the matter about publicizing the fact of your visit to the Vatican to them for their consideration. We have felt for a long time, as you know, that we cannot act as the International Service Board for all the world.[113]

In reply to this letter, Sackville wrote a spirited and detailed response, pointing out that both the New York and Dublin General Service Boards had been informed in advance about the

visit to Rome, and reminding Ann MacFarlane that AA had previously publicized its acceptance of the Steubenville award from
the Franciscan Order, and that Bill Wilson had checked out the
religious acceptability of the Big Book with the Catholic
Archdiocese of New York prior to its first printing.[114] This dispute
was never resolved in any conventional way, since both Ann
MacFarlane and Sackville clung to their respective convictions
about whether the papal audience and the subsequent publicity
were, or were not, in keeping with AA Traditions. Ann
MacFarlane reminded Sackville that she knew her views were her
own and not reflective of AA as a whole, and she did not appeal
to any ultimate authority to validate them: 'Anyway, I do think
that the nice thing about AA is that we can differ in ideas and
opinions but still love one another, and I do love you Sackville
old dear, and have for years as you know.'[115]

While the photograph of Sackville, Travers and Pope Paul VI
is still to be seen at the General Service Office in Dublin (as it is
at the General Service Office in New York), the issue of Catholic
antagonism towards AA seemed to be of less and less significance
from that time onwards. What this chapter has shown is that,
despite the fact that it had its origins in the Protestant Evangelical
tradition of the USA and was generally viewed as being more
readily diffused to Protestant countries, AA had its first European
experience in Catholic Ireland where it successfully negotiated a
modus vivendi with the dominant Catholic Church. The next
chapter will look in detail at the work of its first members in
negotiating a similar relationship with the medical profession and
the health care system.

Chapter Five

AA, Alcoholism Treatment and the Irish Health Care System

If one is to treat alcoholism successfully, whether in hospital or in general practice, one must feel as well as believe that the alcoholic is ill and suffering from a disease just as surely as a diabetic is suffering from his excess blood sugar ... [B]y their acceptance of the disease concept of alcoholism they [doctors] can influence public opinion and help to bring about an attitude whereby the alcoholic is regarded not as a moral degenerate but as a sick man.[1]

SCIENTIFIC CONSENSUS ON THE STATUS OF ALCOHOLISM?

As outlined in Chapters 2 and 3, the nineteenth and early twentieth centuries were marked by considerable controversy and disagreement as to how society should conceptualize and manage those of its members – variously described as *habitual drunkards*, *chronic inebriates*, *dipsomaniacs* and occasionally *alcoholics* – whose drinking was consistently disruptive to their families or to the wider community. Essentially what was at issue was whether problem drinking of this kind should be regarded as illness/disease and therefore be subject to the ministrations of doctors within health care systems, or whether it was more appropriate to see it as a vice to be punished and, ideally, corrected by criminal justice institutions. Neither the USA nor Britain had succeeded in achieving cultural and societal consensus on this matter, and, not surprisingly, Ireland fared no better in this regard. The Intoxicating Liquor Commission of 1925 (the first official committee to review alcohol issues in the Irish Free State) had expressed a preference for the use of criminal justice rather than rehabilitative institutions in the management of problem drinkers, but the commission's punitive recommendations on this matter were never implemented by government. Neither, it should be pointed out, did the public psychiatric system show any great interest in claiming 'ownership' of drinking problems, although some twenty years later the Mental Treatment Act, 1945, included what could be seen as a belated and somewhat begrudging acceptance of responsibility for the management of alcoholics by the Irish mental health system.

Since psychiatrists had consistently been ambivalent about managing alcoholism, it could not be assumed that they would welcome the advent of AA, and this chapter will look in detail at the way in which fellowship members in Ireland negotiated working relationships with psychiatry and later with newer models of alcoholism treatment – all in the context of the broader societal promotion of the disease concept of alcoholism.

Jellinek's (1960) much cited study of the disease concept began by arguing that despite the tendency from about 1940 onwards to refer to this as the 'new approach to alcoholism', it might be more accurate to refer to it as the 'renewed approach';[2] this was because a previous attempt (in the late nineteenth century) to persuade doctors and public policy makers that alcoholism was a disease had failed. Whether this second attempt, which originated in post-Prohibition America and which explicitly represented itself as reflecting scientific advances in this field, would be any more successful than the first remained to be seen. The quote used as an epigraph to this chapter is from a paper published in 1963 by Dr John Cooney, consultant psychiatrist at St Patrick's Hospital, Dublin, and is broadly typical of disease concept rhetoric of this period. It obviously reflects Cooney's personal commitment to the disease concept and its perceived capacity to usher in a more scientific, and less moralistic, societal regime for the management of alcoholism. However, as may be implied from the overall tone of this quote – and particularly the emotive reference to the necessity to 'feel' that the alcoholic is ill in the same way as a diabetic is ill – its author appeared to recognize that neither doctors nor members of the general public would automatically be persuaded by the scientific evidence allegedly underpinning the disease concept. It was pointed out in Chapter 3 that by the early 1960s American social scientists had already begun to look critically at the disease concept, arguing that it was a social construction or social policy initiative rather than a scientific advance. Similarly, British addiction specialist Griffith Edwards, describing an alcohol-focused study tour of North America which he made in 1961, has revealed how ideological splits were already manifesting themselves within the American alcoholism movement; he particularly recalled the vehemence with which Selden Bacon (a sociologist who was then director of the Center of Alcohol Studies at Yale) had denounced Marty Mann's National Council on Alcoholism as a 'crowd of cultists'.[3] What this reveals is that opposition to the disease concept did not, as proponents of the concept tended to suggest, merely reflect populist moralism and ignorance, but could also be expected to come from researchers who questioned its scientific base or who had studied both its anticipated and unanticipated consequences. By the late 1960s biomedical researchers had joined their social science colleagues in expressing strong criticism of the scientific validity and practical utility of the *alcoholism as disease* idea, and by the mid-1970s the WHO had all but renounced it.[4]

Butler (2002)[5] has shown that in Ireland acceptance of the disease concept at public policy level was a slow, cautious process, coming to fruition in the mid-1960s, but almost immediately beginning to unravel as empirical research evidence accumulated to challenge its most basic tenets. By 1984, when an important mental health policy document *The Psychiatric Services: Planning for the Future*[6] was published, the official policy debate had moved on – reflecting the volte-face of the WHO on this issue – to such an extent that in this policy document alcoholism was summarily dismissed as an unhelpful and scientifically unsustainable concept. Instead, official Irish health policy moved gradually to what was becoming the new WHO orthodoxy on alcohol: usually referred to as the total consumption model or the public health perspective on alcohol.[7]

The distinguishing feature of the disease concept which evolved in post-Prohibition America was that it attributed primary causal responsibility for alcohol problems to the putative biological defects (genetic or otherwise) of a minority of consumers, deemed to be predisposed to alcoholism. Implicit in this concept was the idea that within any society drinkers could be divided into two clear categories: *social drinkers*, who made up the vast majority, and *alcoholics*, who constituted an unfortunate minority. From a health service perspective, the obvious expectation arising from acceptance of the disease concept was that alcoholics should be offered treatment befitting their status as sick people. From a more general public policy perspective, however, what was implied in the disease concept was that there was no justification for the imposition by the state of controls or sanctions on social drinkers; this was because it was assumed that however much they drank, social drinkers were never going to become alcoholic. For the state to implement strict control or prohibition of alcohol was – to those who subscribed to the disease concept – equivalent to banning foodstuffs to which a minority of its population was allergic but which could be eaten with impunity by a majority of its citizens.

The public health or total consumption approach, developed and promoted by the WHO from the early 1970s onwards, effectively constituted a repudiation of almost all aspects of the disease concept. The public health approach advocated a return to 'drier' alcohol policies by re-emphasizing the negative properties of alcohol (its toxicity, its addictiveness and its capacity to intoxicate), which were deemed to create risk for all consumers. This new WHO approach drew on epidemiological research to point out that drinking contributed to a spectrum of health and social problems, and not just to alcohol dependence or 'alcoholism'. It also argued, on epidemiological grounds, that the prevalence of these varied alcohol-related problems was directly related to the total volume of alcohol consumed in any given society: in other words, one could expect to find that when alcohol consumption increased so too would the prevalence of related problems. The major policy implication of this model was that, rather than concentrating on the provision of treatment services for 'alcoholics' (which at best was deemed to make only a modest impact on reducing societal alcohol-related problems), the state should prevent problems by implementing strategies aimed at reducing total societal consumption. Furthermore, it was suggested that in order to reduce consumption the state should rely primarily on the implementation of alcohol control measures – for example, raising the price of alcoholic beverages, limiting access to retail outlets, and restricting the advertising and promotion of alcohol. These paternalistic strategies were advocated because evaluative research consistently revealed that, despite their popularity and intuitive political appeal, more liberal approaches – such as school-based alcohol programmes or awareness-raising campaigns aimed at the general public – had no proven effectiveness. Whatever the scientific merits of the public health approach, it was and continues to be politically contentious since it both challenges popular drinking habits and antagonizes the drinks industry; and while numerous policy reports have recommended its implementation, relatively little progress has been made in doing so.[8]

In short, the scientific consensus on alcoholism as a disease failed to grow as had been anticipated, or to provide definitive support for the view that society should see alcoholism as a 'respectable disease' essentially comparable to diabetes. Jellinek's 'renewed approach' to the disease concept largely succeeded in gaining and retaining popular and political support in the USA, its country of origin, but failed to sustain its position in many other countries, including Ireland, where it made an initial impact. Biomedical and social science research did not, as had been expected, provide unequivocal support for the main tenets of the disease concept, thereby bringing to an end moral and political debate about the role of alcohol in society. On the contrary, evaluative research increasingly cast doubt on the conventional wisdom that investing in more intensive (and more expensive) alcoholism treatment programmes would result in better outcomes; and eventually a critical literature was to emerge on alcoholism treatment as an unscientific and largely self-serving 'industry'.[9] Similarly, broader epidemiological research cast doubt on the validity of the distinction between *alcoholics* and *social drinkers*, and made clear the folly of creating the impression that 'non-alcoholic' drinkers – that is, the majority of drinkers in any society – could increase their consumption levels with impunity.

It should be evident from this introduction that for Irish AA members the task of negotiating relationships with the health care system would prove to be far from straightforward, in the context of a complex and constantly changing policy environment. This chapter will look in detail, therefore, at how this task was accomplished and at the tensions and controversies that arose along the way. It is to be expected that, as in the case of its relationships with the Catholic Church, early AA members in Ireland would seek guidance from their American progenitors and also from the fellowship's Twelve Traditions, which suggested that 'the AA name ought never be drawn into public controversy' (Tradition Ten). One could expect, therefore, that just as Bill Wilson and his fellowship colleagues had opted to keep an exclusive focus on helping individual alcoholics while steering clear of alcohol politics, Irish AA would also distance itself from debate on such topics as licensing legislation, alcohol taxation, drink-driving or health service treatment of alcoholism.

DEALING WITH THE DOCTORS

In his talk at the celebration to mark AA's twenty-first birthday in Ireland, Conor Flynn recalled the sense of unease with which he had approached Dr Norman Moore back in November 1946, an unease which was not solely based on his peremptory dismissal by Dr John Dunne on the occasion of his earlier visit to Grangegorman. He was, he said, acutely conscious of the disparity between Norman Moore and himself in terms of their educational backgrounds: Dr Moore was qualified in medicine and had specialist training in psychiatry while Conor, who was presuming to help him with his management of alcoholic patients, had nothing more than what he described as 'high-school' education.[10] Although Norman Moore's response had none of the arrogance and aggression demonstrated by his colleague in Grangegorman, it is understandable that early AA members in Ireland should have experienced some trepidation about how they might establish working relationships with members of the medical profession. In an era where the idea of mutual help between 'sufferers' of various mental health problems was virtually unknown, the AA programme and practice might well have been interpreted as disrespectful of or a challenge to medical authority.

Just as he had played a dominant role as Secretary of the first Dublin AA group in bridge-building with the Catholic Church, Sackville took the lead from mid-1947 onwards in forming alliances between the fellowship and members of the medical profession. He approached this task carefully and tactfully, clearly appreciating the importance of fostering good relationships with doctors, but also – and perhaps in keeping with his status as a member of the 'officer class' – with confidence and without any of the unease expressed by Conor Flynn. However, the overall picture that emerges from his correspondence is that, beneath his innate courtesy and pragmatic acceptance of the importance of getting on well with doctors, Sackville remained deeply sceptical of the value of medical involvement in the management of alcoholics. This scepticism appears to have been primarily based on his personal experience (referred to in Chapter 4) of having been treated by up to forty different doctors, in almost as many hospitals, before he eventually stopped drinking with the help of AA. His irreverence towards psychiatry is reflected, for instance, in a letter of 1947 to two staff members at the AA Foundation in New York telling them of his success in interesting 'a couple of "trick cyclists"'[11] in the fellowship. A year later, while welcoming the fact that a prominent Dublin psychiatrist had publicly expressed support for AA, Sackville drew on his personal experience to raise doubts concerning this doctor's capacity to help alcoholics:

> By the way, I enclose a small cutting from the Dublin Irish Independent – it is our first medical boost. Dr Eustace is one of the mental experts in Dublin, tho' I haven't much time for him personally. He tried to put me on Benzydryns [*sic*] instead of alcohol 2 years ago.[12]

Criticism of psychiatric treatment on the grounds that it simply added dependency on prescribed drugs to dependency on alcohol was a recurring theme throughout Sackville's correspondence; such criticism was expressed in relatively mild terms, however, and was interspersed with empathic comment on the particular problems experienced by members of the medical profession who themselves had succumbed to alcoholism. Writing to his friend Joe D. in Chicago in 1948, Sackville described the tentative overtures made by one Dublin GP, who moved gradually from expressing interest in working collaboratively with AA to admitting that he was an alcoholic himself who had been taking self-prescribed drugs – as an alternative to going to the pub:

> The doctor who has been so good and helpful to us asked me to come out and see him. He told me he was an alcoholic, but has managed to damp it down, and that he had really been

working for the group to help himself as well ... Anyway, he promises to stop taking the stuff [prescribed drugs], to buy a couple of novels for the night instead, and to come to our meeting on Monday and talk. I quite realised that he is in a difficult position, being a doctor, if he wanted to join as a member. It would in fact be his death warrant in Dublin professionally speaking.[13]

About six months later and shortly before a group had been started in Cork, Sackville returned to this theme, telling Joe D. about the correspondence he had been exchanging with a doctor in West Cork:

> The Skibbereen doctor has been landed. I got a letter from him asking to be regarded as a member and saying that he had never realised that it was the first drink that got him down. Physician, cure thyself, indeed. I find most of the alcoholic doctors go in for drugging as well.[14]

On the whole, however, relationships with doctors and with psychiatric hospitals proceeded smoothly, and the archives record no instance of major tension or conflict between AA and any of the institutions with which it sought to establish working relationships. Given that it had facilitated the fellowship's first Irish meeting, it was not surprising that St Patrick's Hospital continued to work collaboratively with AA. What is most interesting, however, is that within a relatively short space of time the dynamic between the psychiatrist and the recovering alcoholic had shifted, to the extent that it was Norman Moore (consultant psychiatrist and medical director) who was seeking professional advice from Sackville (an alcoholic in recent recovery). Writing to Bobbie Burger in June 1948, Sackville explained how this had occurred:

> I had the amusing experience of being asked by a psychoanalyst i/c [in charge] of the mental diseases hospital for my views on his treatment of alcoholism. (He is a very good man, very anxious to improve anything he can.) Rather bravely, I disagreed with a lot of it and have just heard from him that he is willing to try out at least one suggestion. I told him that if he wanted me to see any of his alcs. [sic] I should prefer to do so whilst they were sick and sorry and not as at present 6 weeks afterwards.[15]

What was equally interesting was that less than a year after Conor
Flynn had been told that St John of God's in Stillorgan never
treated *and never would treat* alcoholics, this hospital began to
express interest in having AA members visit its patients. Sackville,
who may not have been aware of Conor's unsuccessful trip to St
John of God's, told Bobbie Burger in October 1947 that he had
heard that the head of this institution was going to ask AA to send
in some members to contact suitable patients; this, Sackville
thought, would be 'a great chance for us to help, and to spread
our influence'.[16] Similarly, it appears that once it had established
a reputation for uncomplicated collaborative work with psychiatric hospitals, Dr John Dunne of Grangegorman appears to have
forgotten his initial dismissal of AA. In early 1950, Sackville
described how he had been invited to speak at a meeting of the
Medical Society (an undergraduate student society) at University
College Dublin, at which John Dunne engaged in some good-
humoured teasing about AA's ideal of lifelong abstinence from
alcohol for its members:

> I spent last night with the Medical Society of National
> University, and it was pretty good value. There were some
> important doctors there, and I was able to give forth about
> AA and its aims and way of going to work for ten minutes
> or so. The RMS of the big Mental Home here [Dr John
> Dunne] suggested that we might imitate the custom of prim-
> itive tribes who go on an orgy occasionally, and then get rid
> of their repressions for a long time to come. What do you
> think? I imagine it might be hard to repatch the group
> together after one of these beanos. However, of course he
> was only in fun.[17]

The most obvious explanation for this establishment of smooth
working relationships between AA and the medical profession is
that Richard Perceval, Sackville and other early members adhered
scrupulously to the fellowship's Twelve Traditions, thereby maintaining clear boundaries between themselves and the doctors. AA
members simply went into those hospitals where they were invited
to establish groups for alcoholic inpatients and, having established
contact with newly detoxified alcoholics, encouraged them to
keep attending meetings following their discharge from hospital.
Early AA members posed no professional challenge to the doctors

with whom they worked because they did not represent themselves as therapists or counsellors, nor did they purport to offer any scientific explanation of alcoholism. In line with established practice in the USA, established members confined themselves to telling their stories – the way they had been; what they had done to change; and the way they were now – with a view to creating a sense of identification between themselves and those alcoholics who were just emerging from recent binges. This storytelling, which has always been at the heart of AA practice, represented a pragmatic approach to the management of alcoholism rather than a scientific model that could be construed as a challenge to the sapiential authority or professional status of members of the medical profession.

What was also important, although it was not to feature significantly in Sackville's correspondence until many years later, was that AA was an entirely voluntary fellowship (Tradition Seven states that 'Every AA Group ought to be fully self-supporting, declining outside contributions') which neither sought nor accepted financial contributions from institutions to which it could be deemed to be providing a service. Thus the fellowship posed no financial challenge to private psychiatric hospitals or to individual consultant psychiatrists who did private practice with alcoholic patients. One of the few early references to the significance of Tradition Seven occurs in the context of a letter Sackville wrote in 1948 to the new, energetic – and soon to be controversial – Minister for Health, Dr Noel Browne. Bringing his friend, Joe D., up to date with developments within the Dublin group, Sackville wrote:

> I got a letter from our Minister of Health wishing us all success. This is promotion for us. I had of course made it clear to him when I wrote and sent him particulars of the group, and its work, that he was quite safe, inasmuch as we didn't want any money or official backing from the Government. This seems to have so surprised him that it took him 3 weeks to reply.[18]

Just as he had continued to build relationships with influential members of the Catholic Church, Sackville worked consistently throughout the 1950s to ensure that contacts with the psychiatric hospitals would maximize opportunities for newly detoxified alcoholics to come into contact with the fellowship. In 1962, by which time there were three AA groups in Dublin, he seemed satisfied with what had been achieved, telling Bill Wilson that 'Hospitals in Dublin are more and more co-operative, and in one we have a special ward for alkies [*sic*] only.'[19] The fact that such good working relationships had been established with psychiatric hospitals did not necessarily mean, however, that the wider proposition that *alcoholism is a disease* had been culturally accepted or enshrined in Irish public policy.The rest of this chapter will look in detail at some of the continuing controversies arising from AA's involvement with the wider 'alcoholism movement'.

ALCOHOLISM AS A DISEASE

Much of what has already been written here about Sackville's role in promoting AA during its early years in Ireland has presented him as shrewd and sure-footed in his understanding of issues and avoidance of problems. During 1948, however, a mild disagreement arose between Sackville and his friends and advisors at the Alcoholic Foundation in New York concerning the wisdom of describing alcoholism as disease. In retrospect, what this contretemps reveals is that Sackville had not fully thought through the implications of an unqualified acceptance of this proposition or of the creation of alliances with non-fellowship groups who appeared to share this perspective. This episode also helps to explain some of the philosophical and political hoops he was to jump through some twenty years later in his dealings with the Irish National Council on Alcoholism (INCA).

As described in Chapter 3, during what was still a formative phase of its development in the USA, the fellowship had opted to distance itself from the National Council on Alcoholism (NCA), which had been founded by Marty Mann, one of the early women members of AA. The decision taken in 1946 was that, in its country of origin, AA should not align itself officially with the NCA or with any other stakeholder group which was involved in the promotion of the disease concept or in lobbying for its incorporation into public policy. Framed in a more positive way, what this decision meant was that the fellowship should maintain a single-minded focus on helping alcoholics, lest it get drawn into political controversy that might endanger its own unity and ulti-

1. Conor Flynn (the Irish-American who introduced AA to Ireland in November 1946) as a young man

2. Sackville (seated in centre with plaque and apparently the captain) with a British army hockey team in India in 1928

3. Bill Wilson, Sackville and Lois Wilson during the Wilsons' visit to Ireland in June 1950

4. Flyleaf of the second edition of the Big Book, containing Sackville's story 'The Career Officer': the inscription from Bill Wilson reads 'Dear Sackville, Among many notable contributions to our cause, I send you special thanks for the one herein. Gratefully Bill' (Aug/3/55)

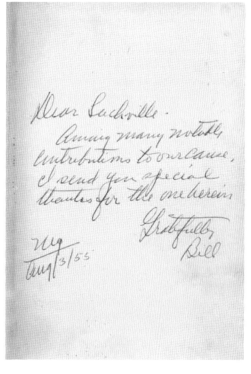

5. AA in Ireland comes of age: Richard Perceval, Conor Flynn and Jimmy R. cut the cake at 21st birthday celebrations in 1967

6. Pope Paul VI meets Sackville and Travers C. (an English member of the fellowship) during their visit to Rome in January 1972

7. Conor Flynn and Sackville during one of Conor's trips to Ireland during the 1970s

8. Marty Mann (one of the first women to get sober through AA in the USA, who later went on to found the National Council on Acoholism and influenced the founding of the Irish National Council on Alcoholism in 1966). The dedication reads 'To Sackville, With love, Marty, July 1976'

9.-15. A selection of the postcards which Dublin AA members sent to 'Joan's Table' in Bewley's Café, Westmoreland St., when Bewleys served as an informal social centre for members during the 1970s

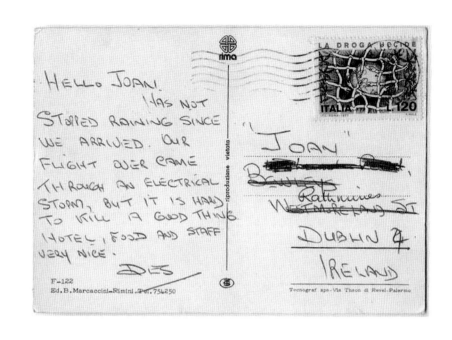

Postcard 1 (back):

HELLO JOAN,
HAS NOT
STOPPED RAINING SINCE
WE ARRIVED. OUR
FLIGHT OVER CAME
THROUGH AN ELECTRICAL
STORM, BUT IT IS HARD
TO KILL A GOOD THING.
HOTEL, FOOD AND STAFF
VERY NICE.

DES

F-122
Ed. B. Marcaccini - Rimini - Tel. 754250

Tecnograf sps - Via Thaon di Revel - Palermo

riproduzione vietata

ITALIA L.120
LA DROGA UCCIDE

"JOAN"
~~BEWLEYS~~
Rathmines
~~WESTMORELAND ST~~
DUBLIN 4
IRELAND

Postcard 2 (back):

500 N.E. 2 AV F.T. LAUDERDALE 20/1/75
Everyone enjoys Hollywood Beach and its boardwalk.
FLORIDA 33301. VIA
DON'T KNOW WHY I MENTION
THE ADDRESS. NOBODY ANS-
WERS ANYHOW. THERE IS
MESSAGE HERE SOMEWHERE.

Photo by Frank Borth

IS EVERYBODY HAPPY?
FOR THE CROSS-WORD
ARTISTS, WHATS A 5
LETTER WORD FOR
AN INEBRIATE? JUST
BEHIND THIS BEACH IN PIC-
TURE WE HOLD AN 11°° A.M MEET-
ING SUNDAYS. THEN PICNIC
+ SWIM ETC. SPENT 3 WEEKS
WITH JOHN DUNN IN HIS NEW
YORK APT, STILL TALKING ABOUT
THE BEE STING AT CHRIST CHURCH
~~HE SENDS~~ HIS REGARDS TO ALL.
GIRLS. IF YOU DRIVE YOUR OLD MAN TO
DRINK DRIVE HIM TO BEWLEYS BRESLYN

POST CARD

Address
JOAN'S TABLE
BEWLEYS RESTAURANT
WESTMORELAND ST
DUBLIN
REPUBLIC O' IRELAND

A. PEARL!
EVERYONE WANTS TO
GO TO HEAVEN BUT
NOBODY WANTS TO
DIE. TEE HEE.

Postcard 1

VIEWS OF ARUBA
1. Historic "Alto Vista" Chapel
2. Cultural Centre
3. Divi-divi tree
4. The Old Dutch Mill

M.T. "CYCLOPS"
AT ARUBA (CARIBBEAN)
FRIDAY 3RD. DEC. 1976
MY DEAR JOAN,
        GIVE MY REGARDS
TO ALL AT THE 'ROUND
TABLE' — WISH YOU WERE
ALL HERE. MISS YOU ALL
VERY MUCH.
        LOVE FROM
            JOHN (SAILOR)

© #1 & 2 D.P.

post card

"JOAN"
'JOAN'S TABLE'
C/O BEWLEYS COFFEE HOUSE
WESTMORELAND ST.
    DUBLIN.
    IRELAND

dp MADE BY
DEXTER PRESS, INC.
WEST NYACK, NEW YORK

Postcard 2

H.M. THE QUEEN: H.M. Portrait Study by Anthony Buckley. Guard Mounting. Tower Bridge. Buckingham Palace.
The Houses of Parliament, London.

Having a nice
holiday here. Plenty
of contact with A.A.S
here who are very
friendly. They don't
have coffee here to
compare with yours!
        Eugene.

Published by I.V.P Ltd. London England.

Printed by United Artists Ltd. Israel

LONDON N.C.
5 8PM
25 JLY
1973

JOAN (A.A. TABLE)
Bewleys Café
Westmoreland St
Dublin 2
IRELAND

222 S

This Space For Writing Messages   LOVE TO ALL

06 NOV. 70

HI JOANIE
        MY SWEET ONE
AS USUAL I KNOW THAT
YOU ARE TAKING EXTRA
SPECIAL CARE OF OUR
CROWD. GIVE MY RE-
GARDS TO ALL AT
OUR VERY OWN TABLE.
HOPE THAT YOU ARE WELL
I'M FINE THANK GOD.
AM WRITING THIS ON
THE BUS BETWEEN STOPS.
HOPE TO GET TO DUB-
LIN THIS SUMMER. LAST
YEAR I GOT A COUPLE OF
TRAIN + BUS RAMBLER
TICKETS + TRAVELLED
FROM DONEGAL TO CORK
TO OVER A DOZEN COUNTIES.
HOPE TO REPEAT NEXT YEAR.

POST CARD

FOR JOAN. THE A.A.
CHAMPION WAITRESS

HERE'S A SPOT OF FLORIDA
SUNSHINE. I'M ON MY WAY TO
A 10.30 AM MEETING ON MIAMI
BEACH. THEN WE ALL GO SWIMMING

This side for the Address only

Printed in U.S.A. by Popular Products, Chicago 60622

1946   ALCOHOLICS ANONYMOUS IN IRELAND   1986
        AA
        1946 • 1986

A souvenir booklet to commemorate forty years of A.A. in Ireland

16. Jacket from the forty years souvenir booklet, 1986. The sketch on the left is of the Country Shop.

mate survival – as had happened to earlier American groups with aims similar to those of AA. This decision not to publicly endorse or lobby for the disease concept also revealed ongoing ambiguity as to whether or not AA believed that alcoholism was a disease. There is no simple answer to this question, since AA is essentially a pragmatic institution which merely suggests helpful practices for people who wish to stop drinking, as opposed to holding or teaching definite beliefs of any kind. Tradition Ten says that 'Alcoholics Anonymous has no opinion on outside issues; hence the AA name ought never be drawn into public controversy'; and within the fellowship the question of whether or not alcoholism is a disease would generally be seen as an 'outside issue' which has the potential to generate controversy. The fact that most AA members informally appear to regard alcoholism as a disease, albeit one which can only be resolved by spiritual means rather than by conventional medical treatments,[20] merely adds to the confusion on this matter.

As part of his general promotion of the activities of AA in Dublin, Sackville had written a little leaflet, a copy of which he had sent on to the Alcoholic Foundation in New York. Having read the leaflet, Bobbie Burger saw fit to urge caution about Sackville's casual assertion that alcoholism was a disease:

> I note in this leaflet that you refer to alcoholism as a disease. This definition is becoming more common but you may have seen we [AA in the USA] still do not use the word 'disease'. The medical profession is arguing about it, and until they come to some kind of decision, we are keeping hands off in line with our policy of staying away from anything of a controversial nature. You will note in our writings we refer to alcoholism as an 'illness' or a 'malady'. This is just a suggestion for you people but do as you please.[21]

This quote is admirably clear and succinct in its general content, but its last sentence exemplifies the fellowship's distaste for top-down authority and its commitment to facilitating the autonomy of individual groups. This was not an edict such as individual Irish bishops might expect to receive from Rome, but simply a suggestion reflecting the experience of American AA members. To Sackville, however, it was not a suggestion that had any relevance to the Irish scene. His reply some weeks later was brief and sardonic:

'I apologise humbly for the word Disease. Please substitute illness or malady wherever necessary. The doctors here have no objection so far to its use, and it makes for simplification.'[22] This response obviously prompted further discussion amongst the staff of the New York office, another of whom (Ann MacFarlane) now entered the fray:

> I will have to join Bobbie and Charlotte in shying away from the word 'disease'. But, of course, what counts is the number of people you are able to reach and help to recovery. For this reason the word 'disease' is not a happy choice because it succeeds in thoroughly frightening and alienating some of those whom we are so anxious to help. I personally find it comforting to think that I am suffering from a disease, but I also know that many of my fellow members feel quite differently about it.[23]

Several letters were exchanged on this subject until Sackville, who appeared to have become bored by it, brought the debate to an end, telling his New York friends that he was 'far too happy in AA to bother whether the correct term is bubonic plague or otherwise'[24]. The tone of his last letter on this subject suggests that Sackville saw his disagreement with the staff of the New York office as nothing more than a semantic quibble or, in more modern terminology, a question of political correctness. However, as he was to discover some twenty years later through his membership of the Irish National Council on Alcoholism, the reservations of his New York friends were shrewd and well founded: unqualified acceptance of the 'alcoholism as disease' rhetoric could lead the fellowship into confusing and potentially compromising relationships with other members of the 'alcoholism movement', as will be discussed in detail later in this chapter.

THE DISEASE CONCEPT AND IRISH PSYCHIATRY

Given its historic ambivalence about the appropriateness of managing problem drinkers within the mental hospital system, it is not surprising that the adoption of the disease concept by Irish psychiatry from the mid-1940s onwards was a somewhat tentative and incremental process. A striking feature of this process, which will be discussed here and which reflects the type of political and economic controversy which AA was generally anxious to avoid, was the manifestly differential response to the disease concept between public and private psychiatry. All psychiatrists, whether employed in the public mental health system or in the much smaller private system, shared a common professional training and education and could therefore be expected to hold broadly similar professional ideologies about alcoholism; from the late 1950s, however, it was the private sector which was to the fore in promoting the disease concept, while the public psychiatric sector was slower to adopt this model and quicker to express reservations about it.

In 1957 a statutory body – the Voluntary Health Insurance (VHI) Board – was established in Ireland with a view to providing a scheme whereby people who because of their high income had no eligibility for free hospital treatment, could insure themselves against the costs of such treatment, and people of middle income could purchase insurance which gave them the option to be treated in private health care settings. This private health insurance scheme was made additionally attractive by virtue of the income tax relief its members could claim against their premiums. VHI came into existence at the end of a turbulent period within the health policy scene in Ireland, during which both the medical profession and the Catholic Church had resisted proposals for an expansion of state-provided health services, comparable to some extent to the recently established National Health Service in Britain. The resistance of the medical profession appears to have been primarily based on fears that the status and earning capacity of doctors would be damaged in a more socialized health care system; Church authorities deemed the idea of 'state medicine' to be offensive to Catholic views on subsidiarity (a social teaching which recommended that activities which could be organized at a lower societal level should not be organized by the state), while also fearing that it might facilitate the entry into the country of specific practices, such as contraception and abortion, to which the Catholic Church was doctrinally opposed.[25] The establishment of VHI made available improved, stable financing for the existing private, voluntary hospitals, most of which were owned and run by religious bodies of one kind or another, and in so doing helped to reduce the ideological and interest group conflict which had been a feature of Irish health care throughout the 1950s. For almost forty years VHI had a monopoly in the Irish health insurance market and was generally viewed as a popular and commercially successful initiative within a mixed health care system frequently characterized by controversy and dissension.

An unanticipated consequence of the establishment and growth of the VHI scheme, which was to have an indirect impact on AA, was that it created financial incentives for private psychiatric hospitals to develop and expand their facilities for alcoholism treatment. This expansion of specialist alcoholism treatment provision within the private psychiatric system, and the more explicit ideological promotion of the disease concept which accompanied it, will now be considered in some detail.

It appears that when first established, VHI had given little thought as to whether or how its scheme might apply to private mental health care, which perhaps was not surprising since there were only two private psychiatric hospitals of any size (St Patrick's and St John of God's – both located in Dublin) in the country at this time. It is worth quoting at some length from a 1992 interview with Dr Desmond McGrath, medical director of St John of God's, in which he describes events in the late 1950s – when he and his counterpart in St Patrick's, Dr Norman Moore, negotiated insurance cover for mental health inpatient care with the VHI's Chief Executive Officer.

> I had a good relationship with Norman Moore although we were inevitably, to some extent, rivals. However, the benefits of cooperation vastly outweighed any rivalry and we were both fundamentally concerned with developing psychiatry in Ireland. We worked together in various ways. For example, when the Voluntary Health Insurance scheme was set up we went together to Noel Burke, who was chief executive of the VHI, and worked out terms for psychiatric patients with him which were vastly better than those with Blue Cross or any other existing insurance scheme. We put it to him that we both worked in non-profit-making hospitals and that our staff were salaried. We could guarantee top quality treatment and he would know exactly what his financial commitments were. He accepted this and agreed initially that the VHI would cover psychiatric patients for

six weeks. After a short time we pushed him to three months and he, himself, because of his satisfaction, ultimately took off all restrictions on psychiatric patients. That is how things were for a long period until the recent cuts were instituted.[26]

While it was quite true that these two hospitals were not-for-profit enterprises and that their medical staff were salaried, this did not mean – as Dr McGrath appears to have suggested rather disingenuously – that all aspects of their management were driven solely by clinical and humanitarian motives and that they were disinterested in maximizing their incomes. At this time in the late 1950s, St Patrick's and St John of God's derived their incomes from a combination of patient fees, philanthropic benefactions and voluntary fundraising, and it would have been unusual if the advent of this new third-party payment scheme was not viewed by hospital managements as an opportunity to put their finances on a sounder footing than had previously been the case. Similarly, it would have been unusual if the consultant psychiatrists employed by private hospitals did not see this increased commitment to alcoholism treatment as an opportunity to develop lucrative private practice with outpatients.

The happy relationship between VHI and private psychiatry described by McGrath lasted for almost thirty years: the 'cuts' referred to presumably being those introduced in 1985 when VHI – on the basis that length of stay and frequency of admission for alcoholism to private hospitals were not clinically justifiable or 'evidence-based' – significantly reduced the amount of inpatient addiction treatment for which it was prepared to pay. While private psychiatry was understandably unhappy with and critical of restrictions on inpatient cover of alcoholism treatment, these changes were broadly in line with what private health insurers had done elsewhere. Given the growth of research evidence critical of the reliance on inpatient rehabilitation of alcoholics, the mystery perhaps was not that VHI unilaterally introduced these changes in 1985, but that it had not done so much earlier.[27]

What appears to have happened is that from the late 1950s, when the two medical directors negotiated the agreement described above, the two private hospitals identified alcoholism treatment as a niche market that had the potential to supply them with a steady stream of relatively uncomplicated patients. These were patients whose physical detoxification could generally be completed quite quickly and whose subsequent management could be left to nurses and other paramedical staff; they presented no major behavioural problems and their bills were guaranteed by VHI, thereby creating a financial cushion for the wider clinical activities of these institutions. The growth and exploitation of this niche market may be inferred from the increasing numbers of alcohol admissions and from the move to establish specialist alcoholism treatment units within private psychiatric hospitals, from this time onwards; it is also discernible, however, in the emergence of an explicit ideological shift to the disease concept of alcoholism on the part of private psychiatrists, at a time when psychiatrists in the public sector appeared to remain unconvinced about the notion of alcoholism as disease.

As described in Chapter 4, Conor Flynn had received no encouragement for his attempts to establish an AA group at St John of God's Hospital when he visited it in late 1946, being told that the hospital never treated and had no plans to treat alcoholics. Despite this, St John of God's continued to admit patients who had drink problems, particularly priests, for a decade or so, but did so without reference to the disease concept and apparently without any great conviction about the value of hospitalization for such patients. Even though AA members were permitted to visit the hospital within a year or so of the establishment of the first Dublin AA group, this did not appear to reflect a general institutional acceptance of the disease concept. For example, one AA veteran later recalled the reception he received when his wife sought to have him treated in the private hospital:

> [I]n 1949 I went out to St John of God's with my wife ... A very tall man came in to see us ... My wife said: 'My husband has a booze problem. We have money and is there anything you can do?' He said: 'Would you get the Grace of God about yourself, go away and take the pledge?'[28]

By the early 1960s, however, St John of God's had shifted to an explicit and apparently unequivocal acceptance of the disease concept, as reflected in its establishment of a specialist alcoholism treatment programme and its commitment to working collaboratively with AA. Dr P.D. McCarthy, the consultant psychiatrist in charge of the hospital's alcoholism treatment programme, spoke on the topic of alcoholism at the 1960 conference on 'The Priest and Mental Health' held in St John of God's (previously discussed in Chapter 4). In this talk to a predominantly clerical audience, he presented the disease concept as one which came with the authoritative approval of such bodies as the World Health Organization and the American Medical Association, but he also acknowledged that there had been confusion and controversy as to where precisely in the health care system alcoholics should be treated. Dr McCarthy's personal preference, exemplified by the creation of an alcoholism unit within St John of God's, was for the establishment of dedicated alcoholism programmes within psychiatric hospitals:

> The question of treatment is an involved one. Basically one must always remember that an alcoholic, even when sober, is always only one drink away from disaster. One problem is the choice of hospital. Alcoholics feel that they have a general hospital problem, but these hospitals are unable, and are not equipped, to deal with them. Alcoholics tend to exaggerate the so-called stigma of psychiatric hospitals, but their problem is basically a psychological one. What seems to me to be a more equitable solution is the formation of a separate alcoholic unit. This should be a joint effort between medical, spiritual and the Alcoholics Anonymous organizations.[29]

In the official history commissioned to mark a century of St John of God Brothers' activity in Ireland in 1979, this conversion to the disease concept is presented solely in scientific and humanitarian terms and – perhaps understandably – no reference is made to the hospital's earlier refusal to collaborate with AA's founding members in Ireland, or to the significance of the new source of funding for alcoholism treatment provided by VHI.

> Alcoholism had replaced TB as the disease most prevalent in Ireland. Older readers will remember how, in the early decades of this century, TB was supposed to 'run in families', and indeed there were cases of entire families contracting the disease. Identification of the bacillus causing it, the development of drugs capable of conquering the virus, a publicity drive to educate the public regarding TB, and the

determined efforts of Dr Noel Browne – all these factors combined to banish the scourge from our country. Alcoholism took its place as a wrecker of health and happiness.[30]

Without in any way calling into question the sincerity of individual clinicians within the St John of God's service who worked directly with alcoholics, this organizational rationale for the order's wholehearted adoption of the disease concept appears singularly unconvincing and somewhat self-serving. Alcohol consumption in Ireland, through the 1950s and into the 1960s, remained low by international standards,[31] and there would appear to be no evidence to support the notion of an epidemic of alcoholism in Ireland at this time. Certainly, if one looks at the limited data on psychiatric hospital admissions available from this period, there is no evidence that the mental health services were inundated with alcoholism admissions. For instance, the Inspector of Mental Hospitals (a statutory office established by the Mental Treatment Act, 1945) in his annual report for 1958 gave a breakdown by diagnosis of all psychiatric admissions during this year, indicating that only 5.7 per cent of admissions had a primary alcohol-related diagnosis.[32] By far the most plausible explanation for the greater demand for alcohol-related admissions into private psychiatric hospitals throughout the 1960s and thereafter is that these hospitals encouraged such admissions, setting up comfortable and welcoming facilities that were a far cry from the squalid and overcrowded public psychiatric hospitals. Middle-class problem drinkers with VHI cover, who would only have sought admission to a public facility *in extremis*, were happy to be admitted to the relatively salubrious facilities on offer from St John of God's and St Patrick's.

While St Patrick's Hospital had facilitated Ireland's first AA meeting and had always been more openly welcoming of alcoholic patients than its Stillorgan counterpart, it was not until VHI funding became available that it considered setting up a specialist alcoholism treatment unit. Following the negotiation of the agreement described above between the private psychiatric hospitals and VHI, Dr Norman Moore appears to have given some thought to the idea of creating a dedicated alcoholism programme within St Patrick's Hospital and, indirectly, he sought the advice of Sackville, who was known to have visited specialist alcoholism units on his trips to the USA. In August 1958, Sackville wrote to Norman Moore, enclosing information on a specialist unit run by Sister Ignatia (a Catholic nun who had worked extensively with Dr Bob Smith, co-founder of AA, in Akron, Ohio) with which he was most impressed:

> Ivor Barry told me you would like some notes on the Alcoholic ward run by the Sisters of St Augustine at Cleveland, Ohio, as seen by me in 1954 and 1956. I am attaching them together with a copy of, in part, some notes I sent to the Department of Health on my return in 1954 at their request ... I would like to emphasise that Sister Ignatia is quite an outstanding woman and that she runs a ward that would be difficult to emulate without someone of her own faith and enthusiasm. That is why I have recommended that if any question of a ward arose in Dublin, the nursing staff should be sent to Cleveland for indoctrination.[33]

It may have been presumptuous of Sackville to think that a traditionally Protestant hospital such as St Patrick's would welcome this effusive promotion of a Catholic-run alcoholism programme, and there is no evidence that Norman Moore acted upon it. However, what is most significant historically is the coincidence of this interest in the creation of a specialist unit with the provision of a funding for alcoholism treatment by VHI. Elizabeth Malcolm, in her 1989 commissioned history of St Patrick's Hospital, presents an uncritical account of the expansion of alcoholism treatment within the hospital, commenting that 'The hospital remains closely associated with AA and INLA [*sic*] to this day, when at least 25 per cent of admissions are for alcoholism.'[34]

In 1966 the Commission of Inquiry on Mental Illness, the first major review of mental health policy since the foundation of the state, issued its report. Amidst its general recommendations for a modernization of mental health services it carried an unambiguous endorsement of the disease concept:

> Alcoholism is a disease and is regarded by the World Health Organisation as a major health problem. The concept of alcoholism as a disease is not new, or even recent, but its general acceptance has been hampered and confused by the

diversity of the causes of alcoholism and the variety of alcoholic behaviour and because some people regard alcoholism merely as a moral problem.[35]

While the report acknowledged that community-based treatment was an option for some alcoholics, the broad thrust of its recommendations in this sphere was for extended provision of psychiatric inpatient care for such patients. Furthermore, the commission accepted that in this regard it was the private sector which had led the way, noting that at this time 'most alcoholics are treated in private hospitals – in particular in St John of God Psychiatric Hospital, Dublin, which has a special unit for alcoholics, and in St Patrick's Hospital, Dublin'.[36] The commission was of the view that public psychiatric hospitals should also, albeit on a regional basis, establish specialist alcoholism treatment units rather than treating alcoholics in wards where they were mixed in with patients with other diagnoses: 'the close association of alcoholic patients in such a setting encourages them more quickly to understand their illness, to help each other and to collaborate with Alcoholics Anonymous'.[37]

ALCOHOLICS ANONYMOUS AND THE IRISH NATIONAL COUNCIL ON ALCOHOLISM

Another significant event which occurred in 1966 in relation to the institutionalization of the disease concept was the establishment of the Irish National Council on Alcoholism (INCA); this was a voluntary body, which was subsequently to receive financial support from the Minister for Health, whose aims were to publicize and promote the disease concept while simultaneously lobbying for improved treatment facilities for alcoholics. The initiative for the establishment of INCA came primarily from the private psychiatric sector, which by the early 1960s had fully embraced the ideology of alcoholism as disease and had identified a need to challenge and reshape what it saw as residual public ignorance and moralism in relation to alcoholism. It was contended, although no specific evidence was adduced in support of this contention, that the establishment of INCA had been hampered by the unwillingness of potential patrons to be associated with alcoholism – such was its alleged stigma. For instance, in 1964 the

Irish Times journalist Michael Viney had concluded a series of articles on alcoholism (which were later published in booklet format) by arguing that one priority for a more rational societal response was

> The establishment of a National Council on Alcoholism, similar to those in Britian and elsewhere, to sponsor research and act as an advisory body. There was an attempt in recent years to establish such a council. One of the key reasons it failed was the reluctance of public figures to have their names associated with it. Even supposedly intelligent and highly educated men were afraid of the stigma they thought would attach to such a patronage. I find this incredible.[38]

A similar reference to the difficulties involved in setting up INCA is contained in the previously cited interview with Dr Desmond McGrath of St John of God's Hospital:

> Then Norman Moore and I, with others, were involved in trying to set up an Irish National Council on Alcoholism ... But we had difficulties the first time around – we couldn't get patrons, that is distinguished public figures who would be willing to be associated with alcoholism.[39]

During 1964, however, Drs McGrath and Moore identified a reputable and high-profile figure in Irish life who was willing to be publicly associated with their planned council: this was Chief Justice Cearbhall Ó'Dálaigh, who would later go on to serve briefly as Uachtarán na hÉireann (President of Ireland) during the 1970s.[40] Towards the end of 1964 plans to establish the council received a significant boost when Marty Mann, director of the National Council on Alcoholism in the USA, visited Dublin where she advised and encouraged those who had been working for some years on this project. Although preparatory work for its establishment went on all through 1965, it was not until 1966 that INCA came into legal existence. The Memorandum and Articles of Association for the new company had just seven signatories: one was INCA's first chairman, Chief Justice Cearbhall Ó'Dálaigh; four were private sector psychiatrists – Drs Moore and Cooney from St Patrick's Hospital, and Drs McGrath and McCarthy from St John of God's; the remaining two were

Sackville O'Conor-Mallins and another AA member, Aiden MacSweeney.[41] It should, however, be pointed out that Sackville and Aiden MacSweeney retained their anonymity in this legal document – with Sackville being described as a 'Retired Army Officer' and Aiden MacSweeney as a 'Chemist' – which made no reference to their membership of the fellowship. From an AA perspective, what was even more important, however, was that the first executive director of INCA was none other than Richard Perceval – co-founder of AA in Ireland back in 1946 – who returned from London where he had been working with the British National Council on Alcoholism. Just as Marty Mann had experienced difficulties in reconciling her membership of the fellowship with her leadership role in the NCA in New York, one could surmise that Richard Perceval too might find this a difficult task.

Sackville's correspondence reveals that, in the years leading up to the establishment of INCA, he was unambiguously positive about the value of such an organization in Ireland: an organization which, as he saw it, would challenge and reshape benighted, moralistic attitudes towards alcoholism and tilt public policy firmly in the direction of the 'new scientific approach' to alcoholism as a disease. He admired the work being done in the USA by Marty Mann's National Council on Alcoholism and, as revealed in his 1948 disagreement with staff in the New York AA office about the wisdom of describing alcoholism as a disease (discussed earlier in this chapter), he had failed to detect the possibility of tensions arising between fellowship members and other stakeholders in the 'alcoholism movement' – all ostensibly committed to the common goal of promoting the disease concept.

In August 1964, in the course of a letter to Bill Wilson in New York, Sackville described a planned visit to Dublin by Marty Mann and his hopes for what the visit might lead to:

> We hope to have a short visit from Marty Mann in November. She is primarily going to London to help on the NCAI work, which is being supervised by Richard Perceval whom you know from meeting in Dublin. We hope to have her in Dublin for 3 days and to use her to advantage ... Of course, we will want her chiefly on the NCAI side to get the Government to do something in the education line and to

impress industry of the benefits it can get from rehabilitation; but we hope to have her as an AA member one of the evenings all to ourselves.[42]

In replying to this letter, Bill Wilson made no comment on Marty Mann's trip to Dublin, but Sackville returned to it in his Christmas Day letter in which, as was his custom, he reviewed the year's activities from an AA perspective: 'I suppose Marty Mann's visit was the main event of the year in one way. It certainly stirred up interest while she was here, but I don't know that it will lead to any concrete result in the near future as far as a National Council on Alcoholism is concerned. We must wait and see.'[43] On this occasion Bill Wilson did comment on the work being done by Marty Mann: the tone of his remarks, however, is subtle and nuanced, seeing the activities of the NCA only insofar as they impacted on AA – in comparison with Sackville's rather more unqualified enthusiasm for national lobby movements outside of the fellowship. Wilson, who had known Marty Mann for several decades, wrote as follows:

> On balance, I think my old friend Marty has done a pile of good. Probably the publicity alone attendant upon her effort has been a channel of public information quite equal to our own, often bringing forward people who would not approach AA directly at first. Almost all other efforts in the general field produce this happy result – they do not themselves sober up a lot of people, but they are drunk traps for us, provided we are friendly to them.[44]

It appears from the correspondence that, despite their expressions of enthusiasm for the establishment of an Irish equivalent to the American NCA, the psychiatrists played no active role in bringing Marty Mann to Ireland, and that it was Sackville who had unobtrusively made all arrangements and set up the agenda for the trip. Marty Mann herself acknowledged this a month before coming to Dublin, when she wrote to thank Sackville for arranging her Irish schedule:

> I must say I think you are terrific! To have the quiet courage to arrange the program and then to disappear is a wonderful measure of your wisdom and grasp of the problem. The schedule you have outlined is first rate, manageable and it

will serve the major purposes of my visit.[45]

Marty Mann's visit to Dublin appears to have given an added fil-lip to the protracted planning process for the establishment of INCA and just a few months later – in February 1965 – Sackville received a letter from Cearbhall Ó'Dálaigh inviting him to serve on the interim committee of this planned body. Again, this letter confirms that the driving force behind INCA was private psychi-atry, but it is also noteworthy that it respected fellowship Traditions in that it neither referred to Sackville as a member nor did it imply that he would be an AA representative on INCA:

> I am writing this letter to ask for your support in launching a National Council on Alcoholism. The nature of the prob-lem of alcoholism in Ireland and what a National Council could do towards helping to solve the problem will, I think, best appear from a perusal of the attached draft circular and from a folder issued by the British National Council.
>
> Four medical experts in the field of alcoholism, Drs Moore and Cooney of St Patrick's Hospital, James's Street, Dublin, and Drs McGrath and McCarthy of St John of God's, Stillorgan, have been discussing this problem with me, and we have decided to invite seven other prominent citizens to join us as a strong committee to launch a National Council on Alcoholism.
>
> Your presence on this steering committee would be a great help indeed, and on behalf of my colleagues and myself I invite you to join us.[46]

Sackville accepted this invitation and may subsequently have been instrumental in getting his fellowship colleague Aiden MacSweeney, an early member of AA in Cork, to become a mem-ber of INCA, on which they served for about five years.[47]

It is clear from Sackville's correspondence, however, that he quickly came to regret his willingness to join INCA, and his let-ters to Bill Wilson and his Chicago friend Joe D. were regularly punctuated with expressions of scorn at its activities (or lack of activity) and bewilderment at how he, as an AA member, had ever allowed himself to become involved with people whose know-ledge and motives he increasingly appeared to distrust. As the years went by, Sackville appeared to become convinced that there was little or no value to be gained for AA – which for Sackville simply meant its existing and potential members – by this attempt to work collaboratively with non-members under the umbrella of INCA. As described in Chapter 4, once he became Secretary of the first Dublin AA group in 1947, Sackville had thrown himself into the role with huge energy and a great sense of urgency, and, consequently, he viewed the more relaxed pace of events within INCA with disbelief and sarcasm. A letter to Bill Wilson, written in July 1965, exemplifies this unhappiness with the speed at which events within INCA were proceeding, while also highlighting Sackville's sense of being (this appears to have been prior to Aiden MacSweeney's membership) the odd man out in this company:

> The proposed National Council seems to be hanging fire just now, but that may be partly due to the fact that the Legal Holidays are on – June to October, apparently – and our Chairman is the Chief Justice of Ireland. He is a nice man, but rather garrulous and determined to make a nice remark about everyone on the committee, which delays proceedings somewhat, as like most people he finds it hard to think of something nice to say about <u>me.</u> I am purely a decorative member of the committee, and have a somewhat unfair advantage over most of them insofar as I have a working knowledge of alcoholism [underlining in original].[48]

This reference to a 'working knowledge' of alcoholism could, of course, be interpreted as nothing other than arrogance on Sackville's part; however, when considered for what it was – a message from one AA member to another – it could equally be interpreted as reflecting Sackville's personal sense of the utter defeat and degradation of active alcoholism and an accompanying moral imperative to respond quickly to the needs of one's peers. In any event, from this time on references to INCA in Sackville's personal correspondence with AA friends in the USA were invariably negative, and he appears to have used this correspondence to vent his spleen while maintaining a superficially untroubled relationship with INCA members and staff back in Dublin. In late 1968, for example, he told Bill Wilson that 'The Irish National Council on Alcoholism is pursuing its so far undistinguished progress, reminding me of Churchill's words, twisted,

"Never has so much money been spent for so little results!" But that is a sentiment I would prefer to keep anonymous!!'[49]

In his 1965 Christmas Day letter to Bill Wilson, only twelve months after he had expressed the hope that Marty Mann's visit to Dublin might consolidate efforts being made to establish an Irish equivalent to her American lobby group, Sackville's views on this topic appeared to have changed totally, and he began to issue what would come to be regular complaints about the way in which Richard Perceval's work as Executive Director of INCA was being given precedence over his AA membership: 'Richard has come back to settle down in Dublin again, and that should be a great help, even if he is involved in the attempt to form a Marty Mann Council over in Ireland![underlining in original]'[50] Four years later, in his 1969 Christmas Day letter to Bill Wilson, Sackville again voiced sharp criticism of Richard Perceval while also making explicit his dislike and distrust of those involved in what he was coming to see as the alcoholism 'industry':

> Richard is concealed in the Irish National Council on Alcoholism and we hardly see him. There is a circus of so-called 'experts' in Europe who go from one good conference, hotel-wise anyway, to pool their knowledge, which has never seemed to me to be very sufficient inasmuch as they can't tell how we develop the disease nor prevent it nor cure it. Richard has joined that crowd as far as he can.[51]

Criticisms of this kind seem unfair to Richard Perceval, who could reasonably be expected to give priority to INCA, of which he was, after all, the paid Executive Director, but such was Sackville's total commitment to AA that he seemed to find it impossible to understand how Richard took INCA seriously. Such criticisms were also expressed in his letters to Joe D. in Chicago, as in a 1967 letter in which he described accompanying Richard to an AA convention in Limerick:

> The Limerick expedition went off well. I had a nice drive down with Richard, though he bored me to tears talking about his Irish National Council on Alcoholism. Although I am a member of the Council, I am not all that interested in it, especially as he related it all to his own activity.[52]

Again, while this criticism of Richard Perceval seems harsh, it should be borne in mind that it may also have reflected a persist-ent fear in the fellowship that members who built up personal careers in the alcoholism industry were at risk of 'reinflating' their egos and reverting to active alcoholism. Over the next few years, Sackville became increasingly dissatisfied with the practice of allowing INCA representatives to speak at AA conventions, arguing – usually unsuccessfully – that the fellowship should not appear to endorse INCA, which in terms of Tradition Six ('An AA group ought never endorse, finance or lend the AA name to any related facility or outside enterprise, lest problems of money, property and prestige divert us from our primary purpose') was an outside enterprise. The distance he had travelled from his orig-inal, uncritical espousal of INCA, and his fears over AA conven-tions being hijacked for promotional opportunities for private treatment centres, may be seen in one final quote from a letter to Joe D. in Chicago:

> I got a request to chair a public meeting held to inform the same Public on <u>Alcoholism.</u> The speakers were to be Richard now of INCA, a doctor and a Brother of St John of God's, the last two non-alcoholics and Richard speaking as Director of the INCA. I turned it down, as I don't believe it is our business to start educating the public about the disease of alcoholism, and I can't see the good of holding a non-AA session at an AA Convention. It is our privilege to pass our Recovery and Hope message to other alcoholics, but surely not to turn ourselves into minnie [*sic*] Marty Manns or doc-tors. Do you think I am right or just old-fashioned and pig-headed? [underlining in original][53]

The style of Bill Wilson's responses to Sackville's tirades about INCA was completely in keeping with AA culture, as set down in the Twelve Traditions: it was not for AA members in New York to tell members in Dublin, or anywhere else in Ireland, how they should handle their relationships with outside enterprises such as INCA. Wilson and his New York colleagues resisted the temptation to say 'I told you so', simply ignoring most of the complaints made by Sackville and, when they chose to acknowledge them, doing so in a mild and non-directive way. An example of Wilson's style can be found in a letter to Sackville written in September 1967:

Concerning your observation about Richard: I might add
that this sort of phenomenon is not new. Wearing two hats
sometimes produces that effect. But by and large AAs who
are working out in the field have done very well on the
whole and I hope that this has been true of Richard's activities.[54]

While the archives contain very little correspondence between
Sackville and Aiden MacSweeney, those letters that do exist confirm that the latter shared Sackville's reservations about INCA
and his distaste at the prospect of the fellowship becoming
involved in professional alcoholism treatment. For example, in a
letter to Sackville from 1967, MacSweeney commented on
Richard Perceval's approach to his position as Executive Director
of INCA: 'Richard is taking his new job very seriously and as
always is very worried about what to do.'[55] A year later, Mac-
Sweeney reported his annoyance when Richard Perceval tried to
enlist his help in getting a paid job with INCA for a mutual AA
friend:

> I had Richard on the phone the other morning asking me to
> suggest to Dr Cooney that Eddie H. be given a job in INCA.
> I found it hard to be diplomatic to him and put over my
> thoughts without being offensive. Eddie is a great guy but I
> don't think jobs should be the reward for 12th step work.[56]

Given these regular expressions of disenchantment, it is not surprising that Sackville and Aiden MacSweeney should have
resigned from INCA, in much the same way as Bill Wilson and
Bob Smith, the fellowship's two co-founders, had severed their
connections with Marty Mann's National Council on Alcoholism
in New York some twenty-five years earlier. The two AA members
appear to have drifted quietly away from INCA from about 1970
onwards, without acrimony and without overt explanation as to
why they were doing so, having tacitly confirmed for themselves
the wisdom of Traditions Six and Ten – which caution against the
fellowship endorsing or lending its name to any outside enterprise or becoming drawn into public controversy. One AA member who joined the fellowship in 1964 retrospectively remarked:
'I came into AA at the stage that St Paul came into the Christian
Church – you know all the old lads were there and there were

giants among them, in their own way'; in the memory of this fellowship member, Sackville's dalliance with INCA was of little
consequence: 'Sackville was with them, but I don't think he
stayed too long.'[57]

While INCA survived until the end of 1988, it never made the
impact or gained the status for which its founders had hoped.[58] The
insight (usually attributed to Brendan Behan) that 'when any Irish
organization is started, the first item on the agenda is the split'
may not apply literally to INCA, but there is evidence that from
early in its existence ideological tensions emerged within the
membership between private-sector psychiatrists who continued
to espouse the disease concept of alcoholism, and public-sector
psychiatrists who became increasingly sceptical of this concept.
Among the public-sector psychiatrists who joined INCA shortly
after its establishment were: Professor Ivor Browne, who had
replaced John Dunne as RMS at St Brendan's Hospital and as
Professor of Psychiatry at University College Dublin; Dr Dermot
Walsh, a consultant psychiatrist with the Dublin Health Authority
and also an epidemiologist with a particular interest in alcoholism; and Dr R.D. Stevenson, another consultant psychiatrist
with the Dublin Health Authority and clinical director of St
Dymphna's, a specialist addictions unit at St Brendan's Hospital.

In its Memorandum and Articles of Association, INCA had
stuck rigidly to the so-called 'new scientific approach' to alcoholism that had characterized Marty Mann's National Council on
Alcoholism in the USA. It was understandable that in post-
Prohibition America lobbyists should have placed maximum
emphasis on the genetic or other biological factors presumed to
be of primary causal importance in alcoholism, while carefully
playing down any negative features of alcohol as a drug. Since
Ireland had never experienced such cultural and legal extremism
in relation to alcohol, INCA's determination to pursue its main
objectives 'without making any judgement upon the consumption
of alcohol per se'[59] seemed unnecessary, and its willingness to
accept funding from drinks industry sources (in its first annual
report, the organization acknowledged the importance for its survival of 'a substantial donation from a world-famous Brewery in
Dublin'[60]) would later be seen as questionable.

In late 1971 INCA hosted an international conference on alcoholism that greatly impressed the then Minister for Health,

Erskine Childers; the minister subsequently wrote to INCA's chairman, Cearbhall Ó'Dálaigh, suggesting that the time was ripe for a major policy initiative on alcoholism to be spearheaded by INCA. This led to a year-long consultation process and the submission of a report by INCA to the Minister for Health in 1973. It was organizationally important for INCA that it capitalize on the Minister's enthusiasm for the disease concept, and it would have been imprudent to highlight the fact that this concept no longer commanded scientific consensus. If one compares the copy of the final report sent to Erskine Childers with a copy of the report retained at INCA's offices in Westmoreland Street, Dublin, it becomes clear that while acknowledging its own internal ideological differences, the organization deemed it prudent to conceal these differences from the minister in the interests of gaining his formal approval and financial support. For example, the report submitted to the minister in January 1973 is unequivocally positive about the disease concept and its alleged value in removing stigma and encouraging alcoholics to seek treatment at an early stage in the disease process; the report retained at INCA headquarters, however, contained this footnote:

> There is a minority viewpoint that over-emphasis on the disease concept has grave disadvantages in that it concentrates too much on individual susceptibility and fails to recognise that quantity, frequency and the use that alcohol is put to by the individual are of greater importance. Moreover, by stressing the disease concept there is the implication that these factors are NOT important. [This footnote was added in November 1973 subsequent to the submission of the report to the Minister for Health.][61]

There were other footnotes added in this fashion (for example, a recommendation that the state should insist on a health warning on all alcoholic beverage containers), indicating that within INCA the 'new scientific approach' no longer had the full support of all members. Although INCA succeeded in gaining ministerial approval and financial support, it would appear that its internal ideological differences remained largely unresolved for the duration of its existence and that these differences were broadly similar to those that characterized alcohol policy debates at national and international levels. By and large, INCA succeeded in containing its internal tensions, with neither side scoring a decisive victory over the other, but the very existence of disagreement of this kind undoubtedly contributed to its failure to become the force within Irish alcohol policy that it had originally promised to be.

THE PSYCHIATRIC SERVICES: PLANNING FOR THE FUTURE (1984)

As indicated earlier in this chapter, the WHO had begun in the early 1970s to move gradually away from its original espousal of the disease concept and its associated support for the value of specialist alcoholism treatment. In Ireland, however, it was not until 1984 that an official health policy document – *The Psychiatric Services: Planning for the Future*[62] – definitively rejected the disease concept and recommended its replacement by a public health or total consumption approach to managing alcohol-related problems in this country. *Planning for the Future* (as this report is usually referred to) was primarily concerned with reviewing progress in the implementation of the mental health service objectives set out in the *Report of the Commission of Inquiry on Mental Illness* (1966), and in doing this it generally reiterated the fundamental importance of shifting public psychiatric services from what had traditionally been an institutional system to a community-based style of service provision. On the specific issue of alcohol-related problems, however, the *Planning for the Future* recommendations constituted a return to the ambivalence that had historically characterized public psychiatric management of such problems; and, in relation to the ideological differences that had emerged within INCA, these recommendations could be viewed as representing victory for the public-sector perspective and defeat for those private-sector psychiatrists who appeared to be still wedded to the disease concept.

Before summarizing and discussing the views and recommendations of *Planning for the Future* on the management of alcohol-related problems by the mental health system, it is useful to look at relevant epidemiological data from 1984 (the year in which this mental health policy document was published) and at the differing ways in which this data could be interpreted.[63] National statistics for 1984 show that exactly 25 per cent of all psychiatric inpatient admissions for this year had been given a primary alcohol-related diagnosis, which clearly represented a dramatic increase on the previously quoted statistic from 1958 when alcohol admissions accounted for less than 6 per cent of all psychiatric admissions. The data can be broken down in various ways: for instance, at a national level, alcohol admissions accounted for 37 per cent of male admissions but only 10 per cent of female admissions, and there are also some regional disparities, with hospitals serving predominantly rural areas reporting a higher burden of alcohol admissions than was the norm for urban areas. In relation to ideological controversies about the disease concept of alcoholism, however, perhaps the most telling statistics are those which relate to individual private psychiatric hospitals. The biggest of these private hospitals, St Patrick's in Dublin, reported that during 1984 alcohol admissions had accounted for 29 per cent of its total admissions, while the second biggest private hospital, St John of God's, Stillorgan, reported that for this year 52 per cent of its admissions had a primary alcohol-related diagnosis. Belmont Park Hospital in Waterford, which was run by the Brothers of Charity, was a more recently established private mental health facility which catered primarily for alcoholics, and for this year 77 per cent (403 out of 524 admissions) were in this category. In the context of national and international debates on the disease concept of alcoholism, these data were open to two completely contradictory interpretations. To those who still espoused the disease concept, these statistics were positive proof that its acceptance at policy level and its dissemination through publicity and awareness-raising campaigns was paying off, in the sense that the stigma had been largely removed from the disease; that those who previously might have remained 'hidden alcoholics' were now coming forward for treatment. To those, however, who no longer saw any validity in the notion of alcoholism as disease, the 1984 admission statistics were merely reflective of a national delusion, in which the public was being misled about the capacity of the mental health services to 'cure' or 'treat away' this condition: a condition which might be better conceptualized as a lifestyle problem, and whose prevalence appeared to reflect shifting population drinking habits rather than mysterious biological vulnerabilities. Implicit in these conflicting perspectives, although rarely discussed openly in polite policy debate, were understandings of the differential financial impact of alcoholism treatment on the public and private sectors. To the public mental health system, which saw itself as chronically under-resourced, the dramatic increase in alcoholism admissions that had occurred in the twenty years prior to *Planning for the Future* was an unwelcome burden. Despite all the rhetoric of science and modernity, there was no evidence that inpatient treatment of alcoholism in public mental hospitals had become any more effective than it had been in the asylums of the late nineteenth and early twentieth centuries, or indeed that it conferred any lasting benefit on its recipients. What was clear, however, was that the greatly increased burden of alcoholism treatment in the public health system diverted scarce resources away from the management of serious mental illnesses – such as schizophrenia and bipolar disorder – which arguably were not self-inflicted conditions in the way that alcoholism was often perceived to be. On the other hand, for the private psychiatric sector alcoholism treatment had become something of a cash cow, an important source of revenue without which the private units would struggle for financial survival. In one of the few explicit and, by the standards of the time, impolite comments on the politics of alcoholism, this author (Butler, 1983) wrote:

> This commitment to alcoholism treatment on the part of the private hospital would appear to be explicable primarily in commercial terms. These hospitals obviously derive a large part of their revenue from alcoholism treatment and, were they to appear less than enthusiastic or discourage this kind of patient, it is doubtful if they could continue in operation for long. These hospitals cater mainly for people in the upper income bracket and for middle-class people who have Voluntary Health Insurance; alcohol abusers from these sectors of society can therefore afford to have themselves admitted and re-admitted for detoxification and treatment ...[64]

To say that *Planning for the Future* (1984) reversed the ideological thrust of the *Report of the Commission of Inquiry on Mental Illness* (1966) on the management of alcoholism within Irish mental health services would be to understate the vehemence with which it rejected each and every tenet of the disease concept. Chapter 13 of *Planning for the Future* (that chapter of the report which dealt with both alcohol and illicit drugs) began with an opening paragraph on definitional matters which clearly flagged the changed policy recommendations to come later in this chapter:

Until recently, the generic term 'alcoholism' has been used to refer to a variety of problems resulting from alcohol abuse. However, because the word is difficult to define satisfactorily and because it suggests a particular type of alcohol problem to the exclusion of others, it is limited in what it covers. The term 'alcohol-related problems', although more cumbersome, is more accurate. This term acknowledges that alcohol can cause, or at least contribute to, an assortment of social and physical problems which include public drunkenness, family violence, absenteeism, road traffic accidents, liver and heart disease and disorders of the central nervous system.[65]

In everyday language, what this indicated was that the authors of *Planning for the Future* had moved beyond traditional debates as to whether or not alcoholism was a disease, arriving at the more radical, but logical, position of saying that alcoholism did not – in any practical or scientific sense – exist. It could be empirically demonstrated that alcohol caused or contributed to the variety of health and social problems listed, but it was illogical in the absence of any supporting evidence to postulate the existence of a discrete disease entity underlying all forms of problem drinking. The remainder of Chapter 13 reflected this fundamental starting point: reverting to commonsense notions that alcohol was an inherently problematic drug; that society could expect to experience more alcohol-related problems when consumption levels increased; and that prevention of such problems could only be done effectively through an integrated alcohol strategy involving all sectors of government, not just the health sector.

In seeking to explain steadily increasing alcohol-related admissions within the Irish mental health system, *Planning for the Future* acknowledged the likelihood that these increases reflected an increased prevalence of problem drinking which, in turn, could be attributed to changes in population drinking habits:

It is now accepted that there is a close relationship between per capita alcohol consumption and the extent of alcohol-related problems. This is certainly borne out by recent Irish experience. Since 1950 there has been an approximate doubling of alcohol consumption in Ireland – from 4.7 litres of 100 per cent alcohol per person aged 15 and over in 1950 to 9.0 in 1982. The most likely explanation for this increase is the growth in disposable personal income in Ireland over the same period. This belief is supported by the downturn in alcohol consumption since 1979 when there was a simultaneous fall in disposable income.[66]

However, the report also voiced a suspicion that increases in the treated prevalence of alcohol-related problems could be attributed to the fact that, under the banner of the disease concept, psychiatric hospitals appeared to have been touting for business: problem drinkers had been explicitly told that their drinking was symptomatic of an underlying disease, and that they could expect to find a welcome on the mat should they seek treatment in any of the country's psychiatric hospitals:

> It is likely that at least some of the increase is due to greater acceptance of the psychiatric hospital as a treatment centre for such problems. Public opinion has also increased pressure on people to seek treatment in hospital in the belief that the problems can be cured.[67]

The report drew on a range of outcome studies and WHO reports, which confirmed suspicions that no discernible improvement could be detected in modern alcoholism treatment services; in particular it was noted that specialist inpatient treatment programmes, such as those which were now the norm in the private hospitals and which were coming to be expected in public psychiatric facilities in Ireland, did not deliver outcomes better than those resulting from less expensive, community-based programmes. Reading through this chapter of *Planning for the Future*, one could easily imagine that its authors had come close to recommending that mental health services should disavow all responsibility for the management of drinking problems. In the end, however, their recommendation was that the mental health system *should* retain a commitment to the treatment of patients experiencing alcohol-related problems, but that such patients should routinely be treated within community-based services and admitted to inpatient care only in exceptional circumstances. From an historic perspective, the wheel could be seen to have turned full circle: this was a far cry from the scientific certitudes of the disease concept that had informed the thinking of the

Commission of Inquiry on Mental Illness less than twenty years earlier, and could, in fact, be seen to represent a return to the begrudging and ambivalent attitudes towards *inebriates* that had characterized Irish lunatic asylums more or less since their establishment. For the authors of *Planning for the Future*, Smith's conclusion about the difficulties facing the inebriate asylums in the early twentieth century still seemed quite appropriate – *Quite bluntly, no one knew how to cure a drunk.*[68]

On the question of the prevention of alcohol-related problems, *Planning for the Future* again followed the considerably drier policy line being advocated by the WHO, which by this time had lost faith in public education and was now advocating alcohol control strategies. It was argued that for effective prevention of alcohol-related problems in Ireland it would be necessary to: introduce higher taxes on alcohol as a means to reduce or stabilize consumption; restrict availability of alcohol at the retail level; have strict enforcement of under-age drinking and drink-driving legislation; impose restrictions on the way in which the drinks industry advertised and promoted its products.[69] It was recognized that the drafting and implementation of a national alcohol policy along these lines could not be undertaken by the health sector acting on its own, but that this would demand an integrated policy response from all the governmental sectors involved with alcohol. It was therefore recommended that an interdepartmental body on alcohol policy be established to co-ordinate all of the relevant bodies, with INCA – 'the primary advisory body in the field of alcohol-related problems in this country' – also being identified as having a role to play in this process. AA was not forgotten either: 'In view of the important role of Alcoholics Anonymous in the support and treatment of persons with alcohol-related problems, this organization should also be represented.'[70] One can assume that the authors of *Planning for the Future* intended this latter recommendation to reflect official approval of AA, but it also reflected official ignorance of how AA works – since the fellowship's Traditions specifically preclude it from becoming involved with policy issues and policy making.

In March 1985, soon after the publication of *Planning for the Future,* a flurry of public debate and controversy arose when the Voluntary Health Insurance organization announced that it was to restrict its cover of inpatient alcoholism treatment: specifying how many days hospital treatment it was prepared to fund for such patients rather than, as in the past, leaving all decision making on the number and length of hospital admissions to the clinical judgement of consultant psychiatrists.[71] These restrictions were apparently introduced without consultation with, and certainly without the approval of, the private psychiatric sector, which responded with indignation to changes in a system that had served it well for almost thirty years. Among those protesting at the decision of VHI to limit its cover of inpatient alcoholism treatment was Dr John Cooney, consultant psychiatrist at St Patrick's Hospital and founding member of INCA. In the course of a public lecture in which he denounced these proposed changes, Dr Cooney reverted to the classic rhetoric of the disease concept, making no reference to the discussion of alcoholism treatment in the recently published *Planning for the Future*:

> Dr John Cooney, Associate Medical Director of St Patrick's Hospital, said in a lecture on 'The Problem Drinker' that the VHI's measures were quite arbitrary and could not be justified, given the natural history of alcoholism and the necessity for properly organised treatment programming designed to achieve recovery rather than mere sobriety.
>
> The VHI organisation would appear to be unaware of the major advances in treatment of latter years in this country, with consequent restoration to health and happiness of so many alcoholics and their families ...
>
> It was also highly disquieting to contemplate the prospect of the alcoholic being forced to go underground and conceal his or her problem, after all these years of painstaking and often frustrating endeavour to remove the stigma of alcoholism.[72]

In light of the apparently authoritative views and recommendations on alcoholism treatment expressed in *Planning for the Future*, which were completely contradictory of Dr Cooney's views, it was not surprising that protests emanating from private psychiatry fell on deaf ears and that the VHI went ahead with its planned restrictions for inpatient cover. INCA, now operating in a policy environment where the disease concept had been scientifically challenged if not entirely discredited, struggled to adapt to this changed external environment and to manage its own internal philosophical tensions. Eventually, in the face of ongoing financial problems during 1988, INCA agreed to wind down and did so at the end of this year.

None of the alcohol policy recommendations contained in *Planning for the Future* proved easy to implement. Admission to the local psychiatric unit had come to be seen as the norm for problem drinkers, so that families, primary care professionals and the Gardai – as well as problem drinkers themselves – were slow to accept that this should change.[73] The recommendations for an integrated national alcohol policy based on public health principles and largely consisting of politically unpopular alcohol control strategies, were repeated in many subsequent health policy documents but never implemented in any consistent or coherent way.[74] What seems especially noteworthy is that *Planning for the Future* (1984) was the last health policy document to use the word *alcoholism*; subsequent reports[75] speak of 'alcohol abuse', 'alcohol-related problems' and 'alcohol dependence' but, despite its continued use in everyday language, the word *alcoholism* had now virtually disappeared from official health policy discourse in Ireland.

Following the withdrawal of Sackville and Aiden MacSweeney from INCA, the fellowship in Ireland appears to have fully grasped the value and significance of its own traditions, which enjoin it to concentrate on its 'primary purpose' – to 'carry its message to the alcoholic who still suffers' (Tradition Five) – while steering well clear of the controversial politics of alcoholism. In accordance with its traditions, the fellowship in Ireland made no comment upon the changed philosophy contained in *Planning for the Future*, neither did it become embroiled in the controversy arising from the decision of VHI to cut back on insurance cover for inpatient alcoholism treatment. Ironically, just as official Irish health policy was becoming sceptical of the value of the disease concept in relation to the management of drinking problems within statutory services, a new and evangelical version of this concept was diffused from its American base and gained considerable popularity within the voluntary sector here. This version of the disease concept, which drew heavily on the AA and is usually known as the Minnesota Model, will now be looked at in the last major section of this chapter.

AA AND THE MINNESOTA MODEL

In the USA, as in many other countries, the mental health system had traditionally managed problem drinkers without much enthusiasm, but with a previously described, fatalistic sense that existing treatment technologies were ineffective and that patients were likely to revert to destructive drinking habits shortly after being discharged from institutional care. From the late 1940s, however, a new and comprehensive approach to alcoholism treatment began to emerge in the State of Minnesota, consisting largely of the application of AA concepts and practices to professional treatment services.[76] This approach, popularly known as the Minnesota Model, was based around the delivery of highly structured treatment programmes, including group therapy, individual and family counselling, and education about alcoholism. Alcoholism counsellors (a new type of health care professional) played a major role in this new regime, and in many instances counsellors were themselves recovering alcoholics and fellowship members. The programmes, typically delivered in specialist alcoholism units within psychiatric hospitals or in free-standing alcoholism treatment facilities, usually began with an intensive period of residential care, lasting for several weeks, followed by a less intensive aftercare regime which could stretch over several years. While in many ways the Minnesota Model shared its core beliefs with the mainstream disease concept, it deviated significantly from the original concept in its assertion that the personality structure of alcoholics was characterized by rigid defence mechanisms, which prevented them from grasping the reality of their condition or taking appropriate remedial action. Since, in the phrase popularized by the Minnesota Model, alcoholics were deemed to be 'in denial', it followed that therapeutic efforts could not afford to be as passive or non-directive as would be the norm for other psychological disorders. On this basis, the model encouraged proactive interventions in which 'constructive confrontation' was expected to play a major role in bringing alcoholics back in touch with reality, preferably before they deteriorated to the point of reaching 'rock bottom'.

In the USA, despite the work of Marty Mann's NCA and other bodies which promoted the disease concept, little change had occurred in service provision until the enactment of the

Comprehensive Alcohol Abuse and Alcoholism Prevention, Treatment and Rehabilitation Act, 1970, facilitated greater funding of alcoholism treatment programmes by state authorities. In the wake of this legislation came an enormous expansion of alcoholism treatment in which the Minnesota Model became the dominant force, following which – through the work of such organizations as the Hazelden Foundation and the Johnson Institute – the model began to be globally diffused.

Since AA had never functioned like a business corporation jealously safeguarding its intellectual property, it was not surprising that it did not react negatively (or, indeed, at all) to the manner in which the Minnesota Model had effectively stolen what might appear to be the key elements of the fellowship's programme for its own use. Clients in residential Minnesota Model treatment systems were introduced to AA and taken through the first five steps of the Twelve-Step AA programme; the educational component of these structured treatment programmes also drew heavily on fellowship ideas, and, as previously mentioned, a major role in treatment was played by counsellors who were themselves fellowship members. This borrowing or adaptation of fellowship ideas and practices was explicit and acknowledged, as may be seen in this quote from Daniel Anderson of the Hazelden Foundation:

> Finally, I would like to comment briefly on what I think is the single most important ingredient in the Minnesota treatment programs. What we have done is successfully integrate the spiritual philosophy of Alcoholics Anonymous into the professional treatment program. And in doing this, something profound has happened. It seems that all we have done is to humanize our programs with the interpersonal mutuality found in most Alcoholics Anonymous relationships. Perhaps the most mutual element in our programs is the opportunity to meet, learn, and grow in small, unstructured peer group relationships.[77]

Although the Minnesota Model was promoted throughout the USA with great enthusiasm and to general approval, it was not without its critics. Senator Harold Hughes, a Democratic Senator from Iowa (who made no secret of the fact that he himself was an alcoholic) had sponsored the federal legislation responsible for the enhanced funding of alcoholism treatment, but appears to have become quickly disenchanted by the events he had set in train. It has been reported that, as early as 1974, Hughes expressed alarm at the expansion of alcoholism treatment and the proliferation of treatment professionals, describing it as 'a new civilian army that has now become institutionalized. The alcohol and drug industrial complex is not as powerful as its military-industrial counterpart, but nevertheless there are striking similarities'.[78] At a popular level, perhaps the most well-known critic was Stanton Peele, a psychologist whose polemic on the 'diseasing of America' challenged all aspects of the Minnesota Model and presented the addiction treatment 'industry' as scientifically spurious and self-serving. From a clinical research perspective, William Miller, a psychologist with particular expertise in treatment programme evaluations, consistently demonstrated that, despite the zeal with which it was promoted, the Minnesota Model was no more effective than anything that had preceded it.[79] Miller also pointed out that, contrary to the claims of proponents of the Minnesota Model, problem drinkers do not have uniquely defensive personality structures, and that their ambivalence about committing themselves to change was no different from that of people with other psychological problems; there was, therefore, no justification for the emphasis on confrontation as a counselling strategy – indeed research clearly showed confrontation to be counterproductive.

Sociologists such as Weisner and Room (1984) argued – as has been argued earlier in this chapter in relation to the impact of VHI funding on Irish alcoholism treatment – that major increases in funding for alcoholism treatment following the 1970 legislation led to an ideological acceptance of the Minnesota Model across the USA. This was because the Minnesota ideas offered a rationale for service expansion based on the perceived necessity to utilize a more aggressive style of intervention with alcoholics still 'in denial', as well as with family members who were increasingly represented as also being in need of treatment. In summary, its critics argued that the Minnesota Model was based on false premises, in the sense that the disease concept was invalid and that problem drinkers could not be shown to be more defensive or 'in denial' than anybody else; more importantly, its critics argued that Minnesota-style treatment programmes were structured along excessively rigid lines and that they owed their popularity more to aggressive marketing than to any demonstrable effectiveness.

While it might be seen as flattering to AA that this professionally delivered model of alcoholism treatment borrowed so heavily from the fellowship's programme of recovery, it was also problematic in that it seemed inevitable that, in the public mind, confusion would arise between AA and the Minnesota Model: indeed, to some it might appear as though AA and the Minnesota Model were one and the same thing. The fact that managers and clinicians within Minnesota-style services were apt to describe their services as Twelve-Step programmes, and that AA members were now working as paid alcoholism counsellors within these programmes, added to the likelihood of such confusion. In formal terms, of course, AA could be expected to regard the Minnesota Model and everything to do with it as 'an outside issue' on which it had no opinion, but such formal dissociation from outside issues did not automatically prevent or resolve difficulties and confusion arising from the similarities between these two institutions.

In Ireland, the first Minnesota-style alcoholism treatment programme to be established was the Stanhope Alcoholism Treatment Centre, a voluntary agency which grew out of the work of a generic social services centre run by the Irish Sisters of Charity in the north inner-city of Dublin. The driving force behind this initiative was Sr Marie Joseph O'Reilly, whose work in this hard-drinking markets' area of the city convinced her that what was most needed was a specialist alcoholism treatment centre. Sr Marie Joseph was familiar with and well disposed towards the work of AA, and was personally friendly with Sackville. For instance, when Bill Wilson, the fellowship's co-founder, died in early 1971, Sr Marie Joseph arranged for a Mass, to which Dublin AA members were invited, to be said in the Stanhope Convent chapel. She responded subsequently to Sackville to say that no thanks were needed for doing this: 'Your letter is on our Community notice board – truly we didn't feel it was due because it was such a pleasure for us to have the Mass for Bill here.'[80]

Sr Marie Joseph, who had previously trained in social care, developed contacts with a number of American services, and arranged for herself and two fellowship members she had earmarked as her first two employees to go for specialist counsellor training in the Minnesota Model. During late 1976 and early 1977 the trainee counsellors from Stanhope St availed themselves of training and work experience with the Christopher Smithers Foundation in New York, and later with the Hazelden Foundation and St Mary's Hospital in Minneapolis. Following this, in late 1977 the Stanhope treatment centre began to operate its own treatment programme. The new service was partially funded by the Eastern Health Board and developed close working relationships with St Dymphna's, the health board's specialist alcoholism treatment unit in St Brendan's Hospital. While the Stanhope service was modelled ideologically and structurally on the Minnesota system, it differed significantly from American programmes in that it was non-residential. Perhaps because its clients had to return home after each therapeutic session, or perhaps because temperamentally Sr Marie Joseph was not comfortable with confrontational counselling, Stanhope never gained the reputation for aggressive confrontation of clients which would later come to be associated with other Minnesota Model agencies in Ireland. Sr Marie Joseph did subscribe, theoretically at least, to the mainstream Minnesota view that alcoholics had to be confronted with reality and that any form of therapeutic molly-coddling was counterproductive. As further Minnesota Model agencies were established in Ireland, these new non-medical agencies effectively became competitors with the specialist alcoholism units within private psychiatry, and one element of ideological tension between competitors was the allegation that private psychiatric units were unhelpfully soft on alcoholics. Sr Marie Joseph was one of the few main players in the alcoholism treatment arena to publicly express this viewpoint, which she did in a letter to the *Irish Times* during the 1985 controversy about VHI restrictions on inpatient alcoholism:

> During my more than 20 years work with alcoholics I have found the greatest obstacle to their recovery to be the people who take responsibility for them and provide for their comforts. No better place to do both than in the private hospital.
>
> If alcoholics are kept secure and comfortable they won't stop drinking no matter how much they want to. They can't.

The best help that can be given is to expose them to the full consequences of their drinking.

To the VHI I would say: 'You have done a good day's work! Stick to it!'[81]

The second Minnesota Model agency in Ireland was the Rutland Centre, a residential unit established in Dublin in January 1978 by Father Raphael Short, a clinical psychologist and member of the Passionist Order.[82] Father Short lobbied the then Minister for Health, Charles Haughey, making extravagant claims about the 'success rate' of Minnesota Model programmes and succeeding in getting substantial statutory funding for his new project. If private psychiatric hospitals were accused of being excessively soft on alcoholics, one of the accusations which became commonplace about Minnesota-style agencies – and about the Rutland Centre in particular – was that they relied too much on aggressively confrontational styles of counselling and on punitive management regimes. Since AA does not have a centralized authority which makes pronouncements about matters outside its own immediate activities, the question of AA approval or disapproval of the Rutland Centre simply does not arise. It is a remarkable irony, however, that after more than thirty years of negotiating relatively trouble-free working relationships with psychiatrists and mental hospitals, AA in Ireland should have experienced unprecedented difficulties in its relationship with the Rutland Centre – a treatment agency which described itself as running a Twelve-Step Programme and which employed several fellowship members as counsellors.

In the course of a general research interview on AA in Ireland, given in 1997, one long-standing fellowship member, Pat H., spoke explicitly and at some length about his experience as chair of the Rathgar AA group, the group that organized meetings for the Rutland Centre (in its original location at Clondalkin) each Sunday and Thursday during the early months of the Rutland's existence. It should be emphasized at the outset that Pat's approach to the task of carrying the AA message to potential members was broadly pragmatic rather than narrowly doctrinaire. For instance, commenting on how some members had been critical of his willingness to speak at Masses in Galway Cathedral during a Redemptorist novena, arguing that he was 'bringing religion into it', he stated bluntly: 'If I'm asked by the proper authorities, I don't give a damn whether I carry AA's message in a cathedral or in a whorehouse.'[83] Some twenty years after these events had occurred, he was equally blunt in describing the difficulties he had encountered in trying to run twice-weekly AA groups in the Rutland Centre. In overall terms, Pat was unhappy with the regime at the Rutland Centre, which, from an AA perspective, he saw as harshly authoritarian and lacking in mutuality. He referred to two counsellors in particular who were themselves members of AA but who, in his view, were almost indescribably aggressive in their management of clients. His conclusion about one of these counsellors was that 'she had no compassion at all'. Of the other, having described in detail the petty restrictions and inconvenience she imposed on one client whom he knew – a nun from rural Ireland – Pat's conclusion was that this counsellor's behaviour was 'pure bloody ridiculous and childish. And I saw the same one, I saw the treatment she got when she came into AA. Lord Jesus almighty, it was so different'.[84]

Pat was clear that, in accordance with its Traditions, outside AA members like himself could continue to run groups in the Rutland Centre regardless of whether or not they approved of this agency's regime; as he saw it, difficulties only arose when some of the therapeutic practices within the centre cut across and interfered directly with the running of AA groups:

> AA was not going to be seen to endorse their type of treatment; we had no opinion on it ... We don't interfere with their treatment. It doesn't matter a damn what they do, but we insist they don't interfere where our meetings are concerned.[85]

The breaking point, as far as Pat was concerned, was when the behaviour of residential clients attending meetings run by outside fellowship members was made to conform to general commitments or injunctions imposed on them as part of their overall management within the Rutland Centre. He cited the example of a young man who had attended an AA group within the centre while wearing a baby's soother around his neck; Pat was later to discover that this was not the fashion statement which he originally thought it to be, but a 'commitment' imposed upon this man by his counsellor to symbolize to himself and others how childish he was. He also described how a young man, previously known to Pat, refused to speak to him at an AA meeting: in this instance one of the other residents explained that this client was under a commitment not to speak to anybody. Pat, whose general view of the Rutland Centre was that he had seen 'more daft suggestions coming out of there than anything I thought the human mind would be capable of', took his complaints to Father Short, arguing that whatever the centre did in its mainstream programme, it should allow AA to run its groups, as it would run them anywhere else, on the basis of equality and mutual respect for all group members. He found Father Short to be 'very dictatorial' and quite unwilling to accede to Pat's request, so that 'eventually we pulled out'. In other words, the Rathgar AA group took the unprecedented step of withdrawing its co-operation with a treatment centre, so that for some time this centre had no AA group. Pat was unclear about what happened subsequently, but knew that at some future time outside AA members had again started to facilitate meetings in the Rutland Centre – 'people probably went in who knew nothing about the Traditions'.[86]

The Rutland Centre was just the first of about a dozen or so residential programmes established in Ireland along Minnesota lines: all voluntary agencies, frequently started by priests, brothers or nuns, and primarily staffed by counsellors. The reputation for aggressive counselling styles, originally associated with the Rutland Centre, no longer appears to be quite as widespread as it was, although these agencies continued to describe their services as 'Minnesota Model/Twelve-Step Programmes'.[87] By and large, these programmes have not published evaluations or outcome studies, which would justify populist beliefs in their superiority over other forms of treatment,[88] but neither has the state made any substantial progress in developing a more rational or coordinated system of voluntary and statutory therapeutic responses to alcohol problems. It is impossible to know definitively the extent to which the Irish public confuses AA with such Minnesota Model practices, but it is likely that some confusion at least exists on this matter. In the USA the emergence of greater research interest in AA led inter alia to an acknowledgement that it was not merely members of the public but academics and researchers – who might be expected to know better – who were regularly confusing AA with the rhetoric and practice of the Minnesota Model, and attributing to AA some of the more aggressive features of the latter. A co-authored paper by William Miller and Ernest Kurtz, the historian of AA, sought to differentiate between AA and other treatment models with which it is often confused, and ended by reasserting the minimalist, pragmatic and essentially spiritual nature of the fellowship:

> AA writings do not assert that: (1) there is only one form of alcoholism or alcohol problem; (2) moderate drinking is impossible for everyone with alcohol problems; (3) alcoholics should be labeled, confronted aggressively or coerced into treatment; (4) alcoholics are riddled with denial and other defense mechanisms; (5) alcoholism is purely a physical disorder; (6) alcoholism is hereditary; (7) there is only one way to recover; or (8) alcoholics are not responsible for their condition or actions. These assertions involve outside economic, political, social, moral, legal and disciplinary issues on which AA takes no stand (although AA members as individuals and political organizations, such as the National Council on Alcoholism and Drug Dependence, do so).[89]

CONCLUSION

If the quote from Cooney used as an epigraph for this chapter is taken as an example of thinking, prevalent in early 1960s Ireland, that medical science had made great strides in its understanding of alcoholism, then this immediately last quote from Miller and Kurtz may be taken as reflecting a more recent view by American alcohol specialists that little scientific consensus has been achieved in what is still a highly controversial aspect of social life. Far from being accepted as a straightforward or 'respectable' disease, as Cooney advocated, alcoholism came over the next forty years to be seen as a conceptual error and a distraction from the more pressing need to focus attention on alcohol control policies at societal level. Such arguments for what is usually described as 'evidence-based' public policy could not, however, get away from the fact that large numbers of people still experienced an inability to manage their drinking and still looked to the health system for help with this problem. What this chapter as a whole has demonstrated is that AA in Ireland, primarily through its adherence to the fellowship's administrative charter, the Twelve Traditions, successfully developed and maintained working relationships with the health care system while avoiding the worst pitfalls of alcohol politics. This process of negotiation was not without its errors and problems, best exemplified perhaps in Sackville's flirtation with INCA. But, paradoxically, it was not AA's contacts with medically dominated treatment systems which proved to be most complicated and difficult, but its contacts with those Minnesota Model agencies which appeared to be ideologically closest to AA. Ultimately, through a realization that AA exists on its own with a single-minded pragmatic focus on being available to those who wish to stop drinking, Irish members succeeded in remaining outside of the ongoing political, economic and scientific controversies which might easily have distracted it from this primary purpose.

Chapter Six

Alcoholics Anonymous: An Irish Institution

I think we will have to decide that the Dublin Group has 'personality'. I don't know how we'd get along without you. In fact, let's not consider that possibility. For a long time before the group started, everyone asked us why there wasn't a group in Ireland – we have so many Irish AAs here, that they couldn't believe you didn't need one.[1]

In their study of AA in eight different societies, Makela and colleagues (1996)[2] confirmed that despite, or perhaps because of, its unusual organizational structures, AA had the capacity to take on a range of features reflecting the social and cultural diversity of the countries to which it had been diffused, while at the same time maintaining a core unitary identity which transcended such international differences. The last two chapters looked at how AA in Ireland created and sustained working relationships with the church and the health care system. The aim of the present chapter is to look more broadly at the work undertaken by early Irish members in getting AA established as an identifiable national institution to which actual and potential members had relatively easy access. In December 1946, just a few weeks into its Irish experience, AA in this country consisted of one group of perhaps no more than fifteen members based in the Country Shop in Dublin, while estimates for the year 2007 indicate that in the thirty-two counties of Ireland the fellowship had about 13,000 members spread across 750 groups.[3] No voluntary body experiences growth of this order without a great deal of hard work by its members, and the aim of this chapter is to outline some of the main events and issues associated with AA's expansion from its modest beginnings in postwar Dublin.

The quote used as an epigraph to this chapter is from a letter written to Sackville by Charlotte Lappen, one of the staff at the Alcoholic Foundation in New York, in April 1948 – when the fellowship was about eighteen months into its Irish existence and when Sackville was just a year into his personal recovery. It can reasonably be assumed that the 'personality' identified and commented upon by the New York office was largely that of Sackville himself; and, as the previous chapter has shown, this was personality which was quite capable of ignoring or resisting advice from the New York office when such advice was deemed to be unhelpful or irrelevant to the Irish scene. It should be remembered, however, that the administrative culture of the fellowship is one which promotes a leaderless or non-hierarchical approach to its own internal management, eschewing both bureaucratic and charismatic leadership styles. It was for this reason that Bill Wilson, as the longest surviving of AA's two co-founders, had worked long and hard to remove himself from a central leadership role so as to ensure that the fellowship would survive should he die prematurely or resume alcoholic-style drinking. This chapter will therefore touch, at least intermittently, upon the dilemmas associated with Sackville's dominant role in putting AA in Ireland on a secure footing. Perhaps the primary dilemma arose from his awareness that he, by virtue of his temperament, organizational skills and leisure time, was ideally placed to contribute to AA's survival and growth in this country, while being simultaneously aware of the risks involved in making the fellowship too dependent upon just one individual. Sackville was also cognizant of the fact that AA's culture of anonymity and its emphasis on 'principles before personalities' (Tradition Twelve) was intended not just to protect the fellowship from individual members who started to take themselves too seriously, but also to protect such individuals from themselves – lest 'ego re-inflation' should lead to a relapse into active alcoholism. On this latter point, it is clear Sackville knew that he had achieved a high profile in international AA circles; but it appears from his correspondence that rather than taking this international reputation seriously, he generally treated it and himself with a high degree of self-mockery. In 1968, for instance, he responded to his friend Joe D., who had apparently been teasing Sackville about becoming a global big shot in the fellowship:

> You fear for my humility? Perhaps you may be right. Someone referred to me at the Scots Convention as the 'British Bill Wilson' [*a handwritten marginal note which is linked to the word 'British' says 'An insult in itself'*]. I feel it is about time people started calling Bill 'The New York Sackville'.[4]

Whatever the risks to Sackville's ego, it should be emphasized that the commitment to growth and expansion by AA members is not comparable to that found in the business world. Twelve-Stepping, or 'carrying the message' to alcoholics deemed to be still suffering, has nothing to do with making a profit, but is seen as a moral responsibility taken on by fellowship members on the basis that by helping others they help themselves: in the words of an AA slogan, 'in order to keep it, you have to give it away'. In the very early days of AA in Dublin, however, members were less concerned with growth and expansion than with survival, and descriptions of the way in which they huddled together for support during that first alcohol-free Christmas of 1946 are reminiscent of the New Testament story of how the apostles clung together for support and survival in the days prior to Pentecost. Richard Perceval's wife, Ruth, has given a vivid account of how during this Christmas the newly sober members lived 'in each other's pockets', sometimes meeting twice a day for mutual support. In addition to formal meetings at the Country Shop, many of these informal meetings were held at the home of Jimmy R., who lived in Adelaide Road and whose wife appears to have been very hospitable to AA members.[5] The Country Shop group struggled for survival following Conor Flynn's return to the United States, but – without attributing Pentecostal qualities to him – it is clear that Sackville's coming reinvigorated the group, quickly giving it the confidence to consider establishing other AA groups in the greater Dublin area and throughout the rest of Ireland.

There was, as described in Chapter 4, some initial discouragement of AA, most obviously in Grangegorman Mental Hospital and in St John of God's Hospital but, once started, the fellowship did not encounter any significant opposition, and it seems fair to say – in the words of a long-serving member, Big Eugene – that 'the Irish took to AA'.[6] Indeed, to the extent that early members experienced opposition to the idea of alcoholism, such opposition appears to have reflected conceptual ambiguity and linguistic practice, rather than genuine ideological antipathy to the fellowship's activities. Nobody denied the existence of drinking problems, merely the use of word *alcoholism* to describe such problems. In the style of politicians who argued that there was no sex in Ireland until television, one AA old-timer remarked that 'there was no alcoholism in Ireland until Conor F. brought it over from America'.[7] One measure of the early recognition of the fellowship within Irish society is to be found in the fact that a letter, written by the relative of a problem drinker in Limerick and addressed simply to 'Dypsomaniacs Anonymous, Dublin', was successfully delivered a few days later to the Country Shop during November 1948.[8] Another incident which suggests that early members had successfully put an Irish gloss on the fellowship occurred in January 1948, when Sackville gave a letter he had received from a member in Arkansas to a new Irish member; this man read and returned the letter to Sackville, saying 'I didn't know they had AA in America.'[9]

AA AS AN ALL-IRISH INSTITUTION

It appears to have been assumed from the outset that, when it came to establishing groups outside of Dublin, AA would be a 32-county institution rather than one which organized itself within the twenty-six counties of the then Irish Free State. Richard Perceval was, after all, from the North of Ireland, and it seemed only natural that he should have an interest in facilitating the introduction of AA to his own part of the country. In January 1948, less than a year into his own recovery and when he was still greatly preoccupied with the problems besetting AA in Dublin, Sackville told one of his New York correspondents: 'Richard and I have great hopes of being able to get things going in Belfast some time, but just now it is difficult to get up there.'[10] Four months later, in May 1948, the first Belfast group was established with the support of Richard and Sackville, and the existence of this new group was almost immediately noted and publicized in the international directory of meetings produced by the New

York Foundation. This provoked a worried response from Sackville to Bobbie Burger:

> Would you please list Irish groups under 'Ireland' and not 'Eire'. Eire is the Irish for Ireland but it is generally taken as meaning the 26 Counties and NOT including Northern Ireland. It may seem childish to you (it does to me), but you might offend Belfast if you list them as Eire![11][capitals in original]

Richard and Sackville were pleased with the manner in which the Belfast group quickly took responsibility for its own destiny, rather than remaining dependent on support from Dublin. A few weeks after the first Belfast meeting, Sackville wrote to Bobbie Burger in New York: 'I heard from Belfast tonight. They had their first solo meeting on Wednesday with 14 there ... Richard and I hope to get up occasionally.'[12] What was also interesting about the Belfast group was that its first secretary was a woman, giving Sackville great hope that this would inspire other women alcoholics to join what had until then been a predominantly male fellowship. This woman (whose name is not recorded in his correspondence) appears to have struck up a close, almost flirtatious relationship with Sackville, whom she regarded as an AA old-timer. In August 1948, in a letter to his friend Joe D. in Chicago, Sackville quoted from a letter he had received from the secretary of the Belfast group:

> The following received this morning from the Belfast lady secretary. It is just one of the 'Ups' of life, if it can be taken seriously.
>
> 'Just for my sake, come up and stay with us. You must realise that you have a big responsibility in me. After all, you were the one to come up and talk about starting the group. You and Richard did all the groundwork and put everything in order. As long as I have you to lean on and Richard to call on I shall try hard to do my best. But if either of you go on a bender, then there will be an excuse for me having one.'[13]

The Belfast group appears to have progressed and matured without any discernible difficulties, and in early 1950 Sackville told Joe D.: 'The Belfast crowd are hoping to open a new group shortly in Bangor, the seaside lung of Belfast, and have asked me to speak there.'[14] Some weeks later he reported: 'I went along to the open-ing open meeting in Bangor with Richard. We both spoke, and in spite of this six men joined and so another infant AA group has been launched on the world.'[15] In 1958 the practice of holding annual All-Ireland AA Conventions began, and the fourth such convention was held in Bangor in 1961.

The original Dublin group had included Catholics and Protestants, and it seems to have been taken for granted that AA in Belfast would have no difficulty in integrating the various religious groupings. In Northern Ireland, as in the Republic of Ireland, AA groups were organized largely on a geographic rather than a religious basis, and there is no evidence that members sought out or tried to develop predominantly Catholic groups or predominantly Protestant groups. It would obviously have been unusual, if not completely unconscionable, for individuals who had been utterly beaten by alcohol and who were now recovering through a spiritually based programme, to engage in sectarian aggression. Nonetheless it is noteworthy that, in a society charac-terized by endemic political and sectarian tensions, AA in Northern Ireland was completely successful in its avoidance of such tensions, so that through the worst years of the 'Troubles' – between 1969 and 1994 – it simply continued to focus on its primary purpose, looking after the common welfare of alcoholics regardless of their religious affiliations or their political alle-giances.

While no controversy arose concerning the decision to run the fellowship as an All-Ireland institution, quite a serious row erupted two years later when, following a trip Bill Wilson had made to Ireland and England, the Alcoholic Foundation in New York suggested that AA might be best advised to organize itself on the basis of a unified AA Foundation serving both the United Kingdom and Ireland. Bill Wilson's trip to Ireland was something that Sackville had long desired; he had begun to correspond with Bill as soon as he joined AA himself in 1947, almost immediately asking: 'Any chance of your visiting Dublin?'[16] Three years later, in June 1950, the visit to Ireland – involving a busy itinerary drawn up by Sackville with military precision – took place. Wilson spoke at a closed AA meeting, attended by more than eighty members, in the Country Shop,[17] and also addressed an open meeting in the nearby Mansion House. Sackville, who had planned the schedule with Helen Brown, Wilson's secretary at the Alcoholic Foundation in New York, wrote to Helen just after the visit to Ireland had ended:

> A line to let you know that Bill has come, seen and con-
> quered ... In the evening [Monday, 26 June] we had the first
> Open meeting of the visit at the Mansion House. It was the
> first really large meeting we had run, so we looked to it with
> a certain amount of dread as to whether anyone would come
> or not. We got about 300 there and Bill spoke for 70 min-
> utes. He got a very good reception.[18]

Bill Wilson also attended open AA meetings in Cork, Limerick and Belfast, as well as visiting St Patrick's Hospital, Dublin, and indulging in some conventional tourist activities, such as kissing the Blarney Stone. His visit was widely reported in the newspapers, and Sackville also arranged for him to record a short interview for a programme called 'Visitors' Book' on the national broad-caster, Radio Éireann.

From an AA perspective, Bill Wilson's visit to Ireland had the significance and sense of occasion that a papal visit would later have for devout Catholics, and at its conclusion Sackville was pleased but, understandably, exhausted. He was greatly apprecia-tive of the co-founder's visit and of the ongoing support of the Alcoholic Foundation in New York, but he believed that by this time the fellowship in Ireland was fundamentally sound and quite capable of standing on its own two feet. He was, therefore, taken aback when some two months later a staff member at the New York office wrote to pass on a suggestion (emanating from discus-sions in New York following Wilson's return) that members in Britain and Ireland should organize themselves into a unified Alcoholics Anonymous Foundation, which would be based in London and comparable to that in New York. This suggestion had its origins in the meetings Wilson had had with members in England, who complained that they were struggling with the costs of running an office and making AA literature (particularly the Big Book) available to members. Reflecting on this, it appeared to the New Yorkers that a single AA Foundation for the 'British Isles' would create economies of scale and, indeed, that such a foundation could itself become the publisher of the Big Book and other AA literature. Despite his friendship with and general deference towards Bill Wilson, Sackville was adamant that, insofar as he could influence events, AA in Ireland would have no truck with such a scheme but would remain as it was – an All-Ireland institution. Sackville was totally committed to the ideal of voluntarism and disliked the notion of establishing a full-time office with paid staff, suspecting that the New York suggestion, if acted upon, would result in Irish AA monies being sent to support paid AA workers in London. He replied instantly and emphatically to Ann Lehman in the New York office:

> The main deterrent from our point of view is the sordid one of funds ... What they care to do over there [in England] is entirely their own affair and has nothing to do with us. We do not propose, however, to join in. The little surplus we have here is going to be devoted to AA in Ireland, not to pay camouflaged salaries to people who have not the work to justify them. The institution of a Foundation, for at most a membership of 5 or 6 hundred members in these islands, seems to us to be completely premature.[19]

This was a relatively polite expression of Sackville's objections to the New York proposal but, as was often the case, he was less restrained in explaining his point of view to his confidant, Joe D. in Chicago:

> I got a royal semi-command to attend a conference in London from the London group. I have refused to go, as I see no particular object in mixing in with them, inasmuch as I disapprove strongly of the way they carry on. Bill wants them apparently to start a Foundation for Britain and Ireland. It would be a waste of time and money at present and for some years to come. He is also anxious for the book to be pub-lished in London. This is also a matter for a fairly distant future. If we set up this format now, all our money will go in paying an English secretary to do sweet fanny adams. All the English groups subscribe heavily at present to pay for a secretary who I am sure does not do as much work as I do.[20]

Bill Wilson and his staff at the New York office appear to have been surprised at the vehemence of the Irish response, and several efforts were made to dissuade Sackville from his outright rejection of the planned foundation. One staff member, Ann MacFarlane, wrote at length, perhaps in the hope that Sackville might be flattered into changing his mind, about the necessity of having a more formal organization in England, since it had no equivalent to Sackville:

> I was disappointed to hear that you are not in agreement with the others about the establishment of a Foundation for the purpose of selling our book ... Another point you made disappoints me a little. You say that English ideas and (I presume) Irish ideas are poles apart on most subjects. This may very well be true, but we are in universal agreement all over the world on one subject, that of alcoholism. We have to be. Our common welfare as alcoholics must come first. All other considerations should be set aside ... Sackville, Ireland is fortunate to have a man like yourself who has the time and the means at his disposal to undertake the wonderful work that you have been doing. It happens that in other parts of the world and under different circumstances, there are simply not people of the right caliber to undertake work of this sort on a purely voluntary basis.[21]

Sackville remained unrepentant on this matter, however, and in further correspondence with Joe D. he expressed fundamental misgivings about the creation of organizational structures which mimicked business practices and which appeared – to borrow a favourite word of Bill Wilson's – 'grandiose'. He preferred, in keeping with the fellowship's Traditions, to see individual groups functioning autonomously, with the minimum of hierarchical structure, and he worried lest the establishment of offices and office holders distract members from their primary purpose and lead to a lack of humility: 'The increasing amount of self-important people coming forward is rather awing.'[22]

But neither was Bill Wilson prepared to give up easily on this idea of a British–Irish foundation, and some weeks into the controversy he took the unusual step of writing in confidence to Richard Perceval, to put the case for such a foundation and to seek Perceval's advice and guidance as to how he might circumvent Sackville's objections. Wilson pointed out that he had not heard anything directly from Sackville, but that the London groups had reported Sackville's refusal to collaborate in the scheme proposed by New York; Wilson also made it clear that he did not 'wish to disturb Sackville or inject any element of controversy into the very happy situation I found in Ireland'.[23] Richard Perceval's reply, handwritten but a model of clear thinking on Sackville, AA and the proposed foundation, may not have been what Wilson had hoped for:

> I do not really think that I can give you much help because Sackville (as you know) does not 'wear his heart on his sleeve', and it is not easy to fathom the workings of his acute mind.
>
> What I think is this – but it is only a matter of thinking. Sackville is a very conscientious member of AA and he has very strong views as to how the principles of AA can be best made known to those who do not know them. He is also aware that he is the Hon. Sec. of the first group to be organised in Great Britain and Ireland, and he feels that this group has a close and very real connection with the Alcoholic Foundation and with the General Service Office. I think he feels – and so do I – that in Dublin we have tried to make AA as democratic as possible, and that we have also tried to stick as closely as possible (subject to our national peculiarities) to the pattern drawn by you and Dr Bob. I think, too, that he feels that London AA is not quite as democratic or as true to pattern as Dublin AA, and that there is a tendency in London to over-emphasise the committee and inter-group aspect to the detriment of the real object of a group, namely the helping and guidance of any alcoholic who wishes to recover. I feel that Sackville fears that acquiescence as regards cooperating with London in the book plan, might lead to interference by London – or at least attempted influence by London – in the general AA work in Ireland.[24] [underlining in original]

Bill Wilson replied to say how much he appreciated Richard's views on this matter, and to reassure him that, in view of the obvious disquiet of Irish members, the proposal to establish a unified British–Irish foundation would now be dropped, reminding Richard that 'In AA nothing is more sure than local autonomy.'[25] From an Irish perspective, this episode was important in that it confirmed that as the fellowship evolved and expanded it would do so on the basis of its original status as an Irish institution. In more general terms, however, it exemplified the priority given within AA to 'local autonomy'; there was no question of the Dublin group (or any other Irish group) simply capitulating to the demands of 'head office', and it is salutary to observe the grace and humility with which AA's co-founder accepted that his preferred administrative scheme for the 'British Isles' was not deemed to be in keeping with AA's Traditions – traditions which, of course, he himself had written.

It seems important to point out that Sackville's emphatic rejection of the proposed British Isles Foundation should not be taken as indicative of isolationist or xenophobic attitudes on his part. On the contrary, through entertaining AA visitors to Ireland, through his own travels to groups in other countries and especially through his correspondence ('The Dublin group, by the way, has achieved special renown because of its world correspondent, Sackville M.'[26]), Sackville had created for himself an unrivalled global network of AA contacts. In the first issue of *The Road Back*, AA's Irish newsletter which he initiated in 1949 and edited for the next twenty-eight years, Sackville reported that '170 groups from Guam, Australia, South Africa, Scandinavia and Iceland have written to us.'[27] It is notable that, despite having spent all his working life as an officer in the British Army, he displayed no loyalty to Unionist ideals, and his writings are completely devoid of jingoistic content – either of the British imperialist or Irish nationalist varieties.

It is clear from the archives that Sackville maintained close, supportive relationships with AA members and AA groups all over Great Britain throughout his time in the fellowship, allowing them to benefit from the experience he had gained in the Dublin group – which was, after all, Europe's first AA group. In 1948, for instance, he became acquainted with Sir Philip Dundas, the founder of AA in Scotland, with whom he struck up a friendship and to whom he acted as advisor. In 1950 he reported to Ann Lehman in New York: 'Here I am back again from Scotland. I had a very good reception there, and no one could have been kinder. I liked Philip Dundas very much, and he has obviously put in an immense amount of work there.'[28] It is difficult at this historic remove to determine how much influence Sackville had on Dundas, but it certainly seems that the latter shared the Irishman's negative views about the consequences of being caught up in an integrated British AA foundation; in 1951, Sackville wrote as follows to Joe D.:

Had a letter from Philip of Scotland, who started AA there. He was breathing fury against London, who apparently had sent him a copy of a Constitution for AA in Great Britain. He will have none of it, believing that AA should not be organised like a city business. He tells me one or two of his own Scotsmen have been bitten with the organisation bug too.[29]

Philip Dundas had expressed private reservations about what he perceived to be the excessive dependence of Irish AA on Sackville, and fears as to the disaster which would befall it should Sackville die suddenly. Ironically, it was Dundas himself – two years Sackville's junior – who died suddenly at the age of 52 in February 1952.[30] Sackville was shocked and saddened at the death of a valued friend who had done so much for AA, but he continued to be involved with the fellowship in Scotland and in England and Wales. Finally, if further proof is needed of his international standing in AA, it should be recalled (see Chapter 4) that, following Bill Wilson's death, Sackville was asked to replace him as keynote speaker at the first European Convention of AA, which was held in Bristol in September 1971.

AA IN THE GREATER DUBLIN AREA

Despite its well-known emphasis on the importance of living 'one day at a time', AA is an institution which greatly values and celebrates history; it is common for individual members to celebrate anniversaries of their personal sobriety, for groups to mark birthdays of their establishment, and for the fellowship as a whole to note and commemorate various other institutional developments. AA in Ireland is no exception to this rule, and Sackville, scarcely six months sober, was the prime mover in organizing a 'First Anniversary Supper' at the Country Shop on 27 November 1947, to which inter alia the staff of the Alcoholic Foundation in New York had been invited with a mock promise to supply air transport – 'Airplanes at 10pm!'[31] A press release later issued to the Dublin newspapers described this event: 'Many of us looked around furtively to see if anyone was noticing us pouring water into our glasses in place of more familiar liquids, and one or two absent-mindedly attempted to blow the froth off the tea.'[32] Since AA in Ireland had started in Dublin, it is not surprising that almost all of its Irish 'creation myths' refer back to these early Dublin experiences. Among the most popular stories which are still occasionally recounted are those about the conviction with which Conor Flynn was told that there were no alcoholics in the Free State, but that some might be found in Northern Ireland; or the story about two brothers, Leo and Matt, each of whom wrote in response to an item in the *Evening Mail,* nominating the other as an alcoholic who would welcome a visit from an AA member; or the story of how Jimmy R. (a cheerful and entertaining man commonly regarded as being co-founder with Richard Perceval of the Dublin group) wandered almost by default into the Country Shop on the night of the first open meeting, primarily with a view to telling this visiting Yank that he should go back home and leave the Irish to drink in peace.[33] One of the other stories which is indicative of the precarious state of the first Dublin group is that concerning the secretary immediately preceding Sackville, who, instead of turning up at the Country Shop, spent the group's postage money on alcohol. Sackville and Jimmy R. tracked the errant secretary down to a city-centre pub where, following an altercation, they succeed in recovering the notebook containing the members' contact information; Jimmy R. was pleased to have retrieved this confidential document, but later commented with mock hurt on the ignominy of being thrown out of this pub when he wasn't even drinking. The group had to cope, however, with the loss of the few shillings which had been so painfully acquired.[34]

Despite these shaky beginnings, the archives reveal that from 1948 onwards AA was sufficiently secure to believe that it could move beyond its comfort zone – one big group based in the Country Shop – and establish locally based groups across the greater Dublin area. Sackville, who actively promoted this idea of decentralization, suspected that some of the resistance to change he encountered might be associated with the fear of some of the lazier members that in a changed regime they might be expected to become more actively and energetically involved in organizing meetings. In October 1948, for instance, in the course of one of his frequent letters to Joe D. in Chicago, he wrote:

> I had a talk last night at our members' meeting about the advisability of making arrangements for splitting up the group into more local groups. However, they all want to

stay with this one. (A compliment to the present management? ... or a nasty feeling that they might be called on to
do some work organising the new groups?)[35]

Even prior to this, however, the first move had been made to
decentralize AA in the greater Dublin area with the establishment
of a new group in Dun Laoghaire on 18 August 1948: 'Fourth
Irish group started off last night at Dun Laoghaire, formerly
Kingstown. It consists at present of about 5 of our members who
live out that way, but there are very good prospects of expansion
there.'[36] Sackville continued to play a strong mentoring role to the
Dun Laoghaire group, whose progress was by no means as swift
or uncomplicated as he had expected. Writing to staff at the New
York Foundation some two months after Dun Laoghaire had been
inaugurated, he informed them that 'The Dun Laoghaire meeting
went off very well as a meeting, but unfortunately they held it on
the night of the local elections, and I expect the hope of free beer
kept the alcoholics away.'[37] A member who showed great promise,
and who was originally identified by Sackville as being most suitable to act as secretary to the Dun Laoghaire group, proved to
be considerably more problematic than anticipated, and despite
consistent support and encouragement, had great difficulty in
remaining sober or in working the AA programme to his advantage. In March 1949, Sackville confided in Joe D.:

> I regret to say that the secretary of the Dun Laoghaire group
> came a bad cropper last week. I met him yesterday when he
> was trying to make up his mind to go back to work. He was
> full of self-pity and rather inclined to take a poor view of me
> for not having slipped yet. 'It's all very easy for you', he said,
> 'you are not married and you have an adequate income to
> live on'.[38]

This Dun Laoghaire member appears to have simply drifted away
from AA, never really establishing any pattern of what is referred
to in the fellowship as 'contented sobriety', and resisting overtures
from members who tried to bring him back to active membership.
In October 1950, Sackville brought Joe D. up to date with the sad
fate of a member for whom he initially had such high hopes:

> You will, I know, be very sorry to hear that Anthony of Dun
> Laoghaire is dead, R.I.P. He gassed himself sometime last

week, and was only discovered some time later, days in fact. He hadn't been with AA properly for over a year, and his wife and family had left him. He was covered in debts. I am deeply sorry, for he was a good speaker and a witty one, had done a lot of work to get the Dun Laoghaire group on its feet, and was intelligent and a very nice man when normal. Unfortunately, he was one of the 25% that AA can do little for.[39]

It cannot have been easy for Sackville to cope with this death, and one must assume that Anthony of Dun Laoghaire was not the only early member to come to such a tragic end. Sackville had no professional training in any area of mental health or psychotherapy and, at this early point in the fellowship's Irish history, did not have an accumulated institutional wisdom and experience to draw on in circumstances such as these. However, despite such setbacks, the fellowship in Dublin continued to prosper. A second Dublin group had been started in Ranelagh in December 1948, and while this group shifted its base periodically across the neighbouring suburbs of Ranelagh, Rathmines and Rathgar, it seems to have experienced none of the problems that had beset the Dun Laoghaire group.

Having been secretary to the Country Shop for more than three years, Sackville eventually stepped down from this position at the end of 1950. He had tried unsuccessfully to do so earlier in the year, reporting to Joe D.: 'As you guessed, I have a further six months to serve in this job before any possible relief. However, I read the riot act to them and told them to start looking for someone else.'[40] On 30 December 1950 he again wrote to Joe D. to tell him that 'I sang my swan song as Secretary of the group last night'; he went on at some length, telling Joe of how in the course of this 'swan song' he had castigated members who did not actively take responsibility for carrying the AA message. He realized that in emotionally purging himself in this way during the course of his final speech he had misbehaved somewhat: 'In fact, I enjoyed myself immensely and should feel ashamed of myself. But I don't.'[41] Sackville had high standards and was not especially enamoured of his replacement as secretary to the first Dublin group,[42] but it is clear he appreciated how necessary it was that he himself should move on, lest the group become excessively dependent on one leader.

Big Eugene recalled that when he joined AA in 1964 there were three Dublin groups – the Country Shop, Ranelagh/Rathmines and High Street. Membership of these three city groups did not appear to be based solely, or even primarily, on their members' place of residence, and Eugene's memory was that the groups – while all broadly similar in relation to the basic fellowship programme – differed from one another in subtle matters of character or temperament. The Country Shop group, by virtue of its history as Ireland's and Europe's first AA group, appeared to see itself in somewhat elitist terms, while the High Street group, with the kind of inverted snobbery sometimes to be found in AA, liked to see itself as consisting of 'real rock-bottom' alcoholics. Eugene did not regard these alleged differences between groups as being of any consequence, and he was particularly sceptical about the High Street group's claim to 'rock-bottom' status; as he recalled it, its members were quite a staid, middle-class bunch, including a Garda inspector and a pharmacist, whose pretensions to skid-row experience were not to be taken seriously.[43] In 1978 the Irish Countrywomen's Association closed the Country Shop and members attending this group replaced it with a number of smaller groups close to this city-centre location. By 2009 the AA website listed almost one hundred Dublin-based groups.

In addition to its formal function of running meetings, AA in Dublin began from relatively early in its history to provide a social outlet for people for whom regular socializing in pubs no longer seemed a prudent option. Teas and coffees were usually served in meeting rooms after the formal business had been concluded, and, as is the case internationally, members welcomed this opportunity for relaxed, informal socializing. The practice of adjourning to coffee shops for further conversation and recreation also became common. Presumably because of its proximity to the Country Shop, the lounge of the Shelbourne Hotel on St Stephen's Green became popular with Dublin-based and visiting AA members, for whom it became an unofficial social centre, even on nights when no meeting was taking place in the Country Shop. Big Eugene remembered times during the 1960s when all of the Shelbourne's lounge would be full of AA members. He particularly recalled an occasion when as he entered the Shelbourne he met Conor Flynn, home on holiday from Philadelphia, who was leaving in disappointment because he had hoped to meet up with some fellowship members in the lounge but found none there; when Eugene brought Conor back in, he was able to identify about half of the tables as being occupied by AA members unknown to Conor.[44]

Another popular venue, from the 1950s until the 1970s, for fellowship members who wished to meet and socialize was Bewley's café in Westmoreland Street; at this time the café was still owned and managed by the Bewley family, a Quaker family with a strong philanthropic bent which took AA under its wing and set aside a table for the exclusive use of members. Denis Murphy, Sackville's nephew, recalled that unless he was travelling outside of the Dublin area, Sackville's morning routine consisted of Mass in the Carmelite church at Clarendon Street, a visit to the bookies, where he bet on carefully selected horses, followed by a trip to Bewley's, where he met up with other fellowship members at the special AA table. For many years this table was served by a waitress named Joan, and Dublin AA members travelling abroad would send postcards and letters simply addressed 'C/o "Joan's Table"' or 'Sackville's Table, Bewley's Café' in the knowledge that such post would reach and be read by individuals or groups socializing in this popular AA haunt in central Dublin.[45]

In November 1967, AA celebrated the twenty-first birthday of the Country Shop group by holding a dinner at the Grand Hotel, Malahide. The following morning, at what was humorously referred to as the 'hangover meeting', several of the founding members of this group – including Conor Flynn and Richard Perceval – recalled the history of the first Dublin group in a series of audiotaped talks. Although Sackville still harboured fears lest Archbishop McQuaid launch a belated attack on the fellowship, the mood of this event was generally buoyant and light-hearted, with a feeling that AA was definitely here to stay. Eva Jennings, who had played an important role in introducing Conor to Dr Norman Moore in St Patrick's Hospital, was living at this time in London, but she had kept up contact with AA and was pleased to attend the celebration at Malahide. Writing to Sackville to confirm that she would attend, she wrote in highly flattering terms that probably reflected the general views of members on the importance of the role played by Sackville in getting the fellowship established here:

> I need hardly say that the Dublin AA to me means you – very personally you. It does not seem like 21 years since I met

Conor in the Abbotsford and Richard, and it is very thrilling
to look back and see the enormous good that came from
their first meeting. Then when you joined, you and Richard
made a wonderful combination. It is almost amusing to
think how in the early stages Richard was credited with your
brains and organising ability, and you were quite content to
remain hidden.[46]

SPREADING AA OUTSIDE THE PALE

Quite distinct from the abstract ideal of establishing AA as a
nationwide fellowship, was the mundane, onerous task of creating
a network of meetings outside the greater Dublin area for a target
client group whose main defining feature was that it was regularly
drunk. Richard Perceval contributed substantially to this task within the limits imposed by the necessity to earn a living, but again it
was Sackville, a retired man with a reasonable pension (and a
motorbike!), who bore the brunt of the work involved in spreading AA outside the Pale (a term used historically in Ireland to refer
to everywhere outside of the Dublin conurbation). In the early
years he did this as Secretary of the first Dublin group, and later
he continued to play an administrative part in AA's nationwide
expansion in his role as editor of *The Road Back*. The diffusion of
AA throughout provincial Ireland was, perhaps inevitably, a hap-
hazard and sometimes chaotic affair rather than a systematically
planned campaign; but Sackville, despite the more ordered nature
of his previous career, appears to have thrived on the challenge.
Requests to speak about and explain the fellowship were received
from all kinds of individuals and institutions right across the country, and groups were started in response to requests that came
directly from problem drinkers themselves, from their families or
from other interested parties – particularly clergymen. Whenever
possible, a Dublin-based AA member would travel to the place
whence this request had come, hold one or more meetings and
offer advice and support until a new local group could 'fly solo'.
Big Eugene, a long-serving member who joined AA in 1964,
described another variant of this process, which involved making
contact with potential members from rural Ireland who came to
be detoxified in St Patrick's or St John of God's hospitals in Dublin;
those interested in starting AA groups in their own localities

following discharge from hospital were encouraged to rent a meeting room, and were then supported by visiting speakers from Dublin until the new local group had gained momentum.[47]

Like a tradesman who advertises that 'no job is too small', Sackville seemed happy to respond to all requests for assistance, even when these requests came from individuals or places whose prospects of establishing a 'critical mass' for the fellowship seemed remote. Nowhere was this more evident, perhaps, than in relation to the Bundoran group, which at the time of its establishment in April 1948 was Ireland's second AA group. Although it is not absolutely clear from his correspondence, it seems likely that in April 1948 Sackville travelled by motorbike from Dublin to Bundoran, County Donegal (a round trip of more than 400 kilometres), in response to a request that he start an AA group there.[48] The scale of this operation was humorously commented upon several times in correspondence with American friends, as in a letter to Bobbie Burger in New York some weeks after the first Bundoran meeting: 'We had a visit from one half of the Bundoran group last week – he is doing fine.'[49] In 1948 communications between Dublin and Bundoran were considerably more difficult than they would be half a century later, and Sackville struggled to maintain contact with and monitor the progress of his Donegal protégés. In early August 1948, for instance, he reported to Joe D. in Chicago that 'James and Fergus of Bundoran were vetted last night and are still dry',[50] but by late September he was less sanguine: 'Bundoran seems to be defunct. I haven't been able to get an answer from them at all.'[51] Despite this breakdown in communications, Sackville was not prepared to abandon the Bundoran alcoholics and some weeks later he told Joe D.: 'I don't understand the reason for the Bundoran Iron Curtain. However, I have a man going their way in a week or so, and I will find out whether they are still alive or not.'[52] By the end of October the situation in Bundoran had been clarified:

> You will be pleased to hear that 50% of the Bundoran group is still dry. The other half wasn't dry enough to escape the police attention invariably centred on a car driven by a man under the influence. He seems to be taking this to heart, and stomach, and it seems to be a toss up at present whether he will revert to dryness or paint Bundoran a rich hue of red.[53]

Despite the fact that for the next four years the Bundoran group consisted of just two members, one at least of whom appeared to be drinking problematically at any given time, Sackville never abandoned hope or interest in these two colourful characters with whose stories he regaled his American friends. By 1952, however, he appeared resigned to the fact that the Bundoran members were neither likely to consolidate AA in their own town nor to inspire problem drinkers in neighbouring towns in the north-western region to start their own groups. In March 1952, Sackville made what seems to have been his final reference to the Bundoran situation:

> No news of the Bundoran duet, though I think one of them is alright. I haven't had any contact down that way lately, but there is a prospect of getting something started nearby in Sligo or thereabouts. Some curate wrote to me this week to say that he had a crowd of alkies [*sic*] in a place called Ballymote, some 20 miles from Sligo. But whether they themselves agree to the description or not, I can't say.[54]

It would be wrong, however, to suppose that the Bundoran experience was unique, and there appear to have been many other places in which the task of getting an AA group up and running proved difficult and frustrating. One such location, whose problems in getting the fellowship started were given considerable publicity, was Cork City. As the second largest city (the 'real capital', as it is often referred to by Corkonians) in what had by then become the Republic of Ireland, one would have thought that Cork would have had a sufficiently large pool of problem drinkers to make the process of starting AA reasonably straightforward, but such was not the case. As mentioned in Chapter 3, the fortunes of AA in the United States had been greatly boosted by an article written in the *Saturday Evening Post* in March 1941 by the well-known journalist Jack Alexander. In April 1950, Alexander published a second article on AA, this time including a discussion of the influence the fellowship was now seen to be exerting outside the United States. This global influence was illustrated by a detailed account of a trip to Cork made by Sackville in October 1949, where he attended an open fellowship meeting – one of Cork's early AA meetings. Sackville is introduced to readers as the 'honorable secretary' of the Dublin group: 'A Sandhurst graduate and a veteran of twenty-six years in the British Army, he is still remembered in some portions of the Middle East for his inspired work with the bottle.'[55] The article goes on to comment on how Sackville had already established a reputation for himself amongst AA members in the USA, with whom he corresponded ('His letters, which are notable for their eloquent understatement, are prized by fellow AAs in this country and are passed around at meetings') before describing the Cork meeting:

This was the honourable secretary's chronological report:

8p.m. The chairman and myself sat alone.

8:05 One lady arrived, a nonalcoholic.

8.15 One man arrived.

8.20 A County Cork member arrived to say he couldn't stay as his children had just developed measles.

8.25 The lone lady departed.

8.30 Two more men arrived.

8.40 One more man arrived, and I decided to make a start.

8.45 The first man arrived, stated that he had to go out and have a drink.

8.50 He came back.

8.55 Three more arrived.

9.10 Another lady, propped up by a companion, arrived, gazed glassily around, collected some literature and departed unsteadily.

9.30 The chairman and I had finished speaking.

9.45 We reluctantly said good night to the new members who seemed very interested.

In summing up, the secretary said: 'A night of horror at first, developing quite well. Think they have good prospects, once the thing is launched.'[56]

Sackville was reasonably pleased with the Jack Alexander article, asking Joe D. to send him on two extra copies of it while simultaneously assuring Joe that his ego had not been inflated by the flattering way in which his work for the fellowship had been portrayed: 'In the meantime, my hat size remains the same.'[57] The secretary's assessment of the prospects for the Cork group appears to have been excessively optimistic, however, and over the next two years the group struggled for survival, in the process evoking uncharacteristically sharp and judgemental comments from Sackville. Writing to Joe D., a year after the *Saturday Evening Post* article was published, Sackville commented: 'There are several members there, but they are all bone lazy, like most Cork people!'[58] A further year on, he wrote:

> Cork AA is still in the doldrums, and I don't see that we can do much for them at present. They are too bone idle to do anything themselves and short of going to reside there, arrange meetings for them AND bring them by main force to those meetings, nothing can be done.[59] [capitals in original]

Given the city's population and the fact that Sackville and Richard gave the fledgling group as much, and probably more, support than they had given to new groups in much smaller locations, it is still not clear why the Cork group should have taken so long to become established. Cork people are the subject of a number of good-humoured stereotypes within Ireland, but laziness is not one of these. A more plausible explanation for these difficulties, albeit one that still remains within the realms of stereotype, is that Cork, often described as the 'rebel county', has a tendency to resent anything it thinks is being imposed from Dublin. In any event, as the 1950s progressed AA in Cork City became firmly established, and Sackville developed a close friendship with one hard-working Cork member, Aiden MacSweeney, who later joined him as a council member on the Irish National Council on Alcoholism (see Chapter 5).

AA membership, insofar as existing statistics are to be trusted, grew rapidly throughout the 1960s: in 1956 total membership for Ireland was estimated to be 1,100, while by 1966 the estimate was 2,250.[60] Sackville continued throughout this decade to play an active role in the diffusion of the fellowship throughout the country, but, as befitted his status as an old-timer, he now could delegate some at least of the travelling to newer and younger members who were dispatched by him to speak at all kinds of events in all parts of the country. One entertaining example of Sackville's determination to miss no opportunity to publicize the fellowship, which was recalled by Big Eugene, concerned a request (apparently in the late 1960s) from a priest in Bunclody, County Wexford, to have an AA speaker perform at a local concert. Against his better judgement, Eugene agreed to speak at this event. However, when the AA turn was due, the priest decided that his target audience had failed to show and so he suspended events while he left the hall, closed two of the local pubs and marched their customers in to hear Eugene, who saw himself as being 'there like a clown'.[61] Whether Eugene's words had any impact on those so aggressively rounded up by the priest is not known, but as of this writing Bunclody has two AA meetings each week.

In 1958, AA began the practice of holding an All-Ireland convention, with the venue rotating annually between the four provinces of Munster, Leinster, Ulster and Connaught. This development reflected the extent to which, just over a decade after it first came to Ireland, the fellowship now viewed itself as an All-Ireland institution. Other institutional developments, which will be looked at in some detail later in this chapter, included the holding of a general service conference in 1968 and the opening of a general service office in Dublin in 1970.

PUBLICIZING IRISH AA

It will be recalled from Chapter 4 that, in addition to winning the approval of the Catholic Church, Sackville had identified publicity as being of central importance in securing the survival and wellbeing of AA in Ireland. Sackville himself again played a dominant role in this sphere, and despite having no formal training or previous experience in public relations, he proved to be remarkably adept as a publicist. Prior to Bill Wilson's visit to Ireland in 1950, for instance, Sackville met the Secretary of the Department of Posts and Telegraphs (the central government department which at this time effectively ran Radio Éireann) and persuaded him to broadcast an interview with Wilson during this visit. Shortly afterwards, he received a letter from the productions director of Radio Éireann, making arrangements for this broadcast and looking for biographical details on Wilson (referred to in this letter as 'Mr William G. Wilson, Founder of the Fellowship of Alcoholics Anonymous') for the programme's producer. Sackville forwarded this letter to New York, but, being acutely conscious of Wilson's sensitivity in relation to anonymity, began his letter: 'Dear Bill, Don't shoot.'[62] Wilson didn't shoot, responded with the necessary biographical information and the interview was broadcast on 1 July 1950.

Although he did occasional radio broadcasts, both in Ireland

and for the BBC, and even did some television work during the 1960s, Sackville's main efforts were directed towards the print media, building on the very positive relationship which Conor and Richard had established with the then popular *Evening Mail*. In March 1949, Sackville produced the first issue of *The Road Back*, a newsletter which he went on to edit – publishing six issues per year – until 1976. *The Road Back* was largely inspired by and reflective of the *AA Grapevine*, a newsletter first published in 1944 by AA in the United States of America and referring to itself as a 'meeting in print'.[63] *The Road Back*, which was primarily aimed at AA members in Ireland, contained a mixture of news items and reflections on various aspects of the Twelve-Step Programme, as well as humour and gossip; the newsletter was also disseminated, however, amongst AA groups in other countries, and in Ireland Sackville sent copies to the newspapers and to other publications (including, for instance, *The Furrow* and *The Pioneer*), for whom he thought it had relevance. As was his custom, Sackville confided in Joe D., reporting both his pleasure at the public relations successes garnered by his newsletter and his fatalistic sense that he would find it difficult to get other members to actively take on responsibility for this project:

> I asked one of our lazier members the other day what he thought of The Road Back. He had done nothing to help it on. He replied 'I am satisfied with it. I am quite satisfied with it'. What higher praise or encouragement could I wish for? I got a paragraph in the Irish Times as a result of its issue. The Times is our snob paper. I also received two copies of The Pioneer, the leading Catholic temperance society here. We are becoming respectable.[64]

The *Irish Times* piece with which Sackville was pleased was an item in 'An Irishman's Diary', written by the well-known journalist Patrick Campbell under the pseudonym 'Quidnunc':

> It is something of a novelty to get an unsigned letter from the secretary of an organisation in which every member wishes to remain anonymous. The honorary secretary of the Dublin Group of Alcoholics Anonymous has sent me the first issue of the group's news sheet 'The Road Back', plus interesting data on the organisation.

Alcoholics Anonymous is a fellowship of men and women started in America fifteen years ago by two men who thought they might help each other to do what they could not do alone ... 'It is not a temperance organisation. Whether a man drinks or not is his own business', writes the honorary secretary. 'We are there to help ourselves, and anyone who wants to join us, to keep off drink ourselves.'

The Dublin Group, the first to be started in Europe, started in November 1946, and has a present membership of 95 men and women. The organisation is non-sectarian, non-political and non-commercial. There is no charge and no subscription, and none of the officers is paid. The only qualification for membership is that the prospective member should admit that he is an alcoholic and should want to recover.[65]

This was indeed a notable public relations success for the Dublin AA group, and Sackville's satisfaction with it was understandable. The archives contain no indication, however, as to whether he was equally happy with a comic piece about AA and alcoholism published in the same paper just a week later, in Myles na gCopaleen's 'Cruiskeen Lawn' column. Myles na gCopaleen was one of many pseudonyms adopted by Brian O'Nolan, a significant literary figure in mid-twentieth-century Ireland whose own alcohol consumption was clearly problematic.[66] This particular Cruiskeen Lawn column was largely based on its author's deliberate and sustained confusion of Ireland's two AAs – Alcoholics Anonymous and the Automobile Association; the piece questioned whether 'we take drink too seriously in this land?' and culminated in the suggestion that, just as the French hold regional wine fairs, the Irish might consider 'a Stout Jamboree during Horse Show Week'. Perhaps some members of Alcoholics Anonymous were offended at what could be perceived as a trivialization of problems that to them were deadly serious. On the other hand, on the basis that all publicity is good publicity and that – however humorously and obliquely it did so – this Cruiskeen Lawn column showed that Alcoholics Anonymous was now being recognized nationally for what it was, the Myles piece may well have been welcomed by fellowship members who read it.

Sackville continued to edit *The Road Back* until 1976, when, at the age of 79, he handed over this responsibility to another member, and five years later the General Service Board of AA in Ireland became its editors. Reflecting on almost twenty-eight years in this role, Sackville pointed out that its circulation had gone from an initial 300 copies per issue to 1,110 and that, as he prepared to step down, it had readers across five continents.[67] Among those who wrote to congratulate Sackville on his work with the newsletter and to wish him well in his retirement, was Father Daniel Dargan, SJ, National Director of the Pioneer Total Abstinence Association, with whom Sackville had built up a close relationship:

> May I offer you my warmest congratulations on the very fine and valuable work you have done as editor of The Road Back during all these years. Through this influential magazine you have done untold good for the cause of sobriety. I have always looked forward to receiving each issue.[68]

By this time, in the late 1970s, AA's position in Irish society could perhaps be deemed unassailable, and its publicity needs were primarily to remind would-be clients that it existed and was available – rather than to sell its programme to a wider society which was ignorant of or antagonistic towards AA. *The Road Back* continues to be published six times per year, but in light of present-day electronic information systems and the more highly developed AA structures which now exist (and which will be discussed in the last section of this chapter), this newsletter may no longer serve the important integrative function which it initially did.

ORGANIZING AA

One of the central paradoxes in AA, a movement in which paradox abounds, is that it has always combined an aspiration to reach and help as many problem drinkers as possible with a determination to avoid hierarchical 'top-down' leadership and all of the conventional trappings of bureaucratic management. As introduced in Chapter 1 and spelt out in somewhat more detail in Chapter 3, AA has developed a system in which front-line groups are accorded priority and deference over what might be seen as superior 'line of command' structures within the movement. Nonetheless, and in common with AA in other countries, the fellowship in Ireland has, over the years, developed a set of organizational structures (see Appendix 3) which members have deemed necessary in order to bring a degree of coherence to what is, after all, a very substantial institution. It can be seen from Appendix 3 that, in line with Tradition Twelve ('AA, as such, ought never be organized; but we may create service boards or committees directly responsible to those they serve'), those structures which in a conventional organizational chart would appear at the top of the chart, are placed at the bottom of AA's organizational chart. What this signifies is that the General Service Office, the General Service Board and the General Service Conference, along with provincial intergroup committees and more locally based area committees, exist to serve the broad membership and *not* to instruct or regulate local groups – which retain almost complete autonomy over their own activities. In fact, it is possible for members to attend 'anchor groups' in their own areas indefinitely without ever being particularly aware of these other organizational elements of the fellowship.

These structures evolved gradually, beginning with the All-Ireland Convention in Dublin in 1958, which went on to become an annual event rotating between the four provinces of Connaught, Munster, Leinster and Ulster.[69] Ten years later, in 1968, the General Service Conference was held in Dublin and this led to the establishment of the General Service Office in Dublin in 1970. This office, which has moved location on a number of occasions, employs a Secretary to the General Service Board as well as other administrative staff who service the needs of the fellowship nationally. These developments do not appear to have changed the essential culture of AA in Ireland in any way, but it must be pointed out that they happened slowly and not without some misgivings on the part of some early members. If this present chapter on AA as an Irish institution were to be summarized, perhaps the main point which has emerged from it concerns the enormous commitment of Sackville in particular to the diffusion of the fellowship across the greater Dublin area and across the thirty-two counties of Ireland. What is also noteworthy, and what has been commented upon both in this and previous chapters, is that despite his officer training and lengthy army career, Sackville showed absolutely no interest in creating a 'line of command' or in introducing any element of hierarchical order to AA in Ireland. On the contrary, while he obviously had great organizational skills, he was happy to allow events to take their own course and to respond to requests for assistance or support regardless of the size of the potential new group or the degree of coherence displayed by those seeking his assistance.

From quite early on in his membership of the fellowship, Sackville started to express the opinion that AA in the United States was becoming preoccupied with the size of meetings, rather than with the basic quality of what went on inside meetings. And, particularly as he read about the holding of big AA conventions, he became convinced that such conventions were tending towards a type of militaristic triumphalism which he considered to be fundamentally at odds with the traditional AA emphasis on anonymity and personal humility. It appeared to Sackville that in seeking to develop beyond the primary group level – and especially in running national and international conventions – AA was starting to ape business or political organizations. As was often the case, he did not express these views directly to Bill Wilson or to any of his other friends at the Alcoholic Foundation in New York, but instead gave full vent to them in his correspondence with Joe D. in Chicago. One such letter, written in July 1950, is savagely critical of the practice of holding large AA conventions, which for Sackville were obviously reminiscent of 1930s Nazi rallies. This letter, which was headed 'Sackville. Day of the International Convention. Heil!', reads as follows:

> I foresee that in traditional style the next Convention will go all out to take the pants off this one. I imagine therefore that the President accompanied by Hearst, Winchill etc. will open the proceedings, escorted by a procession of Cardinals and Bishops all chanting the by then recognised AA school cries ('Ra, Ra, etc.'). This procession will move through streets lined by anonymous members each waving a badge denoting his name and address and period of sobriety. Those with 6 years or more will be in the front rank, the newcomers being put on the outskirts of the city. When the 50,000 have taken their seats in a huge 'auditorium' (how do you Americans manage to find such ugly words?), Bill will appear and the 195? convention will be on. Subjects for discussion will NOT include such tactless points as Humility, the movement being more important than the man, or

Gratitude to God. Dancing will take place to the AA Band and Choir. Fireworks will be set off and pigeons released to all parts of the world. Dinner at the nominal price of ten dollars a stomach will be given to those who have a fashionable Tuxedo ... And a few members will start to wonder what they joined.

Now I feel better. Don't take it too seriously. I am just amusing myself.[70] [capitals in original]

While there is nothing in the archives to indicate that Sackville's views on this subject were ever expressed as explicitly as this to Bill Wilson, it is clear that Wilson was aware that the driving force behind AA in Ireland was at least ambivalent about the tendency to build organizational structures beyond primary group level. For instance, as late as 1963 Wilson himself raised this issue in a letter to Sackville:

Nobody is happier than I that AA really needs very little attention in the way of organization – very little for the group, only a little more for the area. But our world operation does require a pretty definite setup – it has to handle such a mass of business and policy. Here the benign anarchy won't do – paradoxically we have to organize it in order to keep it simple.[71]

Most AA members in Ireland appear to have been happy with the gradual build-up of organizational structures at area, regional and national level, and with the practice of holding national and other conventions; although it is equally safe to assume that those who disagreed with these developments simply had nothing to do with them. It would appear that the only instance where the All-Ireland Convention became controversial was in 1968, when the organizers grossly overestimated the numbers expected to attend the convention being planned for Wexford Town and the dinner that was to take place in nearby Rosslare. Big Eugene recalled these events:

They got the idea down in Wexford that there was going to be a thousand at the dinner, we'll say. And everyone was going to go out to Rosslare for a night. So they hired a huge place – I don't know where it was now – and there was about 200 turned up at the dinner, and there was about 800

vacant places ... They hired a train to bring everyone out and
only three people, I think, travelled on the train. And we
were paying for that train and those dinners for the next few
years, and there was fierce resentment in the fellowship
because the fellowship couldn't be in Stubbs [Gazette]. They
got too big for their boots altogether.[72]

With the exception of this episode, AA in Ireland appears to have
handled the establishment of organizational structures and the
running of conventions smoothly. Even Sackville – having let off
steam to his Chicago confidant – seems to have become happier
with these developments, and Big Eugene, who worked closely
with him over many years, was unaware that he had ever
harboured misgivings of the kind discussed here.

CONCLUSION

By the end of the 1970s, as its founding fathers in this country
began to disappear, AA had become an established and largely
uncontroversial part of the social and cultural fabric of Irish life.
Notices advertising local AA meetings were to be seen in the
porches of churches, the waiting rooms of family doctors and the
foyers of community health centres. New professional services for
alcoholics based on the application of the Twelve Steps were being
set up by voluntary bodies, and the more traditional mental health
services all collaborated with AA in one way or another. Many of
the key ideas of the fellowship appeared to have become part of
the country's conventional wisdom, and a country song called
'One Day at a Time' was popular for several years. At the same
time, however, the WHO had effectively abandoned the disease
concept of alcoholism, reverting to an environmentally based,
public health perspective that emphasized the importance of population drinking habits and the perceived necessity to regulate such
habits through a series of alcohol control policies. And an increasing body of research on treatment outcomes was beginning to
question cherished beliefs about the importance and value
of hospital treatment for problem drinking. In short, the policy
climate, insofar as it related to alcohol problems and their societal
management, was considerably different at the end of the 1970s
from the policy climate of the 1950s and 1960s, when the disease

concept of alcoholism had gradually been gaining acceptance as a modern, scientific development which would finally bring to an end several centuries of benighted moralism on this topic.

Sackville died in Dublin in 1979, about two years after retirement from active participation in AA, and Richard Perceval died in retirement in County Mayo in 1982. Conor Flynn, the youngest of the founders, lived on until 1993, when he died in Philadelphia. These Founding Fathers are obviously remembered and commemorated in the archives of AA in Ireland, but it is probable that most current members know little or nothing of them – which, presumably, is the way these early Irish members would want it.

Chapter 7, the next and concluding chapter of this book, will summarize and offer a final comment on what this study of the history of AA in Ireland can teach us about the role of the fellowship in this country, a decade into the new millennium.

Chapter Seven

The Role of AA in a Nation of Drinkers

> He gave the little wealth he had,
> To build a house for fools and mad:
> And showed by one satiric touch,
> No nation wanted it so much.[1]

When Jonathan Swift, novelist, political satirist and Anglican dean of St Patrick's Cathedral, Dublin, died in the mid-eighteenth century, he left the bulk of his personal fortune for the establishment of the lunatic asylum that was to become St Patrick's Hospital, Dublin – an institution which some two hundred years later would play an important role in the establishment of AA in Ireland. Swift explained his motivation for this bequest in the much quoted sardonic verse which serves as an epigraph to this chapter.

Swift's jaundiced ideas about the mental health, or lack thereof, of the Irish appeared to be borne out by the enormous expansion that took place in public lunatic asylum accommodation, following the establishment of these institutions in the early nineteenth century; and, as late as the 1960s, data compiled for the Commission of Inquiry on Mental Illness indicated that the rate of Irish psychiatric bed occupancy was the highest in the world.[2] The commission was loath, however, to accept this data as objective evidence of a high prevalence of mental illness in Ireland, and subsequent epidemiological research conducted by the Medico-Social Research Board vindicated this scepticism, largely confirming that such high bed occupancy was an artifact – reflecting the legacy of an unusually generous provision of institutional beds in the nineteenth century and an ongoing public administrative culture that favoured institutional care. In an anthropological comment on the persistence, despite solid epidemiological evidence to the contrary, of the stereotypical idea that Ireland has an unusually high prevalence of mental illness, Kane (1986) explored the extent to which such views on the madness of the Irish have become part of the country's national identity. It was, she argued, as though the Irish had become so accustomed to thinking of themselves in this way that they were now almost affronted at the suggestion that they were *not* madder than everybody else.[3]

The other, but closely related, stereotype, which proposes that Irish drinking habits are more extreme and problematic than those of practically all other countries, is not quite as readily resolved, and until comparatively recently it could be argued that it too was largely unwarranted. As recently as 1996, for instance, data compiled for the Department of Health's National Alcohol Policy indicated that the Irish were relatively modest consumers of alcohol, being ranked eleventh in a comparison of per capita alcohol consumption across fifteen EU countries; it was noted, admittedly, that if the data were adjusted to reflect the proportion of children and total abstainers in the population, then Irish drinking habits might not appear so moderate.[4] Data such as these contained in the National Alcohol Policy flew in the face of the widely held stereotype that the Irish are heavy, problematic drinkers, a stereotype that had received a good deal of support from sociological research. Much of this early sociological research (from the 1940s and 1950s), which purported to shed light on Irish alcohol consumption, was, in fact, conducted by American researchers on Irish-American subjects, although it generally tended to seek explanations for what were considered to be unusually problematic drinking habits in this ethnic group by reference back to prevailing cultural factors in its country of origin.[5] It was argued, for instance, that ambivalence towards alcohol within Irish culture was a key variable in explaining a high prevalence of alcohol-related problems amongst the Irish: ambivalence referring to the coexistence of two fundamentally opposed ideologies or value systems towards alcohol – one strongly opposed to and the other highly supportive of drinking.

It was also argued that the repression of sexual behaviour amongst young men, in a culture where sexual activity was normative only within marriage and where marriage was linked to land inheritance, promoted heavy drinking amongst young Irish men.

A later sociological study by Stivers (originally published in 1976 and subsequently published in revised form in 2000) primarily focused on the stereotype of heavy drinking amongst Irish-Americans, tracing the emergence of this stereotype from 'bachelor drinking groups' of nineteenth-century Ireland where, it was argued, drinking was a badge of male identity, to the emigrant experience in America where drinking had become a badge of Irish identity. This intellectually stimulating and well-regarded study was essentially concerned with cultural meanings of alcohol consumption and did not support the generally held view that the Irish are heavy drinkers. In his preface to the revised edition in 2000, the Irish-American sociologist Andrew Greeley commented on how this study finally convinced him that all ideas about the Irish as heavy drinkers were baseless stereotypes:

> The Irish in Ireland are not heavy drinkers. Indeed, they have the lowest per capita alcohol consumption of any people in Europe. If they appear to be heavy drinkers the reason is that they spend so much time in pubs. However, if one keeps an eye on the 'pints' on the table, one notes that not many of them are emptied before the publican announces, with obvious reluctance, 'Time!' The Irish like their 'jar' and some of them consume too many jars, but most of them do not. As a people they empty less jars than do the French or the Italians or anyone else in Europe.[6]

Greeley might have been well advised to look at the most recent data available on Irish alcohol consumption before committing himself to such an unequivocal view on the modest drinking habits of the Irish. A somewhat more cautious perspective on Irish drinking habits had been adopted some years earlier by two Irish economists, Conniffe and McCoy (1993),[7] in a review conducted as part of the policy process leading to the 1996 National Alcohol Policy. While conceding that Ireland, at this time in the early 1990s, did not have a particularly high alcohol consumption rate, these economists had suggested that this situation was unlikely to remain static; Irish alcohol consumption, they pointed out, was highly 'income elastic' (meaning that consumption was especially sensitive to changes in consumers' disposable income), so that increased income could be expected to lead to increased alcohol consumption. By the time Greeley's remarks were published in the year 2000, the dramatic improvement in the Irish economy, colloquially referred to as the 'Celtic Tiger', had been several years in existence, and increases in disposable income – as predicted by Conniffe and McCoy – had already led to unprecedented rises in alcohol consumption. In 2002 another public health document, which reviewed alcohol consumption and associated problems, noted the dramatic changes that had taken place in Irish drinking habits and which were particularly striking at the level of EU comparisons:

> In the last decade, Ireland has seen many changes which have influenced the context and nature of drinking and increased alcohol related harm. Against the backdrop of the fastest growing economy in Europe, Ireland has had the highest increase in alcohol consumption among EU countries. Between 1989 and 1999, alcohol consumption per capita increased by 41%, while ten of the European Union member states showed a decrease and three other countries showed a modest increase during the same period.[8]

A detailed comparative study of Irish drinking habits during the year 2002 (Ramstedt and Hope, 2005)[9] with those of six other European countries (Finland, Sweden, Germany, France, Italy and the United Kingdom) confirmed that while Ireland still had the highest proportion of non-drinkers in its adult population, it also had the highest per capita alcohol consumption, as well as the highest rate of 'binge' drinking – a reference to the risky practice of consuming a lot of alcohol in any single drinking episode. Another study of alcohol consumption in Europe (Anderson and Baumberg, 2006) put Ireland in third place – behind the Czech Republic and Luxembourg – in terms of per capita consumption, but showed that Irish drinkers spent more of their incomes on alcohol than any other European country and were also the most frequent binge drinkers in Europe.[10] In addition to the detailed compilation of negative health consequences of alcohol consumption contained in several health policy documents (for instance, Mongan *et al.*, 2007),[11] researchers have also confirmed the public order and other social consequences of heavy drinking in the context of the urban 'night-life' scene.[12]

All through the Celtic Tiger years, Ireland appeared to celebrate its new-found affluence by drinking excessively. During this period alcohol policy was debated regularly and acrimoniously, with sharp differences emerging between proponents of a public health approach, who called for tougher alcohol controls, and the drinks industry, which considered public education and awareness raising to be sufficient to reduce the prevalence of alcohol-related problems. Senior public figures also contributed occasionally to this debate, as, for instance, when President Mary McAleese, in the course of a speech to an American conference on how affluence had transformed Ireland, commented specifically about money being spent unwisely 'on bad old habits ... the stupid wasteful abuse of alcohol'.[13] It is, of course, to be expected that alcohol consumption will fall in line with decreased disposable income as the economic recession continues to bite, and there are already indications that this is occurring.[14] However, such cyclic declines in consumption cannot be regarded as reflecting any profound change in what would appear to be the fundamentally unhealthy relationship Irish people have with alcohol.

It seems, in short, that while the stereotype of the 'mad Irish' is not supported by properly conducted mental health research, the stereotype of the 'drunken Irish' has considerable validity; when they can afford to – and perhaps even at times when they can't afford to – the Irish tend to drink heavily and problematically. It would certainly be going beyond the evidence to say that they are uniquely problematic in their drinking habits, but it is clear that like many other northern Europeans, the Irish have not evolved a culture in which moderate alcohol consumption is the norm. It is understandable, therefore, that those workers at the Alcoholic Foundation in New York who had observed large numbers of Irish-Americans joining the fellowship during the 1940s should have thought that AA might have something of value to contribute to Irish society. This final chapter of AA's Irish history will attempt to define just what it is that the fellowship has contributed and can continue to contribute to what it clearly a 'drinking society'.

AA AND THE DISEASE CONCEPT OF ALCOHOLISM IN IRELAND

In attempting to summarize AA's contribution to the amelioration of alcohol-related problems in Ireland, it may be useful to revisit the vexed question of the disease concept of alcoholism. Specifically, one may ask to what extent AA explicitly promoted this concept in Ireland, and, conversely, to what extent the effective abandonment of the concept at the level of public policy affected the fellowship – either positively or negatively – in this country?

Perhaps the best place to begin this discussion is by reference back to the 1930s and to AA's origins in post-Prohibition America, as previously discussed in Chapter 3. At this time the United States of America was a society that was understandably anxious to move away from long-standing and bitter divisions between 'wets' and 'drys': that is, between those who saw alcohol as a socially acceptable commodity, and those who saw it as so inherently and obviously problematic that it should be legally prohibited. The development and promotion of the disease concept from this time onwards, but particularly when it picked up pace following the end of the Second World War, had implications both for problem drinkers – those *habitual drunkards, chronic inebriates* and *dipsomaniacs* whose management had posed apparently intractable problems for developed countries for the previous century and a half – and for the broader public policy sphere. In relation to individual problem drinkers, the disease concept purported to base itself on definitive scientific evidence, which demonstrated that such drinkers had a specific disease that could, and should, be managed by the health care system. At the broader public policy level this concept was regarded as bringing scientific closure to the moral debate between wets and drys. With a logic akin to that used by present-day gun lobbyists ('guns don't kill people, people kill people'), proponents of the disease concept argued that the 'problem is in the man, not the bottle'. In other words, it was suggested that alcoholism was not caused by any of alcohol's inherent properties but was, instead, primarily caused by the biological vulnerabilities of a relatively small number of drinkers. In any society, according to this point of view, drinkers could be divided categorically into two populations: the majority which had no vulnerability or predisposition to alcoholism and which could therefore drink with virtual impunity, and the unfortunate minority that would succumb to the disease – sooner or later – once exposed to this substance.

The newly established World Health Organization (WHO) adopted the disease concept in the early 1950s and, largely through the work of E.M. Jellinek, promoted it at international level; member states were urged to develop treatment services for alcoholics but were also told that health authorities need not concern themselves with changes in population drinking habits, since societal prevalence rates for alcoholism would not be affected by increased alcohol consumption.

It is important to remember, however, that AA did not regard the disease concept as an officially binding teaching, and, furthermore, that it enshrined in its Traditions the decision not to formally align itself with any other organizations that lobbied for the acceptance of the disease concept at public policy level. While Bill Wilson and Bob Smith were undoubtedly tempted to get on the alcoholism bandwagon, which must, in the context of 1940s America, have seemed like a perfectly safe and virtually unstoppable vehicle, they decided relatively quickly that AA would be best served by remaining outside of all formal coalitions involved in alcohol politics. As discussed in Chapter 3, the view taken was that formal involvement with the idea of alcoholism as disease would inevitably draw AA into external controversy, create internal dissension and distract it from its primary and pragmatic function of providing mutual aid for those individuals who wished to stop drinking. Bill Wilson, in particular, was keenly aware of the risks incurred by the fellowship in becoming drawn into 'outside issues'; and following a sharp rebuke from the AA grass roots in relation to his own participation in Marty Mann's National Council on Alcoholism, he maintained very clear boundaries between the fellowship and all groups that campaigned politically for the disease concept.

By the late 1960s it was already becoming clear that the anticipated scientific progress which promised to make redundant all moral and political debate about alcohol and its role in society simply had not materialized, and that the disease concept was being widely discredited. For sociologists, to whom the notion of a definitive scientific resolution to complex social problems had always seemed illusory, it came as no real surprise that the disease concept had failed to deliver on its promise. Sociologists generally view the field of alcohol problems as a 'contested' arena; one in which interest groups with conflicting ideologies and value systems fight out their differences with little apparent prospect of ultimate scientific resolution of these differences.[15] For such sociologists the proposition that alcoholism is a disease (or more broadly, that addiction is a disease) is viewed as a *social construction*; that is, an idea which is best explained as having been made up by social actors interacting in a specific set of historic circumstances, rather than a discovery which emerged from objective, value-free science.[16] It was not so much that sociologists took sides in the debate as to whether or not alcoholism was a disease, as that – in a much more fundamental way – they thought that alcoholism did not exist; one American social scientist, Dan Beauchamp (writing in 1980) described alcoholism, in philosophical terms, as a *category mistake*:

> Category mistakes occur when we misclassify a set of phenomena, usually by granting them the status of entities or substances. In Gilbert Ryle's famous example, a visitor to Oxford who asks to see the 'university' after being shown the several colleges is guilty of a category mistake. The visitor mistakenly assumes the term 'university' stands for some separate entity.
>
> The same kind of confusion has arisen around what we commonly refer to as alcoholism or alcohol problems. The terms *alcoholism* and *alcohol problems* are essentially descriptive terms meaning harmful drinking or drinking 'at risk'. While the harm of drinking is the result of specific actions and events, the category mistake occurs when a commentator then moves beyond description by inferring that people drink this way because of the stuff they are made of.[17]

While social scientists such as Beauchamp did not deny the commonsense reality of alcohol-related problems, which impact in varying ways and to varying degrees on individuals and on society, what they were arguing was that no specific or discrete disease existed which invariably underpinned such problems. Their answer to the question 'But is it a disease?' is that there is no 'it'. This critical point of view which, initially at least, seemed heretical to those accustomed to the rhetoric of alcoholism as disease, gradually became widely accepted and orthodox. It is noteworthy, for instance, that *alcoholism* is no longer to be found as a specific disease category in either of the two commonly used diagnostic classification schemes used in psychiatry – the Diagnostic and Statistical Manual (DSM) of Mental Disorders of the American Psychiatric Association, or the International Classification of Diseases (ICD) devised by the WHO. Instead, these classification schemes describe a spectrum of alcohol-related problems, of which alcohol dependency is just one part.[18] And, as described in Chapter 5, the WHO's public health perspective on alcohol, developed in a series of research reports from the 1970s onwards, was one which dropped all reference to 'alcoholism' and argued that the prevalence of a range of social and health problems was causally linked to population drinking levels. Most of these developments occurred following Bill Wilson's death in 1971, but given the clarity and shrewdness of his organizational philosophy for AA, one can reasonably surmise that he would have looked with equanimity at the changing fortunes of the disease concept, which was, after all, an 'outside issue'. And on the specific question of alcoholism as *category mistake*, it seems that Wilson himself had explicitly adopted an almost identical position twenty years before Beauchamp wrote of alcoholism in this way. Replying to a question put to him about alcoholism as disease at the National Catholic Clergy Conference in 1960, Wilson explained:

> We have never called alcoholism a disease because, technically speaking, it is not a disease entity. For example, there is no such thing as heart disease. Instead there are many separate heart ailments, or combinations of them. It is something like that with alcoholism. Therefore we did not wish to get in wrong with the medical profession by pronouncing alcoholism a disease entity. Therefore we always called it an illness, or a malady – a far safer term for us to use.[19]

It would be quite misleading, however, to suggest that the public health model now favoured by the WHO is universally popular or that it has definitively displaced the disease concept either at governmental level or in the hearts and minds of citizens. On the contrary, the public health approach to alcohol policy is at best making a slow impact on national and international policy. Since it attributes primary causal responsibility for alcohol-related problems to alcohol per se and argues that the prevalence of such problems can only be reduced by reducing total societal consumption levels, this approach obviously poses a challenge to the profitability of what is increasingly a globalized drinks industry. Understandably, the drinks industry has mobilized against the public health approach, representing itself as a responsible corporate citizen and advocating prevention strategies which, since they are not reliant on reducing total alcohol consumption, will do less damage to its own profitability.[20] Similarly, since the public health model calls for the extensive use of control strategies – such as regulating the advertising and promotion of alcoholic beverages, raising prices, restricting access and availability at the retail level, and strict enforcement of licensing and drink-driving legislation – this model is difficult to sell to the citizens of democracies who see it as paternalistic or in the 'nanny state' mode.[21]

It is also the case that in the USA, where the disease concept of alcoholism still appears to command uncritical popular support, federal government research on alcohol (and on problems stemming from the use of illicit psychoactive drugs) has, since the late 1990s, renewed its commitment to what is now commonly described as a 'biomedical' focus. Research of this kind, which takes as its starting point that 'addiction is brain disease', relies primarily on scientific progress in the area of genetics and neuroscience, with immediate hopes being pinned on the development of drugs that can dramatically improve treatment of alcohol dependence by reducing cravings in dependent drinkers. This tendency towards biomedicalization is criticized by social scientists who see it as yet another misguided attempt to reduce complex social issues to individual 'disease' issues. Social scientists also point out that highly publicized scientific 'breakthroughs' in this sphere are rarely confirmed by subsequent research to be as significant as originally suggested, and they draw attention to the fact that despite decades of research no effective new medications have transformed alcoholism treatment.[22] In summary, there is still no scientific or policy consensus on how alcohol problems should be conceptualized and managed by society. The two dominant but wildly conflicting models of alcohol-related problems discussed here are the individualized biomedical model, which pins its hopes primarily on developments in the neurosciences, and the public health approach, which believes that progress in this sphere can only come about through environmental changes – involving alcohol control policies and reduced levels of consumption. While these two models each claim to be 'evidence-based' and scientific, the ideological gap between them and the intensity with which the issues are debated is reminiscent of the historical divide between wets and drys in pre-Prohibition USA.

Because of the clarity of its Traditions about not becoming involved in medical scientific controversies about the nature of alcoholism, AA as an international fellowship does not, in general, appear to have been negatively affected by ongoing debates and disputes about the existence or nature of alcoholism. Although most fellowship members routinely, if not invariably, refer to alcoholism as disease, such linguistic usages may be regarded as metaphoric rather than as literal claims to scientific truth, and it would be foolish to view them as evidence that the fellowship has aligned itself with biomedicine in opposition to the public health lobby. As Kurtz (2002) put it, 'the use of that vocabulary no more implies deep commitment to the tenet that alcoholism is a disease in some technical medical sense than speaking of sunrise or sunset implies disbelief in a Copernican solar system'.[23] But perhaps what is most important to bear in mind is that, as discussed in Chapter 3, AA is primarily about *alcoholics* and only very slightly – if at all – about *alcoholism*. Within the framework developed by the fellowship's founders and early members, alcoholics are a self-defining group of people who share a common, subjective experience of being powerless over alcohol and who are mutually supportive of one another's desires to stop drinking. Membership of AA is not based on psychiatric diagnosis or upon any other professionally conducted evaluations, and the fellowship is politely indifferent to such ostensibly scientific activities.

The history of AA in Ireland which has been presented in this book generally shows that the notion of alcoholism as disease was not central to its activities here; it confirms that the fellowship, in keeping with its Traditions, did not actively or explicitly promote the disease concept of alcoholism in this country, nor did it become embroiled in any of the ideological disputes that have periodically surrounded this concept. Chapter 5 has looked in detail at this issue, showing that Richard Perceval (the first Irish resident to become an AA member) moved away from the anonymity of his fellowship activity, when he assumed the director-ship of the Irish National Council on Alcoholism (INCA) in 1966, just as Marty Mann had done when establishing a similar organiza-tion in the USA. What this chapter also revealed, however, was that Sackville, who played a much longer and greater role in AA in Ireland, had come – very gradually, it must be said – to realize that describing alcoholism unequivocally as a disease, and work-ing in collaboration with others to promote the disease concept, was fraught with difficulties. Beginning with his mocking dis-missal of the low-key advice on this subject offered by the Alcoholic Foundation in New York in 1948 (when he ended the discussion by saying that he didn't really care whether 'the cor-rect term is bubonic plague or otherwise'), Sackville moved through a period of conviction that Ireland needed a national organization like Marty Mann's NCA, to an end-state in which he believed that AA members should preserve very clear boundaries between themselves and those who lobbied for the disease concept ('I don't believe it is our business to start educating the public about the disease of alcoholism').

Chapter 5 also detailed the decline of the disease concept in Irish health policy, most pointedly from its high point in 1966, when the Commission of Inquiry on Mental Illness had simply pronounced in its report that 'alcoholism is a disease', to its suc-cessor report *The Psychiatric Services: Planning for the Future* (1984) which – in the manner of Beauchamp discussing category mistakes – dismissed alcoholism as an illogical and redundant concept. It was explained in Chapter 5 that much of the ideolog-ical debate about the disease concept had taken place, as it were, behind closed doors within INCA, with private-sector and public-sector psychiatrists arguing respectively for and against the con-cept, and that the closure of INCA at the end of 1987 had marked a definitive turning point in relation to public lobbying for the idea of alcoholism as disease. While the public psychiatric sector struggled to reduce what it perceived to be an unwarranted burden of alcohol-related hospital admissions, the private sector continued to be more enthusiastic about such admissions and to periodically express support for the disease concept. For instance, Dr John Cooney of St Patrick's Hospital (whose 1963 admonition to fellow doctors to 'feel as well as believe that the alcoholic is ill

and suffering from a disease just as surely as a diabetic is suffering from his excess blood sugar' was used as an epigraph to
Chapter 5) was arguing, as late as 1991, that failure to regard
alcoholics in this way inevitably condemned them to old-fashioned moralistic rejection:

> I am convinced that were it not for the disease concept of
> alcoholism far fewer people would have come forward for
> help, and might not have been encouraged by their families
> and friends to do so. Here in Ireland this concept is being
> threatened at the present time. If we regress to the moralistic
> 'sin' model of long ago, then the victims of alcohol abuse
> will receive the second-class treatment deemed appropriate
> for victims of a bad habit, self-inflicted. This would mean
> that all the ground so laboriously gained over a number of
> years in bringing about the present level of public enlighten-
> ment would be in danger of being lost and alcoholics and
> their families forced to attempt to conceal the problem,
> rather than confront it and seek the assistance so readily
> available in the many treatment centres now functioning
> throughout the country.[24]

The proposition that health and social service responses must either
regard problem drinkers as sick people *or* as moral degenerates is
patently a false dichotomy. It ignores the practical difficulties of simply assigning alcoholics to the passivity of what sociologists refer to
as the 'sick role' – which implies both that they are victims of their
disease and that primary responsibility for their recovery rests with
their doctors. It also ignores the wide range of counselling and
psychotherapeutic options routinely used by mental health professionals in the management of a variety of personal and interpersonal
difficulties: these are treatment approaches that are not explicitly
based on disease models, but which obviously do not start from
the premise that their clients are sinful or immoral. What is most
important in relation to this history of AA, of course, is that the
fellowship also does not operate on this type of logic, neither seeing its members as sick or immoral but simply and pragmatically
suggesting that those alcoholics who wish to stop drinking might
try 'working' the Twelve Steps Programme. As described at various
points throughout this book, this programme is primarily based
on ideas of spirituality, seeing alcoholism as 'an illness which only

a spiritual experience will conquer',[25] rather than as an illness which is remediable by conventional medical or surgical means.

In answering the questions posed at the beginning of this section, it can be concluded, first of all, that AA in Ireland did not promote the disease concept intentionally or explicitly either at the level of popular culture or of public policy, and, secondly, that there is no indication that the effective dropping of this concept from official health policy has had any impact on the fellowship's functioning here. However, just as Kurtz argues in the American context that AA members who commonly use the language of alcoholism as disease 'did have a large role in spreading and popularizing that understanding',[26] so it seems reasonable to conclude that the existence of increased numbers of AA members in Ireland may have contributed to spreading the admittedly ambiguous idea that alcoholism is a disease.

Before concluding this section, which has emphasized that the fellowship did not intentionally promote the disease concept, it seems important to refer to some of the other things which AA in Ireland has *not* done. Although it exists in a drinking society, with a well-established tendency towards extreme patterns of consumption and a high prevalence of related problems, AA in Ireland has never – either on its own or in collaboration with others – sought to educate the Irish public on the risks involved in alcohol consumption. Neither has it alerted the public to the commonsense idea that if it insists on drinking vastly increased amounts of alcohol (as happened during the Celtic Tiger years), it will inevitably pay a serious price by way of a higher prevalence of health and social problems for such increased consumption. AA in Ireland has not contributed to policy debate on the licensing legislation, on the pricing of alcoholic beverages or on the question of alcohol advertising and promotion. It has never sent representatives to sit on governmental committees, and has expressed no views about the way in which the public mental health services have gradually reduced numbers of alcoholism inpatient admissions, while simultaneously shortening lengths of stay for those alcoholics who succeed in being admitted for inpatient care. It could, therefore, be argued that, however unintentionally, AA in Ireland contributed to the notion that alcohol consumption is and should be a normal and everyday practice for most citizens, because only those predisposed to alcoholism will suffer ill effects of such consumption.

It is highly unlikely that AA, in a corporate sense, would choose to respond to these last comments, which could be construed as being critical of the fellowship's contribution to Irish society. Should it do so, however, it would almost certainly point out that its *raison d'être* is simply to provide a source of care and support for individual alcoholics who look for help, and that it has no interest in policy issues. A more developed answer might include reference to the fact that participation in alcohol politics would invariably draw the fellowship into controversy and dispute, thereby threatening its internal unity and impairing its capacity to promote the welfare of alcoholics. Science may yet bring closure to these debates about alcohol and its contributory role in a host of health and social problems, but it certainly has not yet done so; and at the end of the first decade of the new millennium, the intensity of national and international controversies and debates on this topic are very similar to those of a century ago. The decision of Bill Wilson, Bob Smith and the first generation of American members that AA groups 'ought never endorse, finance, or lend the AA name to any related facility or outside enterprise, lest problems of money, property and prestige divert us from our primary purpose' (Tradition Six) would appear to be vindicated by the fellowship's survival and continuing rude health where previous temperance organizations went into decline or completely disappeared. In Ireland, even if one confines one's focus to the acrimonious alcohol politics of the Celtic Tiger era (1994–2008), the wisdom of this decision seems abundantly clear.

ALCOHOLICS ANONYMOUS: DOES IT WORK?

In further exploring the broad topic of what AA can contribute to Ireland, a country with a penchant for heavy alcohol consumption, several specific questions arise concerning the fellowship's effectiveness in helping alcoholics (however they may be defined) to deal with or overcome their problems. Is the fellowship more or less successful than alcoholism treatment methods used by professional addiction therapists? To the extent that it is successful, what is the key to AA's success? And finally, how does AA respond to scientific evaluations of alcoholism treatment outcomes?

Historical reviews of the various methods used to treat problem drinking, since this phenomenon was first conceptualized as ill-ness or disease during the nineteenth century, have revealed an extraordinary diversity of practices, ranging from the use of specialist inebriate asylums where inmates were confined without access to alcohol for variable time periods, to specific medical or psychological techniques which did not necessitate institutional care.[27] In many instances the treatments were presided over by people who could only be described as charlatans, but some treatments at least had the merit of being bizarrely entertaining – for instance, Edwards (2000) reports that 'a Dr Shilo in 1961 advocated a regime which necessitated the consumption of 231 lemons, to be taken by the patient over the course of precisely 29 days'.[28] What all of these, allegedly therapeutic, practices had in common was their abject failure, with such temporary success as was occasionally identified being subsequently attributable to the personality of the therapist rather than to any objective curative factor. Smith's conclusion to her study of inebriate asylums in early twentieth-century Ireland has been quoted several times already in this book, and is an apt comment on the global sense of frustration experienced by those involved in alcoholism treatment up to the last quarter of this century: 'Quite bluntly no one knew how to cure a drunk.'[29]

From the mid-1970s onwards the evaluation of alcoholism treatment became more methodologically sophisticated, and evaluators, clinicians and service managers moved – however grudgingly and falteringly – towards 'evidence-based' service delivery, an ideal which was now being globally promoted throughout all aspects of the health services.[30] The notion of evidence-based health care simply calls for the application of scientific rationality to practice, so that clinical decisions about the management of individual patients, as well as wider decision making about health service delivery, are based on the findings of well-conducted empirical research about what works – rather than on custom and practice, personal preference or the ulterior motives of any individuals or groupings involved in service provision. Alcoholism treatment, with its primary reliance on psychosocial interventions, is not readily amenable to all of the specific methodologies (for example, the so-called 'gold standard' of randomized controlled trials with double-blind assessment[31]), which would be seen as normative in testing the efficacy of new pharmaceutical products.

However, the broad logic of evaluation and the use of pooled findings from many studies can still contribute to a much enhanced understanding of what does and doesn't work in alcoholism treatment.

As indicated briefly in Chapter 5, once properly conducted research into the efficacy of alcoholism treatment began, the findings which flowed from this research were disappointingly, but consistently, unsupportive of conventional approaches to treatment and particularly critical of agencies or services which emphasized the value of lengthy and intensive rehabilitation programmes within hospital or other residential settings. For instance, an early and influential British study (Orford and Edwards, 1977), which compared patients treated intensively over several weeks in a hospital setting with similar patients who were simply given one session of advice on an outpatient basis, found no significant differences in outcome between these groups.[32]

An American study of the 'natural history of alcoholism' by Vaillant (1983),[33] a Harvard psychiatrist with interests in longitudinal research on mental health, was aimed at shedding light on the emergence and resolution of alcohol problems across the lifespan, with a particular interest in exploring the extent to which change or recovery could be attributed to natural healing processes as opposed to formal therapeutic interventions. This study confirmed *inter alia* the much greater tendency of Irish-Americans to develop major alcohol problems, particularly in comparison with research subjects who came from a Mediterranean ethnic background. Of particular relevance to this discussion of AA's effectiveness, however, were its author's disarming remarks on what he referred to as his 'doctor's dilemma'. The dilemma in question arose from Vaillant's attempts to reconcile his enthusiasm for and commitment to clinical work with his equally strong research bent. He evaluated his own treatment programme, which he was initially convinced was 'the most exciting alcohol program in the world',[34] with a view to determining the degree to which treatment led to healing or recovery over and above that which occurred naturally or spontaneously. He found no evidence that treatment in his programme added anything to the recovery process, which led him to ruminate very explicitly about what he perceived to be the real possibility that participation in this professionally run treatment system

might actually have hindered or detracted from the natural healing processes. Ultimately, Vaillant's conclusion, both on his own
programme and on alcoholism treatment generally, was as follows:

> Recently the *Annals of Internal Medicine* editorialized that
> 'the treatment of alcoholism has not improved in any impor-
> tant way in twenty-five years' (Gordis, 1976). Alas, I am
> forced to agree. Perhaps the best that can be said for our
> exciting treatment effort at Cambridge Hospital is that we
> were certainly not interfering with the normal recovery
> process. How can I, as a clinician, reconcile my enthusiasm
> for treatment with such melancholy research data?[35]

On the basis of his findings, Vaillant might well have advised
clinicians simply to confine their activities to the treatment of the
physical and psychological effects of heavy drinking or dependence, and to abandon any broader aspirations they had to help
people with these problems to stop drinking and stay stopped. He
baulked at this radical recommendation, however, but was clear in
his advice to professionals that they be vigilant lest any of their
interventions cut across or interfere with natural healing processes. Of most interest to this book, however, was his identification
of what he perceived to be the main components of recovery from
severe alcohol dependence, and his conclusion that AA membership provided the optimum vehicle for recovery of this type:

> Self-help groups, of which Alcoholics Anonymous is one
> model, offer the simplest way of providing the alcoholic
> with all four components referred to above. First, the con-
> tinuous hope, the gentle peer support, and the selected
> exposure to the most stable recoveries provide the alcoholic
> with a ritualized substitute dependency, and a substitute for
> his drinking companions. Second, like the best behavior
> therapy, AA meetings not only go on daily, especially on
> weekends and holidays, but also single-mindedly underscore
> the special ways that alcoholics delude themselves. Thus, in
> a ritual manner, AA allows the alcoholic, who might uncon-
> sciously be driven to relapse, to remain conscious of this
> danger. Third, belonging to a group of caring individuals
> who have found solutions to the typical problems that beset
> the newly sober alcoholics alleviates loneliness. Fourth, the

opportunity to identify with helpers who once were equally disabled and the opportunity to help others stay sober enhances self-worth.[36]

William Miller, a psychologist at the Center on Alcoholism, Substance Abuse and Addictions in the University of New Mexico, is another internationally recognized researcher who has contributed over the past thirty years to an enhanced scientific understanding of alcoholism treatment and its effectiveness. Running through Miller's work is not only a very clear line on what works and what doesn't, but also a constant, sharp reminder of the way in which treatment services – particularly in his native country – are not especially evidence-based. He has consistently shown that there is an inverse relationship between the demonstrable effectiveness of a particular treatment modality and its popularity; those treatments which are most popular, such as the so-called Minnesota Model, with its base in intensive residential programmes, are not demonstrably successful, while the treatment modalities which emerge positively from the evaluations are rarely to be found in real-world service systems.[37] In general, Miller has been critical of reliance on specialist inpatient alcoholism units, based implicitly on an acute care model (commonly lasting twenty-eight days, since this is the most that American health insurance companies will fund) and relegating ongoing work to the category of 'aftercare'. In a discussion paper (Miller, 2002) in which he questioned whether 'treatment' is a helpful concept to apply to attempts to help people with alcohol or drug dependence, Miller reiterated many of Vaillant's points, particularly those dealing with the need for ongoing and consistent support for people attempting to overcome addiction:

> Where in society does one find such ongoing relationships, where sustained caring and monitoring are feasible? Primary health care is one possibility, wherein a person may see the same physician or team repeatedly for years. People involved in a social service system may see the same social worker, probation officer, or home care nurse over an extended period of time. Pastoral care also provides such a broader relationship context. Pastors, priests and rabbis not only see their parishioners on a regular basis, but also have a role with broad social access, allowing them to make house

calls and initiate contact when concerned. Like religious congregations, the Twelve Step fellowships such as Alcoholics Anonymous can provide a lifelong and pervasive community of support. Unlike acute care specialist treatment, all of these offer the kind of ongoing contact and care that makes sense in addressing addictions.[38]

Unlike Vaillant, who argued strongly for the validity and importance of the disease concept of alcoholism, Miller's work saw this focus on alcoholism as largely irrelevant, and instead viewed the task of professionals as being not one of treating a disease as much as one of helping individual problem drinkers to initiate and sustain personal behaviour change. Miller's work is particularly emphatic about the central importance of personal *motivation* for change, explaining recovery from alcohol dependence as a process that begins when alcoholics convince themselves both that change is necessary and that they are capable of such change. Just as Vaillant recognized the possibility that formal treatment might impede natural recovery, Miller and others who have developed 'motivational interviewing' as a specific form of addiction therapy have highlighted the ways in which professionals can either facilitate recovery or alternatively – albeit unintentionally – reinforce unhelpful patterns of addictive behaviour. Motivational interviewing eschews all aggressive confrontation, whether it be deemed confrontation of the alcoholism or of the alcoholic, in favour of a much gentler style of professional practice which recognizes that no extraneous force can compel alcoholics to stop drinking if they have not committed themselves to this course of action.[39]

For decades it was considered that the effectiveness of AA could not be evaluated, both because of specific methodological difficulties in recruiting self-diagnosed research subjects and appropriate control groups from a loosely organized voluntary association that kept no membership lists, and because of more general perceptions of the difficulties involved in researching an institution which appeared to base its practices on nebulous spiritual beliefs. Since the early 1990s, however, there has been a huge increase in all kinds of research on AA, including research on its effectiveness in helping its members overcome their alcohol dependency.[40] Since such authoritative figures as Vaillant and

Miller had been so positive about the fellowship, it should perhaps come as no surprise that empirical research on its effectiveness generally suggests that 'it works' as well as anything else and better than many conventional treatments. A recent review (Kelly, Magill and Stout, 2009) of its effectiveness starts from the premise that, when it is compared with other professionally developed treatment modalities (such as cognitive-behavioural therapy and motivational interviewing as happened in Project MATCH, a big outcome study funded by the National Institute on Alcohol Abuse and Alcoholism in the USA), 'AA and related 12-step treatment are at least as effective as other intervention approaches.'[41] This review is primarily concerned with finding out how AA achieves its positive outcomes, and concludes:

> AA's effectiveness may not be due to its specific content or process. Rather, its chief strength may lie in its ability to provide free, long-term, easy access and exposure to recovery-related common therapeutic elements, the dose of which, can be adaptively self-regulated according to perceived need.[42]

One specific finding from Project MATCH (Longabaugh, Wirtz, Zweben and Stout, 1998), which would appear to be of considerable relevance to Ireland, was that alcohol-dependent clients with social networks supportive of drinking had better long-term outcomes when they attended AA, regardless of the treatment modality to which they had originally been exposed.[43] In this context the concept of a social network refers to those people who are important to alcoholics and with whom they have regular, ongoing contacts. What the research found was that for alcoholics whose social networks were supportive of regular, heavy drinking AA provided an alternative or buffer that enhanced the prospects of remaining sober. Given the data on Irish drinking discussed earlier in this chapter, perhaps it is not too extreme to argue that most social networks in Ireland are supportive of drinking, so that AA membership may be considered of special value to Irish alcoholics striving to remain sober.

To summarize, the cumulative findings of empirical research on the effectiveness of alcoholism treatment have, since the mid-1970s, succeeded in presenting an increasingly coherent picture of what does and what doesn't work. While there is no suggestion of a 'magic bullet' that has transformed alcoholism treatment, what this body of research tells us is that people who develop major alcohol dependencies can recover when they are personally motivated to do so and when they are linked on an ongoing basis into flexible, non-aggressive support systems. On the other hand, it is clear that acute models of care, which rely on the impact of short-term intensive programmes delivered by addiction specialists in residential settings, have much less positive outcomes.

It sounds somewhat patronizing towards AA to put it this way, but it may now be concluded that modern science confirms the essential soundness and success of its Twelve-Step Programme. One could, alternatively, patronize modern science by concluding that it has finally caught up with AA, since the research broadly confirms that professional alcoholism therapists succeed to the extent that they replicate the attitudes and techniques that have been at the heart of the AA programme since the fellowship's establishment in the 1930s. Accepting this latter perspective, one might fault AA for not being better at teaching the professionals and the wider society about how its programme works, so that the professionals did not take so long to catch up. However, to consider this a fault would be to misunderstand a fellowship that has made it abundantly clear that it has no ambition whatsoever to foist its own practices and beliefs either on health care professionals or on the general public. In a world of 'spin' and aggressive marketing, AA is unusual in that it has absolutely no interest in promoting itself or its programme; in the words of Tradition Eleven, 'Our public relations policy is based on attraction rather than promotion.' As in other matters, AA is indifferent to research and research evidence. The fellowship has no formal mechanisms for exploring the implications of research findings; and, while it may seem hidebound and arrogant, it is impossible to imagine AA modifying any of its traditional practices so as to become more 'evidence-based'.

It should be clear from the research discussed here that research findings have often been controversial and that – contrary to the popular assumption that clinical practice and service delivery will automatically change to reflect research findings – the alcoholism treatment arena has been characterized by intense emotional and ideological struggle. One specific controversy, not previously alluded to in this book, was that which concerned research on the possibility of designing and delivering treatment services which would enable 'alcoholics' to drink in a moderate or controlled way rather than to practise lifelong abstinence. Sobell and Sobell (1995), two American psychologists who were centrally involved in this debate, retrospectively commented that their research 'quickly became a notorious battlefield between scientific- and belief-based views of alcohol problems', and that 'Controlled drinking, in particular, threatened an entire culture based on the philosophy of Alcoholics Anonymous (AA).'[44] It would now appear as though the dust has settled on this once acrimonious subject, largely due to the increased acceptance of the public health idea that personal drinking problems vary in type and severity so that it is illogical to assume that there is only one valid treatment outcome. Sobell and Sobell accept, however, that research indicates 'Recoveries of individuals who have been severely dependent on alcohol predominantly involve abstinence.'[45] What needs to be restated from an AA perspective is that the fellowship neither became embroiled in any way with this research nor did it promulgate the view that total abstinence was the only valid solution to all forms of alcohol-related problems.

The fifth chapter of AA's Big Book, a chapter which has remained unchanged since its original publication in 1939, is headed 'How it Works', a title that might suggest the fellowship views itself from a technical perspective, perhaps in terms of the means–ends logic of evaluative research which underpins all of the research referred to in this section. However, even a cursory reading of 'How it Works' – which sets out the Twelve Steps and presents this programme as belonging essentially in the realms of spirituality – makes it abundantly clear that AA members do not see their programme as a means to an end. AA members do not see the Twelve Steps as a type of technology that assists them in recovering from alcoholism, comparable to the way in which antibiotics assist people with bacterial infections to overcome these infections. Instead, fellowship members see their programme of recovery as an end in itself: a lifelong spiritual process in which they stay sober, remain happy, help others and maintain and develop their 'conscious contact with God *as we understood him*' (Step Eleven). In line with this view of their programme as an indefinite process, AA members generally think of themselves as 'recovering' rather than 'recovered'. Furthermore, the AA programme is based solidly on mutuality, continuing the original shared experience of Bill Wilson and Bob Smith; while they maintain a conventional politeness towards the professional knowledge and skills of addiction therapists, AA members primarily value the experiential knowledge of fellow members and the unique quality of the help one alcoholic can give another. As explained at various points earlier in this book, one of the fundamental ways in which AA members help one another is through the device of storytelling within meetings. By means of such storytelling, members gradually and indirectly learn to construct a new self-identity, moving from the profound negativity of the original alcoholic identity towards the more positive identity of 'recovering' alcoholic, which allows them to make amends for previous wrongdoings, rebuild self-esteem and value their own capacities to help others. Once again, it could be argued (although AA itself would certainly not argue like this) that this type of 'narrative therapy', which is now widely used and popular in many areas of counselling and psychotherapy,[46] is an example of AA practice which was about fifty years ahead of its time.

Despite the fact that it has been increasingly well thought of by scientific researchers, it is still the case that AA's programme is not primarily reflective of western-style scientific logic. The fellowship has little or no interest in defining and understanding alcoholism, and absolutely no interest in defeating it – in the manner of American 'wars' on poverty, cancer or drugs. Instead, AA's basic logic – if one concedes that it has a basic logic – is more akin to that of Zen Buddhism. For instance, it starts with a paradox of seeking to regain a modest and temporary amount of personal power by admitting powerlessness (Step One: 'We admitted that we were powerless over alcohol – that our lives had become unmanageable'); suggests the importance of living in the present; and persists in its view that an individual trying to come to terms with alcohol dependence is more likely to be helped by another falling-down drunk than by an eminent psychiatrist or a devout priest. Long-standing members of AA are also quite likely to announce that they are pleased that they became alcoholic. A paper by two Canadian researchers, Glaser and Ogborne (1982),[47] with the title 'Does AA Really Work?', set out in some detail the specific questions which researchers would need to address and the methodological and research design features of any project which might hope to provide an answer to this question. The authors remained somewhat circumspect, however, as to the prospects of ever answering their title question, and referred on several occasions to the nonsense syllable *MU!*, used by Zen masters to express doubt or poke fun at the possibility of answering seemingly straightforward questions that conceal levels of complexity. Irish AA members when asked (as they have been on occasion by this writer) whether AA really works, tend to say 'Sure what would we know!'

In relating this material on AA – and how and why it works to the extent that it does – to the Irish scene, there are a number of points that should be made in conclusion. Ireland, as discussed earlier in this chapter, is a society in which drinking habits contribute to many personal, familial and communal difficulties. Despite the recurring promise of scientific breakthroughs in biomedicine, there has as yet been no dramatic shift in either scientific understanding of alcohol dependence or in the application of new treatment technologies. Research on the effectiveness of alcoholism treatment, however, basically confirms that alcoholics who wish to stop drinking and remain abstinent may indeed be helped to do so: not by aggressive, high-tech treatments delivered by specialists, but by ongoing, supportive relationships that can be provided by a range of conventional health, social service and pastoral workers. Most researchers are now agreed that, for alcoholics motivated to attend it, the AA programme – in modern parlance – ticks all the boxes in this regard. Despite the weight and clarity of the research findings, neither in Ireland nor elsewhere have health and social services succeeded in transforming services to reflect these findings, and services still appear to have an unjustified faith in acute-style and specialist-led service systems.[48] It seems obvious, therefore, that whether on its own or in collaboration with professionally run treatment programmes, AA has a major contribution to make in helping Irish people who develop serious alcohol problems. The programme is readily available everywhere in the country, offering flexible support at no cost to those who seek its help. And, for those who decide that they wish to stop drinking, the evidence strongly suggests that 'it works'.

In concluding this account of what present-day research findings tell us about the effectiveness of alcoholism treatment, it must be reiterated that such findings do not automatically inform the way in which treatment and rehabilitation services are delivered. On the contrary, it would appear that service delivery is influenced just as much by evangelical zeal and popular enthusiasm as it is by the findings of scientifically conducted outcome studies. It can be argued, furthermore, that alcoholism treatment in Ireland (as elsewhere) often consists of a recycling of previously used models, albeit in a slightly different guise, rather than the implementation of new evidence-based treatment models. For instance, O'Sullivan (2003) in reviewing an edited book on alcohol problems and the law, was struck by the similarity which he discerned between the Ennis inebriate asylum (which operated in the first decade of the twentieth century) and the Minnesota Model Programme run at Harristown House in Castlerea Prison exactly a century later. While the language differed somewhat, each of these institutions reflected an implicit but unwarranted belief in the salutory effects of structured residential programmes in which inmates were, temporarily at least, cut off from access to alcohol. As O'Sullivan put it:

> More interesting is the description of the daily routine of Harristown House (p.369) and the daily routine of the Ennis Inebriate Reformatory at the beginning of the twentieth century in the chapter by Cassidy (p.50). Aside from having to get up earlier in the Inebriate Reformatory, the belief in enforced regimentation and routine as a curative method appears to remain constant.[49]

It remains to be seen whether, or to what extent, professionally delivered services succeed in moving to more evidence-based styles but AA, because of its commitment to independence and neutrality on these 'outside issues', is largely impervious to debate and controversy on these matters.

ALCOHOLICS ANONYMOUS AND ITS CRITICS

At the beginning of this book the television cartoon *The Simpsons* – with its constant references to Homer Simpson's fondness for beer and occasional references to his attempts to seek help from AA – was cited as an example of how well known the fellowship is in popular culture. In bringing the book to a conclusion, it may be appropriate, therefore, to cite another cartoon series, *South Park*, this time as an example at the popular cultural level of the type of criticism which has been levelled at AA at various times and in various places since its establishment in the 1930s. While these two cartoon comedies have a certain amount in common, *South Park* is considerably more biting in its satire and much more likely to evoke protest from individuals, groups or institutions who believe that they have been gratuitously offended by a particular episode. One such episode of *South Park*, which was first screened in late 2005 and is now commonly referred to as the 'Bloody Mary' episode, has a plot revolving around attempts by Randy (father of Stan, one of the programme's main characters) to deal with his alcohol problem. Things come to a head when Randy is caught by the police while drink-driving a car full of children and, under duress from the court, attends AA; at his first AA meeting, he is told unequivocally that he has a disease which only God can cure, information that impels him fatalistically to even heavier drinking. Stan tells his father that AA is a cult, that he doesn't have a disease and that he should take responsibility for his drinking; but Randy remains convinced about his disease and ultimately sets out to look for healing from a statue of the Virgin Mary, which appears to be miraculously bleeding. The episode ends inconclusively, albeit in a style that is comprehensively and magnificently offensive to women, Roman Catholics and AA members, when Pope Benedict XVI visits South Park and declares – in words much too impolite to be repeated here – that the bleeding is not miraculous.

The *South Park* criticism of AA – that it is a cult which saps people's capacity to think rationally or deal responsibly with their own problems – is one which radically contradicts all of the ideas discussed in the previous sections of this chapter, and which sees the fellowship's contribution to all drinking societies in strongly negative terms. As has been made clear repeatedly throughout this book, the AA programme neither encourages irresponsibility nor passivity; members are enjoined to accept responsibility for their shortcomings and 'defects of character' and to 'work' the programme, rather than encouraged to sit around in the hope of a miracle cure. As previously mentioned, however, criticism of this kind has been voiced periodically, and perhaps understandably, all through the fellowship's history. An early sociological study

(Bales, 1944) sought to explain how AA exerted influence over its members, explored the role played by Bill Wilson and identified the measures being taken to ensure that the 'magic' associated with Wilson as the primary founder of AA could be retained within the fellowship's organizational culture following Wilson's death.[50] Bales' analysis of these issues is, however, highly nuanced and stops far short of the conclusion which emerged in subsequent decades that AA may be validly characterized as a cult. Forty years later, two Californian sociologists (Alexander and Rollins, 1984) conducted empirical research into the methods – as opposed to the ideology – of AA, concluding that 'AA uses all the methods of brain washing, which are also the methods used by cults ... The cult offers these alcoholics that which they need: understanding, absolute rules by which to live, and escape from loneliness and isolation.'[51] Over the past twenty-five years AA has been criticized by a range of researchers and journalists in the USA on the grounds that it is excessively and dogmatically religious, and that it prevents its members from exploring a wide number of more rational options in their quests for solutions to drinking problems. Bufe (1998)[52] has written what is probably the most detailed study of AA as 'cult or cure', in which he differentiates between what he terms 'communal AA' and 'institutional AA': the former referring to AA as originally conceived, a voluntary, independent fellowship; the latter to the wider Twelve-Step treatment industry – particularly as it exists in the USA. Bufe goes to considerable trouble working on empirical markers for a cult, and comparing AA with other organizations – such as the Church of Scientology, the Moonies and Syanon (a Californian-based drug-free therapeutic community) – which he considers to be cults. He is not convinced that the divide between communal AA and institutional AA is as clear cut as communal AA would claim it is, and sees many of the professionally run Twelve-Step Programmes as 'fronts' for communal AA. Nonetheless, his conclusion is that communal AA does not satisfy his criteria for cult status, and that it merely has cult-like tendencies.

Criticism of AA on the grounds that it is a cult generally implies that it is a social grouping to which its adherents belong with unusual intensity and perhaps to the exclusion of other personal, social and familial relationships. Criticism of this kind is perhaps best considered in light of the description of AA used consistently throughout this book, namely that it is a *fellowship*. What is implied in this phrase is that, through a process of identification with one another, AA members find themselves uniquely at home and understood at meetings or in less formal gatherings of others who shared the experience of losing control of their alcohol consumption. Bill Wilson's personal history (recounted in Chapter 3) is a good example of someone who felt displaced socially and psychologically and for whom alcohol initially appeared to provide all the answers; while his dramatic conversion experience set him on the road to recovery, it was Wilson's meeting with Dr Bob Smith that persuaded him of the importance of mutuality – he felt at home with Smith, realized that he could help this man with his drinking problem and, significantly, that in the process of helping him he was also helping himself. As the *fellowship* evolved, therefore, its primary defining feature was this mutuality, which helped troubled drinkers long accustomed to feeling displaced to sense that here was a social grouping in which they were understood and which provided them with a base from which to build recovery. It is clearly not the intention of AA, that members should withdraw from other social groupings – such as family, neighbourhood, religious or occupational groupings – since the Twelve Steps is aimed at rebuilding relationships with other people generally, rather than just with other alcoholics. Whether, on the basis that some members give priority over all other relationships to relationships within the fellowship, AA can be considered a cult is obviously a moot point.

In 1986 a Californian social worker, Jack Trimpey, founded Rational Recovery (RR) as a support system for people with alcohol dependence who disliked AA and wished to have some alternative to what was seen as its virtual monopoly of the American recovery scene. RR has a cognitive therapeutic orientation and drew initially on the theory of Rational Emotive Therapy,[53] closely related to Cognitive Behavioural Therapy (CBT), which is now a standard form of therapy for a wide range of substance misuse and mental health problems. RR obviously places a high value on rationality, while being dismissive of the value of religiosity in recovery from alcohol dependence, and is extremely critical of the disease concept of alcoholism. Given the fact that CBT is strongly supported by outcome studies, it is not surprising that research on RR (Galanter, Egelko and Edwards, 1993) has found that outcomes were good for clients of RR who continued to use this support system over time.[54] What is particularly striking about RR, however, is the explicitly ideological style in which it presents itself as a challenge and alternative to AA – most vividly expressed perhaps in the title of a book written by its founder, *The Small Book*.[55]

In the main, controversies of this kind about the status of AA appear to reflect what Stanton Peele has called the 'Diseasing of America',[56] which, in the context of a generalized therapeutic culture, refers to the emergence of an aggressively buoyant addiction treatment industry in the USA, involving vastly increased numbers of clients being coerced into homogenized, fee-paying treatment programmes. And the allegation is that AA, either on its own or in conspiracy with other 'recovery zealots', is committed to imposing its own dogmas and rigid practices on this gigantic process. By and large, AA does not respond to public criticisms of this kind but, as mentioned in Chapter 5, an academic paper by William Miller and Ernest Kurtz (1994) was specifically aimed at clarifying the fact that AA is not part of this wider 'diseasing' movement, that it does not see itself as having a monopoly on effective alcoholism treatment and that it does not approve of coercive treatment.[57]

There has been little or no suggestion in Ireland that AA is a cult or that it has fuelled irrational public anxieties about the entire country succumbing to the ravages of the disease of alcoholism. If uncritical deference towards the founder is regarded as a feature of cults, it is salutary to recall (as detailed in Chapter 6) that when Bill Wilson attempted to set up a unified AA foundation for Britain and Ireland, he was defeated in this venture by Sackville and other Irish members, who told him that they did not want this and that the Traditions gave them the right to make their own decisions. It was also noted in Chapter 6 that Bill Wilson took this rebuff with good grace, and that it neither altered his relationship to AA in Ireland nor his personal friendship with Sackville. In relation to Bufe's notion of 'institutional AA', it is worth recalling that, as detailed in Chapter 5, AA members in Ireland were scrupulous in maintaining the fellowship's autonomy, carefully avoiding co-optation into any wider 'alcoholism' movement. And specifically in relation to professionally run Twelve-Step treatment services being a 'front' for AA, it should be recalled that the fellowship in Ireland negotiated relationships in a relatively smooth and unproblematic way with a range of hospitals that detoxified and treated alcoholics, paradoxically only running into conflict with the Rutland Centre – the country's first residential Twelve-Step treatment programme.

AA in Ireland, as elsewhere presumably, is sometimes criticized in an anecdotal way for replacing one dependency with another: the argument being that families who previously suffered the loss of company of a member who was usually in the pub now continue to experience a similar loss when the recovering alcoholic is constantly attending AA meetings. Criticisms are also occasionally voiced about sexual misbehaviour between AA members, and the 'Thirteenth Step' is a euphemism commonly used (in Ireland and elsewhere) to refer to illicit sexual liaisons – particularly predatory sexual activity by older men in AA towards recently arrived young women. Behaviour of this kind, which is obviously damaging to these vulnerable young women, is clearly at odds with the Twelve Steps; men within the fellowship are regularly warned that they too are at risk of relapse (in AA parlance 'a slip') should they behave in this way. Within the predominantly male fellowship in Dublin, men were traditionally warned that 'beneath every skirt there's a slip'. Such politically incorrect language should not be taken as evidence that members trivialize behaviour of this kind, which deviates from the moral and spiritual standards that they have set for themselves. What appears to characterize the spirituality of AA, however, is the struggle – which members discuss within meetings and with their sponsors – to live up to these standards, while at the same time avoiding being overwhelmed by a strong sense of their own imperfection. The spirituality of AA has been described as a 'spirituality of imperfection'.[58] Recent revelations concerning the extent of physical and sexual abuse of children and young people by Catholic priests, brothers and nuns who worked in Irish childcare institutions have made it clear that failure to live up to high moral standards is not uniquely an issue for AA.

However politically incorrect the adage 'beneath every skirt there's a slip' may be, it does exemplify the central role played by humour in AA, a feature of the fellowship which its critics sometimes seem to miss. It is to be hoped that readers will have at least occasionally spotted in the earlier chapters of this history of AA in Ireland that, despite the fact that it deals constantly with personal misery, ill health, suicide and disrupted family and work lives, the fellowship is frequently a venue for fun, jokes and inter-personal teasing. Criticism of AA as cult may be particularly prone to portraying the fellowship as consisting of constant pious adherence to a set of beliefs by po-faced members, an image most members would not recognize as reality. Critics who take particular umbrage at the suggestion made to agnostic or atheistic members that they regard AA itself as their Higher Power, should perhaps be told that in Dublin AA it is sometimes recommended to such members that they might consider regarding the 46A bus as their Higher Power – 'it seems to be able to go past pubs a lot better than we can'. AA meetings, through their use of storytelling, allow members to construct a new and healthier sense of self or personal identity, and members routinely entertain one another with self-deprecating humour in meetings.[59]

ALCOHOLICS ANONYMOUS IN IRELAND: A CONCLUSION

Ireland is a drinking society, in the sense that alcohol consump-tion is and has been part of its culture since time immemorial but also in the sense that it accepts – apparently quite stoically – a high prevalence of alcohol-related problems. What this book has shown is how AA, a novel approach to the management of such problems, came to Ireland in 1946, took root in what was poten-tially an inhospitable social and cultural clime, and has survived the vicissitudes of Irish life ever since.

In practical terms, AA in Ireland had to negotiate working relationships with the Catholic Church and with the health care system, the two institutions which, however uneasily, had tradi-tionally 'owned' drinking problems in the country. In doing this, it was fortunate in that its early members, particularly Sackville O'Conor-Mallins, displayed considerable strategic abilities, tact-fully building alliances and avoiding conflict. Since the AA Twelve-Step Programme is primarily spiritual in terms of its con-tent, with members who have repeatedly failed to solve their own problems turning to a Higher Power to restore their sanity, early fears were that the Catholic Church might take umbrage. At the end of the first decade of the new millennium, when the Catholic Church in Ireland is in disarray over a variety of church-related, child abuse scandals, it is not easy to understand the influence it had in 1940s Ireland, or the personal power wielded by

Archbishop John Charles McQuaid of Dublin. These, however, were the realities with which early AA members had to deal, and it is greatly to their credit that they did so as effectively as they did. From the perspective of the health care system, what was original about AA was that it was entirely based on mutual help; in this instance, the potential challenge was to the medical profession, since AA – implicitly at least – took the view that an alcoholic *in extremis* was more likely to benefit from a conversation with another alcoholic than with a doctor. Again from our vantage point ten years into the new millennium, when mutual-help or self-help groups are commonplace in the health care system, it may not be immediately obvious why doctors might regard AA members as upstarts. This, however, was the situation facing original fellowship members and one which – following initial rejections in Grangegorman and St John of God's Hospital – they handled tactfully and successfully. In managing these institutional connections, the fellowship in Ireland benefited obviously from guidance provided by the then Alcoholic Foundation in New York, but most importantly it benefited from the Twelve Traditions, which provided it with a highly original administrative template. These Traditions have ensured that AA has preserved its unique status as a democratic, bottom-up fellowship, which has just one primary purpose – that of helping individuals who wish to stop drinking – and which has no opinion on alcohol policy or any other 'outside issue'.

Perhaps the discovery of the alcoholic gene is just around the corner, and with it new forms of biomedical technology that will provide an effective and definitive clinical answer to the problem of alcoholism. This is, however, an unlikely eventuality. But should it happen, there is no reason to believe that AA would regard this development as making its programme redundant; instead, it would almost certainly regard it as an 'outside issue' on which it would hold no opinion, while it would continue offering its Twelve Step Programme to those who sought its assistance. One way or another, the fellowship in Ireland seems set to perpetuate the work which began in November 1946 when Richard Perceval was allowed out of St Patrick's Hospital to meet with Conor Flynn, and which continued with such style when Sackville O'Conor-Mallins stumbled drunkenly into the Country Shop in April 1947.

Appendix One

Chronology of Main Events in the History of AA in Ireland

1935   Alcoholics Anonymous founded in Akron, Ohio

1946   Conor Flynn, home on holiday from Philadelphia, is introduced to Richard Perceval, a patient in St Patrick's Hospital, leading to the holding of Ireland's (and Europe's) first AA meeting

1947   Conor returned to America in January of this year, but in April Sackville O'Conor-Mallins attended his first AA meeting at the Country Shop, stayed sober and quickly took over as secretary of the Country Shop group

1948   Second Irish AA group started in Bundoran, County Donegal

1949   Sackville edited the first issue of *The Road Back*, an AA magazine which he continued to edit until 1978

1950   Bill Wilson and his wife Lois visited Ireland

1958   The first All-Ireland AA Convention is held in Dublin

1967   21st birthday celebrations of AA in Ireland, at which the founders' reminiscences are recorded

1968   A General Service Conference of AA held its first meeting

1970   AA in Ireland opened its first General Service Office at Essex Quay, Dublin

1978   Establishment of General Service Board for AA in Ireland

1979   Death of Sackville O'Conor-Mallins

1982   Death of Richard Perceval

1987   General Service Office moved to South Circular Road, Dublin

2008   General Service Office moved to Santry in North Dublin

Appendix Two

The Twelve Steps and Twelve Traditions

THE TWELVE STEPS OF ALCOHOLICS ANONYMOUS

1 – We admitted we were powerless over alcohol – that our lives had become unmanageable. 2 – Came to believe that a Power greater than ourselves could restore us to sanity. 3 – Made a decision to turn our will and our lives over to the care of God *as we understood Him*. 4 – Made a searching and fearless moral inventory of ourselves. 5 – Admitted to God, to ourselves, and to another human being the exact nature of our wrongs. 6 – Were entirely ready to have God remove all these defects of character. 7 – Humbly asked Him to remove our shortcomings. 8 – Made a list of all persons we had harmed, and became willing to make amends to them all. 9 – Made direct amends to such people wherever possible, except when to do so would injure them or others. 10 – Continued to take personal inventory and when we were wrong promptly admitted it. 11 – Sought through prayer and meditation to improve our conscious contact with God *as we understood Him*, praying only for the power to carry that out. 12 – Having had a spiritual awakening as a result of these steps, we tried to carry this message to alcoholics, and to practise these principles in all our affairs.

THE TWELVE TRADITIONS OF ALCOHOLICS ANONYMOUS

1 – Our common welfare should come first; personal recovery depends upon AA unity. 2 – For our group purpose there is but

one ultimate authority – a loving God as He may express Himself in our group conscience. Our leaders are but trusted servants; they do not govern. 3 – The only requirement for AA membership is a desire to stop drinking. 4 – Each group should be autonomous except in matters affecting other groups or AA as a whole. 5 – Each group has but one primary purpose – to carry its message to the alcoholic who still suffers. 6 – An AA group ought never endorse, finance or lend the AA name to any related facility or outside enterprise, lest problems of money, property and prestige divert us from our primary purpose. 7 – Every AA group ought to be fully self-supporting, declining outside contributions. 8 – Alcoholics Anonymous should remain forever non-professional, but our service centres may employ special workers. 9 – AA, as such ought never be organized; but we may create service boards or committees directly responsible to those they serve. 10 – Alcoholics Anonymous has no opinion on outside issues; hence the AA name ought never be drawn into public controversy. 11 – Our public relations policy is based on attraction rather than promotion; we need always maintain personal anonymity at the level of press, radio and films. 12 – Anonymity is the spiritual foundation of all our traditions, ever reminding us to place principles before personalities.

Appendix Three

Structure of the Fellowship

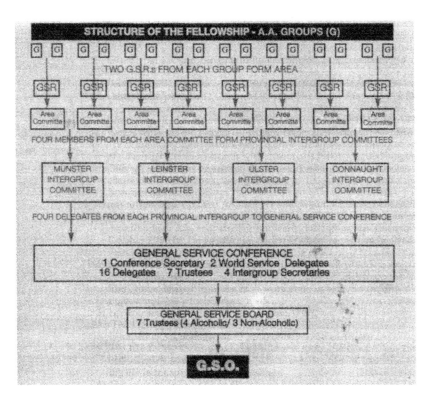

STRUCTURE OF THE FELLOWSHIP - A.A. GROUPS (G)

TWO G.S.R.s FROM EACH GROUP FORM AREA

FOUR MEMBERS FROM EACH AREA COMMITTEE FORM PROVINCIAL INTERGROUP COMMITTEES

MUNSTER INTERGROUP COMMITTEE

LEINSTER INTERGROUP COMMITTEE

ULSTER INTERGROUP COMMITTEE

CONNAUGHT INTERGROUP COMMITTEE

FOUR DELEGATES FROM EACH PROVINCIAL INTERGROUP TO GENERAL SERVICE CONFERENCE

GENERAL SERVICE CONFERENCE
1 Conference Secretary 2 World Service Delegates
16 Delegates   7 Trustees   4 Intergroup Secretaries

GENERAL SERVICE BOARD
7 Trustees (4 Alcoholic/ 3 Non-Alcoholic)

G.S.O.

Bibliography

A Dublin Member of Alcoholics Anonymous (1972), 'The Vatican and Alcoholics Anonymous', *The Furrow* (March), 181–3.

'A Member' (1953), 'Alcoholics Anonymous', *The Furrow* (November), 139–46.

Alcoholics Anonymous (1955) (2nd edn, 1973), *Alcoholics Anonymous: The Story of How Many Thousands of Men and Women have Recovered from Alcoholism* (The Big Book) (New York: AA World Services).

Alcoholics Anonymous (1957), *Alcoholics Anonymous Comes of Age: A Brief History of AA* (New York: AA World Services).

Alcoholics Anonymous (1960), *Twelve Steps and Twelve Traditions* (New York: AA World Services).

Alcoholics Anonymous (1984), *'Pass It On': The Story of Bill Wilson and how the AA Message Reached the World* (New York: AA World Services).

Alcoholics Anonymous (1986), *Alcoholics Anonymous in Ireland – 1946–1986: A Souvenir Booklet to Commemorate Forty Years of AA in Ireland* (Dublin: AA General Service Office).

Alcoholics Anonymous (1988), *The Language of the Heart: Bill W.'s Grapevine Writings* (New York: AA Grapevine Inc.).

Alcoholics Anonymous (1996), *Fifty Years a Growing: A Souvenir Booklet to Celebrate Fifty Years of AA in Ireland* (Dublin: AA General Service Office).

Alexander, F. and Rollins, M. (1984), 'Alcoholics Anonymous: The Unseen Cult', *California Sociologist*, vol. 7, 33–48.

Anderson, D.J. (1981), *Perspectives on Treatment: The Minnesota Experience* (Center City, Minnesota: Hazelden).

Anderson, P. and Baumberg, B. (2006), *Alcohol in Europe* (London: Institute of Alcohol Studies).

A Vision for Change: Report of the Expert Group on Mental Health Policy (2006) (Dublin: Stationery Office).

Babor, T., Caetano, R., Casswell, S. *et al.* (2003), *Alcohol – No Ordinary Commodity: Research and Public Policy* (Oxford: Oxford University Press).

Bales, R. (1944), 'The Therapeutic Role of Alcoholics Anonymous as Seen by a Sociologist', *Quarterly Journal of Studies on Alcohol,* vol. 5, 267–78.

Barrington, R. (1987), *Health, Medicine and Politics in Ireland 1900–1970* (Dublin: Institute of Public Administration).

Beauchamp, D. (1980), *Beyond Alcoholism: Alcohol and Public Health Policy* (Philadelphia: Temple University Press).

Bretherton, G. (1987), 'Irish Inebriate Reformatories, 1889–1920: A Small Experiment in Coercion', *Contemporary Drug Problems,* vol. 13, 473–502.

Brown, G. (1973), 'The Mental hospital as an Institution', *Social Science and Medicine,* vol. 7, 407–24.

Browne, I. (2008), *Music and Madness* (Cork: Atrium Press).

Bruun, K., Edwards, G., Lumio, M. *et al.* (1975), *Alcohol Control Policies in Public Health Perspective* (Helsinki: Finnish Foundation for Alcohol Studies/World Health Organization).

Bufe, C. (1998), *Alcoholics Anonymous: Cult or Cure?* (2nd edn) (Tucson, Arizona: See Sharp Press).

Butler, S. (1983), 'The Politics of Alcoholism', *Irish Social Worker,* vol. 2, no. 1, 12–15.

Butler, S. (2002), *Alcohol, Drugs and Health Promotion in Modern Ireland* (Dublin: Institute of Public Administration).

Butler, S. (2009), 'Obstacles to the Implementation of an Integrated National Alcohol Policy in Ireland: Nannies, Neo-Liberals and Joined-Up Government', *Journal of Social Policy,* vol. 38, 343–59.

Carty, F.X. (2007), *Hold Firm: John Charles McQuaid and the Second Vatican Council* (Dublin: Columba Press).

Cheever, S. (1999), 'The Healer: Bill W.', *Time Magazine* (14 June), 115–17.

Cheever, S. (2004), *My Name is Bill: Bill Wilson and the Creation of Alcoholics Anonymous* (New York: Simon & Schuster).

Cochrane, A. (1972), *Effectiveness and Efficiency: Random*

Reflections on Health Services (London: Provincial Hospitals Trust).

Conniffe, D. and McCoy, D. (1993), *Alcohol Use in Ireland: Some Economic and Social Implications* (Dublin: Economic and Social Research Institute).

Cooney, J. (1999), *John Charles McQuaid: Ruler of Catholic Ireland* (Dublin: O'Brien Press).

Cooney, J. G. (1963), 'Alcoholism and Addiction in General Practice', *Irish Medical Journal*, vol. 53, 53–5.

Cooney, J.G. (1991), *Under the Weather: Alcohol Abuse and Alcoholism – How to Cope* (Dublin: Gill & Macmillan).

Cronin, A. (1976), *Dead as Doornails: A Chronicle of Life* (Dublin: Richview Press).

Cullen, B. (2008), *A Study of the Management and Treatment of Alcohol Problems in a Regional Health Board in Ireland* (unpublished PhD thesis, Trinity College Dublin).

Davidson, R. (2002), 'The Oxford Group and Alcoholics Anonymous', *Journal of Substance Use*, vol. 7, 3–5.

Directory of Alcohol, Drugs and Related Services in the Republic of Ireland 2000 (Dublin: Health Promotion Unit, Department of Health and Children).

Dunn, J. (1986), *No Tigers in Africa: Recollections and Reflections on 25 Years of Radharc* (Dublin: Columba Press).

Dunn, J. (1994), *No Lions in the Hierarchy: An Anthology of Sorts* (Dublin: Columba Press).

Dunne, E. (2006), *The Views of Adult Users of the Public Sector Mental Health Services* (Dublin: Mental Health Commission).

Edwards, G. (2000), *Alcohol: The Ambiguous Molecule* (Harmondsworth: Penguin).

Edwards, G. (2008), 'Visiting America: Notes from an Alcohol-Focused Study Tour made in 1961', *Addiction*, vol. 103, 1939–47.

Edwards, G., Marshall, E. and Cook, C. (2003), *The Treatment of Drinking Problems: A Guide for the Helping Professions* (4th edn) (Cambridge: Cambridge University Press).

Ellis, A. and Powers, M. (1975), *A New Guide to Rational Living* (Hollywood, California: Wilshire Book Company).

Epstein, E. (2001), 'Classification of Alcohol-Related Problems and Dependence' in Heather, N., Peters, T. and Stockwell, T. (eds), *International Handbook of Alcohol Dependence and*

Problems (Chichester: John Wiley & Sons), 47–70.

Ferriter, D. (1999), *A Nation of Extremes: The Pioneers in Twentieth-Century Ireland* (Dublin: Irish Academic Press).

Finnane, M. (1981), *Insanity and the Insane in Post-Famine Ireland* (London: Croom Helm).

Fitzgerald, R. (1995), *The Soul of Sponsorship: The Friendship of Fr Ed Dowling, S.J., and Bill Wilson in Letters* (Center City, Minnesota: Hazelden).

Foucault, M. (1977), *Discipline and Punish: The Birth of the Prison* (London: Allen Lane).

Galanter, M., Egelko, S. and Edwards, H. (1993), 'Rational Recovery: Alternative to AA for Addiction', *American Journal of Drug and Alcohol Abuse*, vol. 19, 499–510.

Gallagher, R. and Cannon, S. (eds) (1998), *Sean O'Riordan – A Theologian of Development: Selected Essays* (Dublin: Columba Press).

Glaser, F. and Ogborne, A. (1982), 'Does A.A. Really Work?', *British Journal of Addiction*, vol. 77, 123–9.

Grant, M. and O'Connor, J. (eds) (2005), *Corporate Social Responsibility and Alcohol: The Need and Potential for Partnership* (New York: Routledge).

Greeley, A. (2000), Foreword to Stivers, R., *Hair of the Dog: Irish Drinking and its American Stereotype* (rev. edn) (New York: Continuum).

Gusfield, J. (1963), *Symbolic Crusade: Status Politics and the American Temperance Movement* (Urbana: University of Illinois Press).

Gusfield, J. (1996), *Contested Meanings: The Construction of Alcohol Problems* (Madison: University of Wisconsin Press).

Hartigan, F. (2001), *Bill W.: A Biography of Alcoholics Anonymous Cofounder Bill Wilson* (New York: St Martin's Press).

Healy, D. (1992), 'Interview: In Conversation with Desmond McGrath', *Psychiatric Bulletin*, vol. 16, 129 –37.

Hope, A. (2007), *Alcohol Consumption in Ireland 1986–2006* (Dublin: Health Service Executive – Alcohol Implementation Group).

I.G.S. (1957), 'The American Church and A.A.', *The Furrow* (February), 79–86.

Inglis, T. (1998), *Moral Monopoly: The Rise and Fall of the*

Catholic Church in Modern Ireland (2nd edn) (Dublin: University College Dublin Press).

Intoxicating Liquor Commission Report (1925) (Dublin: Stationery Office).

Jellinek, E. (1960), *The Disease Concept of Alcoholism* (New Haven: Hillhouse Press).

Jensen, G. (2000), *Storytelling in Alcoholics Anonymous: A Rhetorical Analysis* (Carbondale: Southern Illinois Press).

Johnstone, G. (1996), 'From Vice to Disease? The Concepts of Dipsomania and Inebriety, 1860–1908', *Social and Legal Studies*, vol. 5, 37–56.

Jordan, A. (2000), 'Alcoholics Anonymous in Ireland' (unpublished M.Litt. thesis, Trinity College Dublin).

Jordan, A.J. (2008), *The Good Samaritans: Memoir of a Biographer* (Dublin: Westport Books).

Journal of the Medical Association of Éire (1945), 'Mental Treatment Bill, 1944' (editorial), vol. 16, 8.

Joyce, J. (2008), *Ulysses* (the 1922 text) (Oxford: Oxford University Press).

Kane, E. (1986), 'Stereotype and Irish Identity: Mental Illness as a Cultural Frame', *Studies* (winter), 539–51.

Kelly, J., Magill, M. and Stout, R. (2009), 'How do People Recover from Alcohol Dependence? A systematic review of the research on mechanisms of behaviour change in Alcoholics Anonymous', *Addiction Research and Theory*, vol. 17, 236–59.

Kerrigan, C. (1992), *Father Mathew and the Irish Temperance Movement 1838–1849* (Cork: Cork University Press).

Kilcommins, S. and O'Donnell, I. (2003), *Alcohol, Society and the Law* (Chichester: Barry Rose Law Publishers).

Kurtz, E. (1991), *Not-God: A History of Alcoholics Anonymous* (Center City, Minnesota: Hazelden).

Kurtz, E. (2002), 'Alcoholics Anonymous and the Disease Concept of Alcoholism', *Alcoholism Treatment Quarterly*, vol. 20, 5–40.

Kurtz, E. and Ketcham, K. (2002), *The Spirituality of Imperfection: Storytelling and the Search for Meaning* (New York: Bantam Books).

Lean, G. (1985), *Frank Buchman: A Life* (London: Constable).

Leane, M. and Powell, F. (1994), *Courage to Change: An Evaluation of an Irish Addiction Programme* (Cork: Social Policy Research Unit, University College Cork).

Leshner, A. (1997), 'Addiction is a Brain Disease and it Matters', *Science*, vol. 278, 45–57.

Levine, H.G. (1978), 'The Discovery of Addiction: Changing Conceptions of Drunkenness in America', *Journal of Studies on Alcohol*, vol. 40, 143–74.

Levine, H.G. (1992), 'Temperance Cultures: Concern about Alcohol Problems in Nordic and English-Speaking Cultures' in Lader, M., Edwards, G. and Drummond, D. (eds), *The Nature of Alcohol and Drug Related Problems* (Oxford: Oxford University Press), 15–36.

Longabaugh, R., Wirtz, P., Zweben, A. and Stout, R. (1998), 'Network Support for Drinking, Alcoholics Anonymous and Long-Term Matching Effects', *Addiction*, vol. 93, 1313–33.

Lynch, D. (2005), *The Rooms* (Dublin: Hot Press Books).

Makela, K., Arminen, I., Bloomfield, K. *et al.* (1996), *Alcoholics Anonymous as a Mutual-Help Movement: A Study in Eight Societies* (Madison: University of Wisconsin Press).

Malcolm, E. (1986), *'Ireland Sober, Ireland Free': Drink and Temperance in Nineteenth-Century Ireland* (Dublin: Gill & Macmillan).

Malcolm, E. (1989), *Swift's Hospital: A History of St Patrick's Hospital, Dublin, 1746–1989* (Dublin: Gill & Macmillan).

Mann, M. (1979), *Primer on Alcoholism* (reprint of original 1950 edition) (London: Gollancz).

McCarthy, J. (1950), 'Alcoholics Anonymous', *Irish Ecclesiastical Record*, vol. 73, 258–9.

McCarthy, P.D. (1962), 'Alcoholism 1' in O'Doherty and McGrath (1962), 136–41.

McCoy, D. (1991), 'Issues for Irish Alcohol Policy: A Historical Perspective with Some Lessons for the Future' (paper read for the Statistical and Social Inquiry Society of Ireland, 24 October).

McCrady, B. and Miller, W. (eds) (1993), *Research on Alcoholics Anonymous: Opportunities and Alternatives* (New Brunswick, NJ: Rutgers Center of Alcohol Studies).

McMahon, D. (2001), Review of *John Charles McQuaid: Ruler of Catholic Ireland*, *Catholic Historical Review*, vol. 87, 345–7.

Menand, L. (2001), *The Metaphysical Club: A Story of Ideas in America* (New York: Farrar, Straus & Giroux).

Michels, R. (1968), *Political Parties: A Sociological Study of the*

Oligarchical Tendencies of Modern Democracy (New York: Free Press).

Midanik, L. (2004), 'Biomedicalization and Alcohol Studies: Implications for Policy', *Journal of Public Health*, vol. 25, 211–28.

Miller, W. (2002), 'Is Treatment the Right Way to Think about It?' in Miller and Weisner (2002), 22–7.

Miller, W. and Heather, N. (1986), *Treating Addictive Behaviours: Processes of Change* (New York: Plenum).

Miller, W. and Kurtz, E. (1994), 'Models of Alcoholism used in Treatment: Contrasting AA and Other Perspectives with which it is often Confused', *Journal of Studies on Alcohol*, vol. 55, 159–66.

Miller, W. and Rollnick, S. (2002), *Motivational Interviewing: Preparing People for Change* (2nd edn) (London: Guilford Press).

Miller, W. and Weisner, C. (eds) (2002), *Changing Substance Abuse through Health and Social Systems* (New York: Kluwer Academic).

Miller, W., Brown, J., Simpson, T. *et al.* (1995), 'What Works? A Methodological Analysis of the Alcohol Treatment Outcome Literature' in Hester, R. and Miller, W. (eds), *Handbook of Alcoholism Treatment Approaches: Effective Alternatives* (Boston: Allyn & Bacon), 12–44.

Miller, W., Zweben, J. and Johnson, W. (2005), 'Evidence-Based Treatment: Why, What, Where, When and How?', *Journal of Substance Abuse Treatment*, vol. 29, 267–76.

Mongan, D., Reynolds, S., Fanagan, S. and Long, J. (2007), *Health-Related Consequences of Problem Alcohol Use: Overview 6* (Dublin: Health Research Board).

National Alcohol Policy – Ireland (1996) (Dublin: Stationery Office).

Nielsen, J. (2004), *The Myth of Leadership* (Mountain View, California: Davies-Black Publishing).

O'Connor, J. (1978), *The Young Drinkers: A Cross-National Study of Social and Cultural Influences* (London: Tavistock).

O'Connor, P. (1942), 'Some Dangers in Alcoholics Anonymous', *Ecclesiastical Review*, vol. 106, 285–8.

O'Doherty, E.F. and McGrath, S.D. (eds) (1962), *The Priest and Mental Health* (Dublin: Clonmore & Reynolds).

O'Hare, A. and Walsh, D. (1987), *Activities of Irish Psychiatric Hospitals and Units 1984* (Dublin: Health Research Board).

O'Riordan, S. (1952), 'Round the Reviews: Grace is Sufficient – Why Alcoholics Anonymous?', *The Furrow* (January), 31–40.

O'Riordan, S. (1962), 'Alcoholism 111' in O'Doherty and McGrath (1962), 150–4.

O'Sullivan, E. (2003), Review of Kilcommins and O'Donnell (2003), *Irish Jurist*, vol. 38, 414–17.

Orford, J. and Edwards, G. (1977), *Alcoholism: A Comparison of Treatment and Advice with a Study of the Influence of Marriage* (Oxford: Oxford University Press).

Peele, S. (1995), *Diseasing of America: How We Allowed Recovery Zealots and the Treatment Industry to Convince Us We are Out of Control* (2nd edn) (New York: Lexington Books).

Pollner, M. and Stein, J. (2001), '"Doubled Over in Laughter": Humor and the Construction of Selves in Alcoholics Anonymous' in Gubrum, J. and Holstein, J. (eds), *Institutional Selves: Troubled Identities in a Postmodern World* (Oxford: Oxford University Press), 46–63.

The Psychiatric Services: Planning for the Future (Report of a Study Group on the Development of the Psychiatric Services) (1984) (Dublin: Stationery Office).

Purcell, M. (1979), *A Time for Sowing: The St John of God Brothers in Ireland – A Centenary Record, 1879–1979* (Dublin: Hospitaller Order of St John of God).

Quinn, J. (2002), *Father Mathew's Crusade: Temperance in Nineteenth-Century Ireland and Irish America* (Amerherst: University of Massachusetts Press).

Ragge, K. (1998), *The Real AA: Beyond the Myth of 12-Step Recovery* (Tucson, Arizona: See Sharp Press).

Ramstedt, M. and Hope, A. (2005), 'The Irish Drinking Habits of 2002: Drinking and Drink-Related Harm in a European Comparative Perspective', *Journal of Substance Use*, vol. 10, 273–83.

Reinarman, C. (2005), 'Addiction as Accomplishment: The Discursive Construction of Disease', *Addiction Research and Theory*, vol. 13, 307–20.

Report of the Commission of Inquiry on Mental Illness (1966) (Dublin: Stationery Office).

Report of the Inspector of Mental Hospitals, 1958 (1959)

(Dublin: Stationery Office).

Reynolds, J. (1992), *Grangegorman: Psychiatric Care in Dublin since 1815* (Dublin: Institute of Public Administration).

Ritzer, G. (1993), *The McDonaldization of Society: An Investigation into the Changing Character of Social Life* (London: Pine Forge).

Scull, A. (1979), *Museums of Madness: The Social Organization of Insanity in Nineteenth-Century England* (London: Allen Lane).

Seeley, J. (1962), 'Alcoholism as a Disease: Implications for Social Policy' in Pittman, D. and Snyder, C. (eds), *Society, Culture and Drinking Patterns* (New York: John Wiley), 592–9.

Seymour, M. and Mayock, P. (2009), 'Ireland' in Hadfield, P. (ed.), *Nightlife and Crime: Social Order and Governance in International Perspective* (Oxford: Oxford University Press), 77–98.

Smith, B. (1989), 'Ireland's Ennis Inebriates' Reformatory: A 19th Century Example of Failed Institutional Reform', *Federal Probation*, vol. 53, 53–64.

Sobell, M. and Sobell, L. (1995), 'Controlled Drinking after 25 Years: How Important was the Great Debate?', *Addiction*, vol. 90, 1149–53.

Spicer, J. (1993), *The Minnesota Model: The Evolution of the Multidisciplinary Approach to Addiction Recovery* (Center City, Minnesota: Hazelden).

Strategic Task Force on Alcohol: Interim Report (2002) (Dublin: Department of Health and Children).

Strategic Task Force on Alcohol: Second Report (2004) (Dublin: Department of Health and Children).

Townend, P. (2002), *Father Mathew, Temperance and Irish Identity* (Dublin: Irish Academic Press).

Trimpey, J. (1995), *The Small Book: A Revolutionary Alternative to Overcoming Alcohol and Drug Dependence.*(New York: Dell Publishing).

Vaillant, G. (1983), *The Natural History of Alcoholism* (Cambridge, MA: Harvard University Press).

Valverde, M. (1997), '"Slavery from Within": The Invention of Alcoholism and the Question of Free Will', *Social History*, vol. 22, 251–68.

Valverde, M. (1998), *Diseases of the Will: Alcohol and the*

Dilemma of Freedom (Cambridge: Cambridge University Press).

Valverde, M. and White-Mair, K. (1999), '"One Day at a Time" and other Slogans for Everyday Life: The Ethical Practices of Alcoholics Anonymous', *Sociology*, vol. 33, 393–410.

Viney, M. (1964), *Alcoholism in Ireland: An Inquiry by Michael Viney* (Dublin: Irish Times).

Walsh, D. (1983), 'Alcohol Problems and Alcohol Controls in Ireland' in Davies, P. and Walsh, D. (eds), *Alcohol Problems and Alcohol Controls in Europe* (London: Croom Helm), 90–105.

Walsh, D. (1987), 'Alcohol and Ireland', *British Journal of Addiction*, vol. 82, 118–20.

Walsh, D. and Daly, A. (2004), *Mental Illness in Ireland 1750–2002: Reflections on the Rise and Fall of Institutional Care* (Dublin: Health Research Board).

Waters, J. (2008), *Lapsed Agnostic* (London: Continuum).

Weisner, C. and Room, R. (1984), 'Financing and Ideology in Alcohol Treatment', *Social Problems*, vol. 32, 167–84.

White, M. and Epston, D. (1990), *Narrative Means to Therapeutic Ends* (New York: W.W. Norton).

Whyte, J. (1971), *Church and State in Modern Ireland 1923–1970* (Dublin: Gill & Macmillan).

Wiener, C. (1981), *The Politics of Alcoholism: Building an Arena Around a Social Problem* (New Brunswick, NJ: Transaction Books).

Wren, J. (2000), *Sir Philip Dundas (Founder of Alcoholics Anonymous in Scotland) and His Brothers – The Missing Generation of Arniston* (Kidderminster: M. & M. Baldwin).

Notes

CHAPTER ONE

1. Statistics quoted on the website of the General Service Office of AA in Ireland.
2. See, for example, Lynch (2005) and Waters (2008).
3. Ritzer (1993).
4. See Appendix 2 page 217 for the Twelve Steps and Twelve Traditions. AA's suggested programme of recovery for its members is summarized in its Twelve Steps, while its administrative philosophy is contained in its Twelve Traditions. See Alcoholics Anonymous (1960).
5. Michels (1968).
6. Bill Wilson, co-founder of AA in 1935, said at a convention to celebrate the fellowship's 20th birthday that 'AA can be likened to a temple supported by three pillars: one is religion, another is medicine and the third is our own experience as people who have suffered from alcoholism': Alcoholics Anonymous (2000), 236. For a more theoretical study of AA that bases itself on this 'hybrid terrain' idea, see Valverde and White-Mair (1999).
7. For a much-cited sociological presentation of these ideas, see Levine (1992).
8. Malcolm (1986).
9. Ferriter (1999).
10. See Levine (1992); also Makela *et al.* (1996).
11. Inglis (1998).
12. See Appendix A ('Alcoholics Anonymous and "Absolutes": The Spiritual as Growth or Perfection') in Kurtz (1991).
13. Ragge (1998), 154.
14. Whyte (1971)
15. Cooney (1999).
16. See Edwards (2000).
17. Levine (1978).
18. One of the best-known and most influential accounts of the disease concept is that of Jellinek (1960).
19. Waters (2008), 81.
20. Makela *et al.* (1996), 140–1.
21. Jensen (2000).
22. See White and Epston (1990).
23. For a chronological summary of the main events in the history of AA in Ireland, see Appendix 1 page 215.

CHAPTER TWO

1. Smith (1989), 64.
2. See Edwards (2000), 29.
3. See, for instance: Malcolm (1986); Kerrigan (1992); Quinn (2002); and Townend (2002).
4. McCoy (1991), 4.
5. See references in note 2 above.
6. Malcolm (1986), 135–7.
7. Gusfield (1963).
8. Ferriter (1999).
9. Malcolm (1986), 312–13.
10. Ibid., 312.
11. See Chapter 2, 'Foundations', in Ferriter (1999).
12. Levine (1992), 16.
13. Foucault (1977).
14. Malcolm (1989).
15. Reynolds (1992).
16. Finnane (1981), 26.
17. Ibid., 226 (Table A).
18. Walsh and Daly (2004).
19. The establishment of medical hegemony within the Irish asylums is described in Finnane (1981), 39–47; for a detailed analysis of the same process within the English system, see Scull (1979).
20. Controversies and disputes about the legitimacy of the medical model are reflected, for instance, in Chapter 2 ('Policy Framework') of Ireland's most recent mental health policy document: *A Vision for Change: Report of the Expert Group on Mental Health Policy* (2006).
21. See Valverde (1997) and Valverde (1998).
22. Finnane (1981), 146–50.
23. Smith (1989), 57.
24. See ibid. and Bretherton (1987).
25. Johnstone (1996).
26. See Smith (1989), 64.
27. *Intoxicating Liquor Commission Report* (1925).
28. Ibid., 4.
29. Ibid., 2.
30. Ibid., Minutes of Evidence, 6 April 1925.
31. Ibid., Minutes of Evidence, 24 March 1925.
32. Ibid., Minutes of Evidence, 23 March 1925.
33. See, for instance Babor *et al.* (2003).
34. *Intoxicating Liquor Commission Report* (1925), Minutes of Evidence, 5 May 1925.
35. Ibid., 19.
36. *Mental Treatment Acts 1945–1961: Statutory Provisions, Regulations, Explanatory Notes* (Part B, Section 3) (Dublin: Stationery Office), 19.
37. *Journal of the Medical Association of Éire* (1945).
38. *Dáil Debates* (1945), Vol. 96, column 1009.
39. Ibid., col. 1012.
40. Walsh (1987).
41. For relevant statistics and a discussion of the burden which alcohol had become for the mental health services, see Chapter 13 ('Alcohol and Drug-Related Problems') in *The Psychiatric Services: Planning for the Future* (1984).
42. The concept of 'ownership' of social problems refers to the way in which a particular institution (e.g., health care, criminal justice or religion) claims or is given primary societal responsibility for its management: see Gusfield (1996).

CHAPTER THREE

1. Kurtz (1991), 164.
2. The Kurtz (1991) history of AA was based on full access to the fellowship's archives in New York and – since its author is a professional historian – is generally regarded as being more objective and balanced than some of the writings published by AA itself. While somewhat hagiographical, the following two AA publications (the first compiled by Bill Wilson, co-founder of the fellowship, and based on the fellowship's 'coming of age' convention in St Louis in 1955; the second – a biography of Bill Wilson – written by AA General Service Office staff some fifteen years after his death) provide useful detail on the founding of AA: Alcoholics Anonymous (2000 but originally published in 1957), *Alcoholics Anonymous Comes of Age: A Brief History of AA*; Alcoholics Anonymous (1984), *'Pass It On': The Story of Bill Wilson and how the AA Message Reached the World*
3. Alcoholics Anonymous (1984), 56.
4. *Alcoholics Anonymous: The Story of How Many Thousands of Men and Women have Recovered from Alcoholism* (New York: AA World Services, 1955). This is the 'Big Book', the first edition of which was published in 1939.
5. See Appendix 1 for the Twelve Steps and Twelve Traditions.
6. See 'How AA's World Services Grew: Part 1' in *The Language of the Heart: Bill W.'s Grapevine Writings* (New York: AA Grapevine Inc., 1988), 142–50 (originally published by Bill Wilson in *The Grapevine* in May 1955). The Jack Alexander article, entitled 'Alcoholics Anonymous' was published in the *Saturday Evening Post* in March 1941.
7. First published in *The Grapevine* (AA's official newsletter) in 1947.
8. See, for example, Dunne (2006); this research reports on service user consultation with patients of adult mental health services, who would traditionally have been regarded as characterized by irrationality and, therefore, incapable of offering ideas or suggestions likely to be of value to professional clinicians or public sector managers.
9. Makela *et al.* (1996), 143.
10. See Miller and Kurtz (1994).
11. Alcoholics Anonymous (1955) (The Big Book), 44.
12. Alcoholics Anonymous (1984), 121.
13. Ibid., 123.
14. For a recent study of how James developed his thinking about pragmatism in the context of a wider philosophical group in post-civil war USA, see Menand (2001),
15. Ibid., 372.
16. Alcoholics Anonymous (1955), 28.
17. Alcoholics Anonymous (1984), 124.
18. 'The Bill W. – Carl Jung Letters' in *The Language of the Heart* (1988), 279 (originally published in *The Grapevine* in January 1963).
19. Ibid., 281.
20. Lean (1985).
21. Davidson (2002).
22. AA (1984), 172.
23. AA (1984), 173.
24. Kurtz (1991), 47.
25. Fitzgerald (1995), 2.
26. Kurtz (1991), 52.
27. For instance, in 1942 one of Ed Dowling's fellow Jesuits published such an attack in an American Catholic publication; see O'Connor (1942).
28. The following all provide useful academic accounts of the disease concept of alcoholism as it emerged in post-Prohibition USA: Beauchamp (1980); Edwards (2000), Gusfield (1996). For a polemical presentation of the disease concept written by Marty Mann – one of the early American AA members, who was later to be a direct influence on policy events in Ireland – see Mann (1979).
29. Jellinek (1960), *The Disease Concept of Alcoholism*, 1.

30. Kurtz (1991), 118–19.
31. Kurtz (2002), 5.
32. Seeley (1962), 593.
33. The first WHO publication (sometimes referred to as the 'Purple Book') to reflect this new 'public health' perspective on alcohol was Bruun *et al.* (1975).
34. See Kurtz (1991), 20–1.
35. Bill Wilson, cited in Kurtz (1991), 51.
36. Cheever (1999), 115–17.
37. See Hartigan (2001) and Cheever (2004).
38. See, for instance, Nielsen (2004).
39. 'Will AA ever have a Personal Government?' in *The Language of the Heart* (1988), 41 (originally published in *The Grapevine,* January 1947).
40. Kurtz (1991), 63–4.
41. Ibid., 66–7 and 92–3.
42. See, for instance: 'The Book is Born' in *The Language of the Heart* (1988), 9–12 (originally published in *The Grapevine*, October 1945); and 'Dangers in Linking AA to Other Projects' in *The Language of the Heart* (1988), 43–6 (originally published in *The Grapevine*, March 1947).
43. Inglis (1998).
44. The fullest biographical study to date of Archbishop McQuaid is that written by J. Cooney (1999). While this book has been criticized by some – for example, see its review by D. McMahon (2001) – as being unscholarly and as presenting a crude stereotype of McQuaid, it contains enough detailed and well-substantiated information on his style of leadership to explain why AA in Ireland feared an attack from this source.

CHAPTER FOUR

1. *Alcoholics Anonymous Comes of Age* (1957), 83.
2. Letter from Bobbie Burger to Father Senan Moynihan, 22 August 1944 (New York: Alcoholics Anonymous Archives).
3. *Alcoholics Anonymous in Ireland – 1946–1986: A Souvenir Booklet to Commemorate Forty Years of AA in Ireland* (Dublin: Alcoholics Anonymous, 1986).
4. The Dunlea interview was published in the now defunct *Dublin Evening Mail* on 5 October 1946, and the Conor Flynn interview on 1 November 1946.
5. Alcoholics Anonymous (1986).
6. See Reynolds (1992).
7. Like all of the original nineteenth-century lunatic asylums established in Ireland, Grangegorman had grown enormously in size. When it was opened as the Richmond Asylum in 1814, it had a bed capacity of 250, but by 1904 it had 3,218 beds – see Appendix A in Finnane (1981).
8. For a discussion of the authority of the Resident Medical Superintendents, see ibid., 176–85.
9. See, for instance, Scull (1979) and Brown (1973).
10. Reynolds (1992).
11. Browne (2008), 104.
12. Audiotape of talk by Conor Flynn at AA's 21st birthday celebration in Dublin (AAAD, 1967).
13. Ibid.
14. Ibid.
15. Ibid.
16. Joyce (2008), 281
17. See Purcell (1979), which is the authorized history of the work of the St John of God brothers in Ireland. This history contains a detailed account of the evolution of its psychiatric hospital in Stillorgan, but fails to mention its rejection of Conor Flynn in 1946. The only reference to AA (page 118) is in connection with the hospital's development of a specialist alcoholism treatment facility from the early 1960s onwards.

18. Healy (1992) presents an interview with Dr Desmond McGrath, former medical director of the St John of God Hospital in Stillorgan. It is worth noting that Dr McGrath's comments on alcoholism treatment occurred at a point in this interview when the interviewer asked: 'There has always been a particular association between St John of God Hospital and alcoholism. Why is this?' Effectively, Dr McGrath's answer conceded that such an association always had existed.
19. See Malcolm (1989), which is the authorized history of St Patrick's Hospital, Dublin.
20. Ibid., 278.
21. Ibid.
22. 'Significant Dates in the History of AA in Ireland' in Alcoholics Anonymous (1996), 15.
23. Audiotape of talk by Conor Flynn.
24. Audiotape interview of Ruth Perceval (widow of Richard) by Tony Jordan (28 June 1998) for M.Litt. research at Trinity College Dublin. Further information on Richard Perceval's family background and early life is also taken from his obituary in the *Irish Times* (1 January 1983).
25. Letter from Richard Perceval to AA Foundation, New York, 23 November 1946 (AAANY).
26. Letter from Richard Perceval to Bobbie Burger, 11 December 1946 (AAANY).
27. Ibid.
28. Letter from Bobbie Burger to Richard Perceval, 20 December 1946 (AAANY).
29. Letter from Sackville O'Conor-Mallins to Joe D., 11 August 1948 (AAAD).
30. E. Jennings, 'How I Got Involved in AA' in Alcoholics Anonymous (1996), 25.
31. Letter from Richard Perceval to Bobbie Burger, 6 May 1947 (AAANY).
32. Letter from Bobbie Burger to Richard Perceval, 15 May 1947 (AAANY).
33. There are many sources on which to draw for an understanding of Sackville's biography. Perhaps the most obvious written source is his own potted biography, 'The Career Officer', which was written at the request of Bill Wilson for inclusion in the second edition of the Big Book, first published in 1955. There are also many biographical facts recorded in the letters that he wrote to fellowship members, particularly his letters to Joe D., a Chicago AA member with whom he corresponded for about twenty-five years. There are short accounts of Sackville's life in the souvenir booklets produced by Irish AA, and, last but not least, this author was given an interview on 22 October 2008 by Denis Murphy, Sackville's nephew, whom he lived with for the last years of his life.
34. Letter from Sackville to Joe D., 23 September 1948 (AAAD). Sackville's explanation of the family name *O'Conor Don* is almost certainly incorrect; the word *Don* is more likely to be derived from the Irish word *donn*, which means 'brown', than it is a corruption of *Dhu*, which means 'black'.
35. Letter from Sackville to Joe D., 17 June 1966.
36. 'The Career Officer', 523.
37. Letter from Sackville to Joe D., 2 February 1966 (AAAD).
38. The late Paddy K., to whom Sackville was sponsor from the late 1960s, inherited all of Sackville's army photographs, which suggests that he had a busy social and sporting life in his various military postings.
39. Text of talk given by Sackville to an AA group in Manchester, 23 July 1975 (AAAD).
40. 'The Career Officer', 529.
41. Ibid., 530.
42. Audiotape interview of Ruth Perceval.
43. Since Ireland had remained neutral during the Second World War, the period between 1939 and 1945 was officially referred to as the 'Emergency'.
44. Audiotape interview of Paddy K. by Shane Butler, 04.03.2008.
45. 'The Career Officer', 526.
46. Audiotape interview of Denis Murphy by Shane Butler, 22.10.2008.
47. Alcoholics Anonymous (1986).
48. Letter from Sackville to Lucy at the Alcoholic Foundation, 24 August 1949 (AAANY).
49. Letter from Sackville to Bill Wilson, 6 January 1950 (AAANY).

50. Letter from Sackville to Joe D., 10 December 1949 (AAAD).
51. McCarthy (1950).
52. Letter from Sackville to Joe D., 23 February 1952 (AAAD).
53. See Carty (2007), 47–9.
54. See Gallagher and Cannon (1998).
55. O'Riordan (1962).
56. Ibid., 36.
57. Letter from Sackville to Bill Wilson, 16 February 1952 (AAANY).
58. Letter from Sackville to Ann Lehman, 19 February 1952 (AAANY).
59. Letter from Bill Wilson to Sackville, 5 March 1952 (AAANY).
60. 'A Member' (1953).
61. I.G.S. (1957).
62. It seems likely that this was a reference to a letter Sackville had received in 1949 and had held on to with a view to making the best possible use of it at some future time. 'I had a grand letter from the Chancellor of the Detroit Archdiocese, giving me his own, and therefore Cardinal Mooney's views on AA. I hope it will be very useful to me for working on the bishops here' – Letter from Sackville to Joe D., 17 November 2008 (AAAD).
63. I.G.S. (1957), 86.
64. Letter from Father John C. Ford to Sackville, 18 October 1955 (AAAD).
65. Letter from Sister M. Ignatia to Sackville, 13 November 1956.
66. Letter from Professor J.G. McGarry to Sackville, 8 December 1956 (AAAD).
67. Letter from Fernand Picard (Domremy Maison D'entrade, Quebec City) to Dublin AA Group, 24 April 1959 (AAAD).
68. Letter from Carlos Camara Evia (Secretary Groupo 'Lucerna' AA, Mexico) to Dublin AA Group, 31 October 1959 (AAAD).
69. Jordan (2000).
70. Positive relationships between AA and the religious orders are evident throughout the archival material and have also been confirmed by fellowship members interviewed by Tony Jordan during the 1990s. See Jordan (2000).
71. Ferriter (1999), in his history of the Pioneers, touches on the attitudes of this Catholic temperance association towards the newly arrived AA and towards the concept of alcoholism as a disease.
72. Letter from Sackville to Joe D., 18 July 1950 (AAAD).
73. Letter from Sackville to Joe D., 21 November 1950 (AAAD).
74. Letter from Archbishop Joseph Walsh to Eva Jennings, 12 November 1953 (AAAD).
75. Cooney (1999).
76. McMahon (2001).
77. Carty (2007).
78. Dunn (1986) and (1994).
79. Dunn (1986), 25.
80. For example, in a letter to Dunn dated 1965, McQuaid expressed umbrage at the fact that the Italian priest, Father Mario Borelli, well known for his work with street children in Naples, had visited Dublin without contacting him as the local bishop: 'I see he has lunched at the Nunciature and addressed social workers in my city' (Dunn, 1986, 32).
81. Cooney (1999), 163–5.
82. P. McGarry, 'Dublin Samaritans plan viewed with suspicion by archbishop', *Irish Times*, 28 October 2008. See Jordan (2008).
83. O'Doherty and McGrath (1962).
84. O'Riordan (1962), 152.
85. Carty (2007), 46.
86. The only references to AA to be found in the McQuaid Papers at the Dublin Diocesan Archive are dinner invitations to the archbishop from the fellowship dating from the late 1960s.
87. Audiotape interviews by Tony Jordan for M.Litt. research at Trinity College Dublin: interview with Ruth Perceval, 28 June 1998; interview with Donal X., 6 October 1997.

88. Letter from Sackville to Bill Wilson, 28 April 1961 (AAANY).
89. Letter from Sackville to Joe D., 27 January 1967 (AAAD).
90. Audiotape interview with Big Eugene.
91. Cited in Malcolm (1986), 317.
92. See Ferriter (1999),
93. See Chapter 6 for a fuller discussion of *The Road Back*.
94. The archives of the Pioneer Total Abstinence Association are now held in the University College Dublin archives at the School of History and Archives.
95. Information on Father John Mulligan, S.J., from the Irish Jesuit Archive, Leeson St, Dublin (JAD).
96. Minutes of the meeting of the St Francis Xavier Council of the PTAA, 24 August 1960 (PTAAUCD).
97. Minutes of the meeting of the St Francis Xavier Council of the PTAA, 28 February 1964 (PTAAUCD).
98. Minutes of the meeting of the St Francis Xavier Council of the PTAA, 27 May 1966 (PTAAUCD).
99. Minutes of the meeting of St Francis Xavier Council of the PTAA, 26 May 1967 (PTAAUCD).
100. Minutes of the meeting of the St Francis Xavier Council of the PTAA, 30 May 1969 (PTAAUCD).
101. Minutes of the meeting of St Francis Xavier Council of the PTAA, 27 June 1969 (PTAAUCD).
102. Letter from Father Cecil McGarry, S.J. (Jesuit Provincial) to Father John Mulligan, S.J., 24 September 1969 (JAD).
103. Audiotape interview with Big Eugene.
104. Letter from Sackville to Cardinal William Conway, 23 January 1972 (AAAD).
105. Letter from Sackville to Joe D., 3 January 1972 (AAAD).
106. Letter from Archbishop Enrici to Travers C., 10 November 1971 (AAAD).
107. Letter from Sackville to Cardinal William Conway, 23 January 1972 (AAAD).
108. Letter from Sackville to Joe D., 19 January 1972 (AAAD).
109. A Dublin Member of Alcoholics Anonymous (1972), 182.
110. Letter from Cardinal William Conway to Sackville, 25 January 1972 (AAAD).
111. Letter from Robert Hitchins, AA General Service Board, New York, to Sackville, 1 February 1972 (AAAD).
112. Letter from Lois Wilson to Sackville, 16 April 1972 (AAAD).
113. Letter from Ann MacFarlane, AA General Service Board, New York, to Sackville, 1 May 1972 (AAAD).
114. Letter from Sackville to Ann MacFarlane, New York, 11 May 1972 (AAAD).
115. Letter from Ann MacFarlane, AA General Service Board, New York, to Sackville, 19 May 1972 (AAAD).

CHAPTER FIVE

1. Cooney (1963), 54.
2. Jellinek (1960), 1.
3. Edwards (2008), 1944.
4. As previously indicated, the first major WHO report to reflect this change of perspective was Bruun *et al.* (1975).
5. Butler (2002).
6. *The Psychiatric Services – Planning for the Future: Report of a Study Group on the Development of the Psychiatric Services* (1984).
7. For a comprehensive statement of this public health–total consumption model by the WHO, see Babor *et al.* (2003); for an application of this perspective to the Irish alcohol policy scene, see *Strategic Task Force on Alcohol: Interim Report* (2002).
8. See Butler (2009).
9. See Peele (1995) for a controversial and well-known attack on America's commitment to the disease concept.

10. Audiotape of talk by Conor Flynn at AA's twenty-first birthday celebration in Dublin (AAAD, 1967).
11. Letter from Sackville to Bobbie Burger and Charlotte Lappen at the Alcoholic Foundation, 1 October 1947 (AAANY).
12. Letter from Sackville to Bobbie Burger at the Alcoholic Foundation, 22 May 1948 (AAANY).
13. Letter from Sackville to Joe D., 2 October 1948 (AAAD).
14. Letter from Sackville to Joe D., 14 May 1949 (AAAD).
15. Letter from Sackville to Bobbie Burger at the Alcoholic Foundation, 5 June 1948 (AAANY). Sackville's description of Norman Moore as a psychoanalyst is inaccurate.
16. Letter from Sackville to Bobbie Burger, 20 September 1947 (AAANY).
17. Letter from Sackville to Joe D., 14 February 1950 (AAAD).
18. Letter from Sackville to Joe D., 20 August 1948 (AAAD).
19. Letter from Sackville to Bill Wilson, 10 November 1962 (AAANY).
20. Kurtz (2002), 5.
21. Letter from Bobbie Burger to Sackville, 15 June 1948 (AAANY).
22. Letter from Sackville to Bobbie Burger and Ann MacFarlane, 21 September 1948 (AAANY).
23. Letter from Ann Lehman to Sackville, 6 October 1948 (AAANY).
24. Letter from Sackville to Bobbie Burger, Charlotte Lappen and Ann Lehman, 11 October 1948 (AAANY).
25. For a detailed discussion of this period in Irish health policy and the establishment of the VHI scheme, see Barrington (1987), Ch. 10.
26. Healy (1992).
27. For a detailed discussion of the controversy surrounding the 1985 restrictions on VHI cover of inpatient alcoholism treatment, see Butler (2002), 60–2.
28. Veteran AA member, Terry, cited in Jordan (2000), 111.
29. McCarthy (1962), 139–40.
30. Purcell (1979), 117.
31. See, for instance, Walsh (1983). The Commission of Inquiry on Mental Illness in its 1966 report commented : 'It is also of interest to note that the per capita consumption of alcoholic drink in Ireland is one of the lowest for all countries for which reliable statistics are available' (*Report of the Commission of Inquiry on Mental Illness*, 1966, 80).
32. *Report of the Inspector of Mental Hospitals, 1958* (1959).
33. Letter from Sackville to Dr Norman Moore, St Patrick's Hospital, 28 August 1958 (AAAD).
34. Malcolm (1989), 278. The reference to INLA, which appears to hint at an affiliation between St Patrick's and one of the more violent paramilitary groups of the 'Troubles', is presumably intended to refer to INCA (the Irish National Council on Alcoholism), which had in fact been wound up at the end of 1987.
35. *Report of the Commission of Inquiry on Mental Illness, 1966*, 77.
36. Ibid., 79.
37. Ibid., 82.
38. Viney (1964), 49.
39. Healy (1992), 136.
40. Cearbhall Ó'Dálaigh resigned from the office of Uachtarán (President of Ireland) in 1976 in protest at what he saw as a scurrilous verbal attack on him by the Minister for Defence, Patrick Donegan. It has occasionally been remarked that since Donegan was generally regarded as an alcoholic and was certainly drunk at the time he delivered this verbal onslaught, Ó'Dálaigh as first Chair of the Irish National Council on Alcoholism might have been more understanding.
41. *Memorandum and Articles of Association of The Irish National Council on Alcoholism* (1966).
42. Letter from Sackville to Bill Wilson, 14 August 1964 (AAANY).
43. Letter from Sackville to Bill Wilson, 25 December 1964 (AAANY).
44. Letter from Bill Wilson to Sackville, 5 January 1965 (AAANY).

45. Letter from Marty Mann to Sackville, 16 October 1964.
46. Letter from Chief Justice Cearbhall Ó'Dálaigh to Sackville, 19 February 1965 (AAAD).
47. It is impossible to say precisely when the two AA members resigned their INCA membership, since a full set of INCA papers was not preserved following its closure at the end of 1988. It would appear, however, that they had resigned prior to October 1971, when INCA held an international conference in Dun Laoghaire, following which it was asked by the Minister for Health, Erskine Childers, to submit a report on alcoholism in Ireland.
48. Letter from Sackville to Bill Wilson, 24 July 1965 (AAANY).
49. Letter from Sackville to Bill Wilson, 19 November 1968 (AAANY).
50. Letter from Sackville to Bill Wilson, 25 December 1965 (AAANY).
51. Letter from Sackville to Bill Wilson, 25 December 1969 (AAANY).
52. Letter from Sackville to Joe D., 10 February 1967 (AAAD).
53. Letter from Sackville to Joe D., 11 April 1968.
54. Letter from Bill Wilson to Sackville, 26 September 1967 (AAAD).
55. Letter from Aiden MacSweeney to Sackville, 8 February 1967 (AAAD).
56. Letter from Aiden MacSweeney to Sackville, 10 May 1968 (AAAD).
57. Audiotape interview with 'Big Eugene' (AA member since 1964) by Tony Jordan (01.07.1997) for M.Litt. research at Trinity College Dublin.
58. For a full account of INCA's travails, see Butler (2002), *Alcohol, Drugs and Health Promotion in Modern Ireland* (Dublin: Institute of Public Administration), especially Chapter 3, pp.44–74.
59. *Memorandum and Articles of Association of the Irish National Council on Alcoholism* (1966), 2e.
60. *Irish National Council on Alcoholism Annual Report, February 1967–February 1968.*
61. Butler (2002), 51–2.
62. *The Psychiatric Services: Planning for the Future* (1984).
63. All of the statistics quoted here are drawn from O'Hare and Walsh (1987). In the reports compiled by the Health Research Board, psychiatric diagnoses are recorded in accordance with the World Health Organization's International Classification of Diseases (ICD); categorization of alcohol-related problems within the ICD system has changed over the years, but in 1984 these problems were categorized as 'Alcohol Abuse and Alcoholic Psychoses'.
64. Butler (1983). While nobody from the private mental health sector chose to offer written replies to this article, the author received a considerable amount of informal feedback that was highly critical of the views he had expressed and indignant at his impertinence in setting such views down on paper.
65. *The Psychiatric Services: Planning for the Future* (1984), 104.
66. Ibid., 105–6.
67. Ibid., 105.
68. See Chapter 2 above.
69. *The Psychiatric Services: Planning for the Future* (1984), 108.
70. Ibid., 113.
71. See Butler (2002), 60–2.
72. *Irish Press*, 22 March 1985.
73. See Cullen (2008).
74. See Butler (2009).
75. For instance: *National Alcohol Policy – Ireland* (1996); *Strategic Task Force on Alcohol: Interim Report* (2002); *Strategic Task Force on Alcohol: Second Report* (2004).
76. For 'insider' presentations of this model, see Anderson (1981) and Spicer (1993). For more critical 'outsider' views of the model, see Weisner and Room (1984) and Peele (1995).
77. Anderson (1981), 29.
78. Senator Harold Hughes, cited in Wiener (1981), 3.
79. See, for instance: Miller and Heather (1986); Miller *et al.* (1995); Miller and Rollnick (2002).

80. Letter from St Marie Joseph to Sackville, 23 April 1971 (AAAD).
81. *Irish Times*, 2 April 1985.
82. For a detailed account of the events leading up to the establishment of the Rutland Centre, see Butler (2002), 56–9.
83. Audiotape interview with Pat H. (AA member since 1967) by Tony Jordan for M. Litt. research at Trinity College Dublin.
84. Ibid.
85. Ibid.
86. Ibid. All other quotations are taken from this source.
87. See, for instance, *Directory of Alcohol, Drugs and Related Services in the Republic of Ireland 2000* (2000), in which many of the services listed describe themselves as providing Twelve-Step or Minnesota Model Programmes.
88. An exception is the published evaluation of the Aiséirí programme in Cahir, Co. Tipperary – Leane and Powell (1994) – which is methodologically limited and does not provide an evidence base for programmes such as this.
89. Miller and Kurtz (1994).

CHAPTER SIX

1. Letter from Charlotte Lappen (Alcoholic Foundation, New York) to Sackville, 20 April 1948 (AAANY).
2. Makela *et al.* (1996).
3. The estimate of membership of the Country Shop group in December 1946 is that of Richard Perceval (see Ch. 4 note 26), and the estimate of 2007 membership is from AA's national website (see Ch. 1 note 1).
4. Letter from Sackville to Joe D., 5 November 1968 (AAAD).
5. Audiotape interview of Ruth Perceval.
6. Audiotape interview with 'Big Eugene'.
7. Audiotape interview of Paddy M. by Tony Jordan, 28 July 1997. (The idea that there was no sex in Ireland until television is usually attributed to the Fine Gael politician, Oliver Flanagan).
8. This letter, dated 10 November 1948, is still in the AA Dublin Archive.
9. Letter from Sackville to Charlotte Lappen, 14 January 1948 (AAANY).
10. Ibid.
11. Letter from Sackville to Bobbie Burger, 25 May 1948 (AAANY).
12. Letter from Sackville to Bobbie Burger, 5 June 1948 (AAANY).
13. Letter from Sackville to Joe D., 18 August 1948 (AAANY).
14. Letter from Sackville to Joe D., 28 February 1950 (AAANY).
15. Letter from Sackville to Joe D., 10 March 1950 (AAAD).
16. Letter from Sackville to Bill Wilson, 28 August 1947 (AAANY).
17. *Dublin Evening Mail*, 28 June 1950.
18. Letter from Sackville to Helen Brown at the Alcoholic Foundation, New York, 2 July 1950 (AAANY).
19. Letter from Sackville to Ann Lehman at the Alcoholic Foundation, New York, 26 August 1950.
20. Letter from Sackville to Joe D., 21 August 1950 (AAANY).
21. Letter from Ann McFarlane to Sackville, 31 August 1950 (AAANY).
22. Letter from Sackville to Joe D., 25 August 1950 (AAAD).
23. Letter from Bill Wilson to Richard Perceval, 18 September 1950 (AAANY).
24. Letter from Richard Perceval to Bill Wilson, 28 September 1950 (AAANY).
25. Letter from Bill Wilson to Richard Perceval, 13 October 1950 (AAANY).
26. Bill Wilson: see epigraph to Chapter 4 above.
27. *The Road Back*, issue 1, March/April 1949.
28. Letter from Sackville to Ann Lehman, 2 February 1950 (AAANY).
29. Letter from Sackville to Joe D., 4 March 1951 (AAAD).
30. See Wren (2000), 83.
31. Letter from Sackville to Bobbie Burger, 22 October 1947 (AAANY).

32. Press release, 28 November 1947 (AAANY).
33. These stories may be found in written format in the two anniversary publications previously cited above.
34. This story is told, for instance, in 'How it Began in Ireland', *AA Grapevine*, January 1996.
35. Letter from Sackville to Joe D., 10 October 1948 (AAAD).
36. Letter from Sackville to Joe D., 19 August 1948.
37. Letter from Sackville to Bobbie Burger, Charlotte Lappen and Ann Lehman, 11 October 1948 (AAANY).
38. Letter from Sackville to Joe D., 30 March 1949 (AAAD).
39. Letter from Sackville to Joe D., 20 October 1950 (AAAD).
40. Letter from Sackville to Joe D., 8 February 1950 (AAAD).
41. Letter from Sackville to Joe D., 30 December 1950 (AAAD).
42. Sackville described his replacement as pompous and hard to like: 'He is to me the outstanding example of the man one must love but cannot like.' Letter from Sackville to Joe D., 24 March 1951 (AAAD).
43. Audiotape interview with 'Big Eugene'.
44. Ibid.
45. Audiotape interviews with 'Big Eugene' and Denis Murphy.
46. Letter from Eva Jennings to Sackville, 19 November 1967 (AAAD).
47. Audiotape interview with 'Big Eugene'.
48. Denis Murphy, Sackville's nephew, thought that Sackville did not own a motorbike until the early 1950s, and the story that Denis heard within his family circle was that this trip to Bundoran was made on a pushbike (audiotape interview with Denis Murphy by the author, 22.10.2008).
49. Letter from Sackville to Bobbie Burger, 5 June 1948 (AAANY).
50. Letter from Sackville to Joe D., 3 August 1948 (AAAD).
51. Letter from Sackville to Joe D., 9 September 1948 (AAAD).
52. Letter from Sackville to Joe D., 10 October 1948 (AAAD).
53. Letter from Sackville to Joe D., 26 October 1948 (AAAD).
54. Letter from Sackville to Joe D., 22 March 1952 (AAAD). While the archives don't indicate whether the Bundoran group survived continuously, it should be noted that at present there is an active AA group in this town and that it still has an historic claim as the first place in Ireland – outside of Dublin – to host AA.
55. J. Alexander, 'The Drunkard's Best Friend', *Saturday Evening Post*, 1 April 1950.
56. Ibid.
57. Letter from Sackville to Joe D., 11 April 1950 (AAAD).
58. Letter from Sackville to Joe D., 8 April 1951 (AAAD).
59. Letter from Sackville to Joe D., 10 January 1952 (AAAD).
60. Alcoholics Anonymous (1996), 18.
61. Audiotape interview with 'Big Eugene'.
62. Letter from Seamus Kavanagh, Productions Director, Radio Éireann, to Sackville (undated copy); letter from Sackville to Bill Wilson, 2 May 1950 (AAANY).
63. Summary information on *The Road Back* may be found on AA's Irish website (www.alcoholicsanonymous.ie); more detail is available in its fiftieth anniversary issue – *The Road Back* (March/April 1999, issue no. 301) (Dublin: AA General Service Office).
64. Letter from Sackville to Joe D., 22 April 1949 (AAAD).
65. *Irish Times*, 18 April 1949.
66. *Irish Times*, 25 April 1949. For a detailed account of Brian O'Nolan's literary achievements and alcohol consumption, see Cronin (1976).
67. *The Road Back*.
68. Letter from Father Daniel Dargan, S.J., to Sackville, 3 November 1977 (AAAD).
69. A chronological account of the evolution of these structures and of other significant events in the history of AA in Ireland is contained in Alcoholics Anonymous (1996), 15.
70. Letter from Sackville to Joe D., 29 July 1950 (AAAD).
71. Letter from Bill Wilson to Sackville, 3 January 1963 (AAAD).
72. Audiotape interview with 'Big Eugene'.

CHAPTER SEVEN

1. Malcolm (1989), 3.
2. For statistical data on the expansion of district lunatic asylums in Ireland during the nineteenth century, see Finnane (1981), 227; for comparative mental health data compiled in the 1960s, see *Report of the Commission of Inquiry on Mental Illness* (1966), 21–5.
3. Kane (1986).
4. *National Alcohol Policy – Ireland* (1996), 15–16.
5. For a review of this research by an Irish sociologist, see O'Connor (1978).
6. Greeley (2000).
7. Conniffe and McCoy (1993).
8. *Strategic Task Force on Alcohol: Interim Report* (2002), 5.
9. Ramstedt and Hope (2005).
10. Anderson and Baumberg (2006).
11. Mongan *et al.* (2007).
12. See, for instance, Seymour and Mayock (2009).
13. Speech by President Mary McAleese at the 'Re-Imagining Ireland Conference', Charlottesville, Virginia, 7 May 2003.
14. Hope (2007).
15. See, for instance, Gusfield (1996).
16. For an example of sociological literature that sees the idea of addiction-as-disease as a social construction rather than an objective science, see Reinarman (2005).
17. Beauchamp (1980), 94.
18. For a useful summary of how mental health specialists have attempted to classify alcohol-related problems, see Epstein (2001).
19. Cited in Kurtz (2002), 7.
20. As an example of how the drinks industy has worked at portraying itself as a model of corporate social responsibility, see Grant and O'Connor (2005).
21. For a detailed account of the controversies and conflicts that have characterized the recent Irish alcohol policy debate, see Butler (2009).
22. For a well-known paper advocating this renewed biomedical focus ('Addiction is a brain disease and it matters'), see Leshner (1997). For a critical sociological view of the policy implications of the biomedical approach, see Midanik (2004).
23. Kurtz (2002), 6.
24. Cooney (1991), 7–8.
25. Alcoholic Anonymous, 'The Big Book' (1955; 2nd edn, 1973), 44.
26. Kurtz (2002), 6.
27. See, for instance, Chapter 1, 'The History of Treatment for Drinking Problems' in Edwards, Marshall and Cook (2003), 3–15.
28. Edwards (2000), 118.
29. Smith (1989), 64
30. The text that is usually credited with starting the current interest in systematic and methodologically sophisticated reviews of outcome studies, as part of the wider commitment to evidence-based health care, is Cochrane (1972).
31. In a randomized controlled trial of a new drug, half of the patients in the trial are randomly allocated to the experimental group, which is given the drug being tested, while the other half is given a placebo or inert drug; in a single blind trial the patients are unaware of whether they are receiving the new product being tested or the placebo, while in a double-blind study both the patients and those professionals assessing the impact of the drug are unaware of which patients are in the experimental group and which are in the control group. This method is used to differentiate between the pharmacological effect of the drug and the psychological effect of being treated and involved in a study of a new product.
32. Orford and Edwards (1977).
33. Vaillant (1983).
34. Ibid., 284.

35. Ibid., 285. The Gordis paper cited by Vaillant is: E. Gordis, 'Editorial: What is Alcoholism Research?', *Annals of Internal Medicine,* vol. 85 (1976), 821–3.
36. Vaillant (1983), 301.
37. See, for instance, Miller *et al.* (1995); also Miller, Zweben and Johnson (2005).
38. Miller (2002).
39. Miller's work on motivational interviewing as a style of addiction counselling has been developed since the early 1980s; for an authoritative account of this perspective and its effectiveness, see Miller and Rollnick (2002).
40. See McCrady and Miller (1993).
41. For a recent overview of the research literature on the mechanisms of change within the AA programme, see Kelly, Magill and Stout (2009).
42. Ibid., 236.
43. Longabaugh *et al.* (1998).
44. Sobell and Sobell (1995).
45. Ibid., 1149.
46. One influential text on narrative therapy (which, incidentally, makes no reference to AA) is White and Epston (1990).
47. Glaser and Ogborne (1982).
48. This criticism is not unique to Ireland, in the sense that no country has successfully developed rational, comprehensive approaches to tackling addictions through health and social service systems. See Miller and Weisner (2002).
49. O'Sullivan (2003), 417.
50. Bales (1944).
51. Alexander and Rollins (1984).
52. Bufe (1998).
53. The founding father of Rational Emotive Therapy was the New York psychologist, Albert Ellis (1913–2007); see, for instance, Ellis and Powers (1975).
54. Galanter, Egelko and Edwards (1993).
55. Trimpey (1995). As a sardonic marker of how categorically different his approach to recovery was from that of AA, Trimpey called this publication 'The Small Book'.
56. Peele (1995).
57. Miller and Kurtz (1994).
58. The idea of spiritual imperfection, which is central to the AA programme, is presented in narrative or storytelling form in Kurtz and Ketcham (2002).
59. An academic paper that describes AA humour (without, it must be said, many laughs) is Pollner and Stein (2001).

Index

(Entries marked with a P before a page number refer to Plates)

Ireland's 'Moral Hospital'
The Irish Borstal System 1906–1956

Conor Reidy

Clonmel borstal in county Tipperary was the first and only such institution in Ireland and opened in 1906 for the purpose of reforming male offenders aged between sixteen and twenty-one years. The book also provides comparisons between the administration of the system by the British government prior to Independence and the Irish state after 1921. Two key periods, from 1922–24 and from 1940–46, when the borstal was removed from Clonmel for military purposes, are examined.

The book explores the renewed government interest and investment in the borstal in the aftermath of the *'Father Flanagan controversy'*, following its return to Clonmel in 1946. With signs that the system might finally be on course to fulfill its potential, a number of factors ensured that this optimism was to be short-lived and in 1956 Clonmel borstal ceased operations and the institution was transferred to Dublin. Reidy utilises primarily unpublished official sources to analyse the daily operation of Clonmel borstal.

2009   272 pages
978 0 7165 2980 4   cloth   €60.00/£45.00/$69.95
978 0 7165 2981 1   paper   €24.95   (Ireland only)

Music in Irish Cultural History

Gerry Smyth

This collection of essays on the subject of music and Irish identity covers a number of different musical genres and periods, produced in a coherent volume representing a significant intervention within the field of Irish music studies. The main essays include the (re-)establishment of music as a key object of Irish cultural studies; the theoretical limitations of traditional musicology; and the development of new methodologies specifically designed to address the demands of Irish music in all its aspects.

With chapters ranging from the politics of betrayal in the songs of Thomas Moore to the use of music in the award-winning film *Once, The Dancer From The Dance*, the book offers an analysis of key moments from Irish cultural history considered from the perspective of music.

2009   272 pages
978 0 7165 2984 2   cloth €60.00/£40.00/$69.95
978 0 7165 2985 9   paper €24.95   (Ireland only)

A Nation of Extremes
The Pioneers in Twentieth Century Ireland

Diarmaid Ferriter

Explores the extraordinary relationship the Irish have with alcohol from the point of view of the group who were intent on reducing alcohol consumption through membership in the Pioneer Total Abstinence of the Sacred Heart. The Pioneers was formed in 1898, by the mid 1950s the association was to claim a membership of nearly half a million, identifiable by the wearing of a pin, the outward expression of an internal and deeply personal piety. It was a startling figure for such a small country but the stereotype of the Irish as a nation of heavy drinkers continued unabated, aided by vast expenditure on alcohol. As the century progressed two diametrically opposed cultures – abstinence and heavy drinking – were lying alongside each other.

Ferriter makes use of previously unpublished sources, examines the Irish temperance movement in the context of Irish society as a whole and attempts to tease out some of the intricacies and ambiguities associated with these two cultures. Although the leaders of this temperance crusade insisted that it was primarily a religious movement, given the pervasiveness of the Irish drink culture it was inevitable that in their desire to transform attitudes they would have to involve themselves in the wider, and more material debates about the role of drink in Irish society. The fact that the movement was founded at a time of intense cultural nationalism gave these debates an added potency, particularly as it had often been contended that increased sobriety was essential for any self-respecting self-governing nation. After Independence, the quest for sobriety and an initially robust Catholic crusade ultimately led to confrontation and confusion.

April 2008   304 pages
978 0 7165 2623 0 cloth €55.00/£40.00/$69.50
978 0 7165 2986 6 paper €22.95/£19.95/$32.95